Dirk Schnelle

Context Aware Voice User Interfaces for Workflow Support

Dirk Schnelle

Context Aware Voice User Interfaces for Workflow Support

Voice Based Support for Mobile Workers

VDM Verlag Dr. Müller

Imprint

Bibliographic information by the German National Library: The German National Library lists this publication at the German National Bibliography; detailed bibliographic information is available on the Internet at http://dnb.d-nb.de.

Cover image: www.purestockx.com

Publisher:
VDM Verlag Dr. Müller Aktiengesellschaft & Co. KG , Dudweiler Landstr. 125 a, 66123 Saarbrücken, Germany,
Phone +49 681 9100-698, Fax +49 681 9100-988,
Email: info@vdm-verlag.de

Zugl.: Darmstadt, TU, Diss., 2007

Produced in USA and UK by:
Lightning Source Inc., La Vergne, Tennessee, USA
Lightning Source UK Ltd., Milton Keynes, UK
BookSurge LLC, 5341 Dorchester Road, Suite 16, North Charleston, SC 29418, USA

ISBN: 978-3-8364-8874-7

Wissenschaftlicher Werdegang des Verfassers[2]

10/1989–06/1995 Studium der Informatik an der Friedrich-Alexander-Universität
Erlangen-Nürnberg

07/1993–10/1993 Studienarbeit am Lehrstuhl für Mustererkennung
Friedrich-Alexander-Universität Erlangen-Nürnberg
Automatische Erkennung von prosodischen Phrasengrenzen

06/1993–12/1994 Diplomarbeit am Lehrstuhl für Mustererkennung
Friedrich-Alexander-Universität Erlangen-Nürnberg
Grundfrequenzbestimmung mit künstlichen Neuronalen Netzen

04/2003–09/2006 Wissenschaftlicher Mitarbeiter an der Technischen Universität
Darmstadt

---

[2]Gemäß §20 Abs. 3 der Promotionsordnung der TU Darmstadt

Abstract

Audio is a significant factor in the design of the human computer interface in ubiquitous computing. The characteristics of the medium allow for a hands-free interaction without the need to switch the focus to a display (eyes-free). Moreover, determining the graphical capabilities of the wearable device to adapt the output to the device is not needed. But audio based interfaces are also challenging, since humans are visually oriented.

The ubiquitous computing community recognized the advantages of the audio channel, but the restrictions inherent to the medium are mostly ignored. Authors of such systems who know about these challenges often look for a solution by using additional modalities, preferably visually oriented.

This thesis analyses these challenges with respect to the humans cognitive capabilities and shows a possible solution using audio design patterns.

Users on the move face additional challenges, since wearable devices do not have the computational power and storage capacity of desktop PCs which are required to use speech recognizers and speech synthesizers off the shelf. Thus recognition and synthesis software running on such a device does not have the capabilities of their desktop size counterparts. Streaming technologies can use high-end voice technology on a server at the cost of network dependency. This thesis introduces a new approach combining both worlds.

In order to aid the user best, context information is used, location at first place. The context information is obtained from the current environment and from the task that she wants to accomplish. workflow engines are a standard for storing and controlling tasks as processes. Additionally, workflow engines consider the data flow which is a fundamental aspect of each process. Initial approaches to using context information in workflow engines exist but they lack a reusable concept. This thesis introduces such a concept. The process descriptions in workflow engines are modality independent in order to have reusable business logic. Modality dependant specifications of the current activity reside outside the workflow engine and are stored in a meta format that can be used to address multiple modalities. The user interfaces are generated by code generators at run-time. Current concepts consider neither a separation of modality independent business logic nor do they regard data flow. If a user is working on multiple processes in parallel, she needs support in returning into the context of an interrupted process. The challenges inherent to audio are not well suited to aid her resuming the task efficiently. In this thesis, we introduce a first concept of an audio-only support for task resumption.

Zusammenfassung

Im Ubiquitous-Computing-Umfeld ist Audio eine wesentliche Komponente bei der Gestaltung der Mensch-Maschine-Schnittstelle. Die Eigenschaften des Mediums ermöglichen eine Interaktion ohne Zuhilfenahme der Hände (hands-free) und ohne den Blick von der Haupttätigkeit abzuwenden (eyes-free). Daneben müssen auch die grafischen Möglichkeiten der tragbaren Geräte nicht ausgelotet werden, um die aktuelle Ausgabe an diese Fähigkeiten anzupassen. Da der Mensch jedoch hauptsächlich visuell ausgerichtet ist, bringt die Gestaltung von audiobasierten Schnittstellen eine Reihe von Herausforderungen mit sich.

Dennoch werden die Vorteile des Audiokanals in den meisten Arbeiten im Bereich Ubiquitous Computing als solche erkannt. Die damit einher gehenden Einschränkungen werden jedoch häufig gänzlich ignoriert. Autoren, die die technischen Beschränkungen audiobasierter Schnittstellen erkennen, suchen oft eine Lösung durch das Hinzuziehen weiterer Modalitäten, vorzugsweise visueller Art.

In dieser Arbeit werden die Herausforderungen unter Berücksichtigung kognitiven Fähigkeiten von Benutzern rein audiobasierter Anwendungen systematisch analysiert und Möglichkeiten zu ihrer Bewältigung mit Hilfe von Design Patterns aufgezeigt.

Für die mobile Benutzerin ergibt sich zudem die Problematik, dass mobile Geräte nicht über das Leistungspotenzial, insbesondere in Bezug auf Rechenleistung und Speicherkapazität, wie Desktop PCs verfügen, die die Verwendung von Standardsoftware zur Spracherkennung und Sprachsynthese erst ermöglicht. Sprachsoftware, die auf den tragbaren Geräten läuft, verfügt deswegen nicht über die Leistungsfähigkeit der Standardsoftware. Streamingtechnologien hingegen nutzen höherwertige Sprachsoftware auf dem Server auf Kosten von Netzabhängigkeiten. In dieser Arbeit wird ein neuer Ansatz vorgestellt, der beide Welten miteinander verbindet.

Um die Benutzerin effizient unterstützen zu können, werden Kontextinformationen, insbesondere der Aufenthaltsort der Benutzerin, genutzt. Diese werden zum einen aus der aktuellen Umgebung der Benutzerin gewonnen und zum anderen aus dem Kontext der zu erledigenden Aufgabe. Eine standardisierte Form zur Speicherung und zur Ablaufsteuerung dieser Aufgaben ist in Form von Prozessen einer Workflow Engine gegeben. Zudem haben Workflow Engines den Vorteil, dass sie auf einen durchgängigen Datenfluss, der immer zu einem Prozess gehört, Wert legen. Erste Ansätze zur Nutzung von Kontextinformationen in Workflow Engines existieren, es fehlt jedoch ein wiederverwertbares Konzept. In dieser Arbeit wird ein solches Konzept vorgestellt. Die Beschreibung des Prozesses in der Workflow Engine wird Modalitäten unabhängig gehalten, um so Widerverwendbarkeit zu erreichen. Eine Modalitäten abhängige Konkretisierung des aktuellen Prozessschrittes wird außerhalb der Workflow Engine in einem Metaformat gespeichert. Mit Hilfe eines Codegenerators wird hieraus die verwendete Benutzungsschnittstelle zur Laufzeit erzeugt. Bisherige Konzepte haben hier weder eine solche Trennung vorgesehen, noch den Datenfluss aktiv unterstützt. Arbeitet eine Benutzerin an mehreren Prozessen gleichzeitig, so muss sie bei der Wiederaufnahme eines Prozesses aktiv unterstützt werden, um effizient weiter arbeiten zu können, was durch die speziellen Eigenschaften des auditiven Mediums erschwert wird. In dieser Arbeit wird erstmalig ein Konzept zur aktiven Unterstützung dieser Wiedereinführung in den Aufgabenkontext präsentiert.

viii

Danksagungen

Die vorliegende Arbeit entstand während meiner Tätigkeit als wissenschaftlicher Mitarbeiter an der Tbsechnischen Universiät Darmstadt im Fachgebiet Telekooperation. An dieser Stelle möchte ich mich bei allen bedanken, die mich bei der Erstellung dieser Arbeit geholfen haben und ohne deren breite Unterstützung und Hilfe diese Arbeit nicht zustande gekommen wäre.

An erster Stelle möchte ich mich bei Prof. Dr. Max Mühlhäuser für den Mut bedanken, sich auf das Experiment einzulassen, einen Mitarbeiter aus dem industriellen Umfeld als wissenschaftlichen Mitarbeiter zu einer Promotion zu führen. Weiterhin bedanke ich mich für die Freiheiten, die er mir gewährt hat, meine Ideen zu entwickeln.

Herrn PD Dr. habil. Elmar Nöth danke ich für seine Bereitschaft das Koreferat zu übernehmen und die Unterstützung im Bereich Spracherkennung.

Einen beträchtlichen Beitrag zum Gelingen dieser Arbeit und zum angenehmen Verlauf dieser Dissertation haben die vielen freundlichen Mitarbeiterinnen und Mitarbeiter des Fachgebietes Telekooperation geleistet, die mir in guter Erinnerung bleiben werden: Besonders gilt dieser Dank Herrn Prof. Dr. Jussi Kangasharju für konstruktive Gespräche und wertvolle Unterstützung bei Publikationen, Fernando Lyardet bei der Entwicklung von Ideen im Pattern Umfeld und Erwin Aitenbichler für die Unterstützung beim Einsatz von MundoCore.

Weiterhin möchte ich mich bei Melanie Hartmann, Tao Wei, Marcus Ständer, Hidir Akhan, Alexander Hannappel und Falko Radke bedanken, die im Rahmen ihrer Diplomarbeiten und Studienarbeiten wesentliche Bausteine für Prototypen realisiert haben oder Benutzerstudien durchgeführt haben, die Grundlage vieler Ergebnisse dieser Arbeit waren.

Meinem Bruder Detlef Schnelle und Bríd Phelan sei für die stilistischen und orthographischen Korrekturvorschläge gedankt.

Großen Dank schulde ich meiner Freundin Simone Walka, die mich in einer schweren Zeit so viel weiter getragen hat und die mir insbesondere in der letzten Phase Geduld, Unterstützung und Aufmunterung entgegen gebracht hat.

Auch möchte ich meinen Kindern Aron-Samuel, Jesse-Elias und Noah Gabriel danken, die mich auch mal auf andere Gedanken gebracht haben, so dass ich wieder frisch an den Entwicklungen meiner Ideen arbeiten konnte.

Viele Personen, die mir ebenfalls bei dieser Arbeit geholfen haben, sind ungenannt geblieben. Auch Ihnen möchte ich an dieser Stelle danken.

Contents

List of Figures

List of Tables

Chapter 1

Introduction

1.1 Motivation

"Reports and theses in speech recognition often begin with a cliche, namely that speech is the most natural way for human beings to communicate with each other"

This statement from Hunt in [Hun92] is still true and the question arises, why do we see so little use of voice interfaces in today's human-computer interaction.

Speech is certainly one of the most important means of communication for humans [WRM75]. It has been used from the beginning of mankind to transfer customs and knowledge from one generation to the next. Although new technologies have been developed throughout history, speech remains a very efficient way of communication. But is this also true for the computer as the counterpart?

It can be concluded from Hunt's statement that the expectation, that a computer can be treated like a human, led to the vision of the patiently listening homunculus [Sil14] in a computer's shape. As a result, less pretentious, but more realistic and helpful applications were of low interest for academic research.

A prominent representative of such a homunculus is the computer HAL 9000 in Stanley Kubrick's famous movie *2001 A Space Odyssey* [Kub64]. HAL, the navigation computer, has an artificial intelligence and speaks with Dave Bowman, the commander of the space ship, like a human.

Dave Bowman: Hello, HAL do you read me, HAL?
HAL: Affirmative, Dave, I read you.
Dave Bowman: Open the pod bay doors, HAL.
HAL: I'm sorry Dave, I'm afraid I can't do that.
Dave Bowman: What's the problem?
HAL: I think you know what the problem is just as well as I do.
Dave Bowman: What are you talking about, HAL?
HAL: This mission is too important for me to allow you to jeopardize it.
Dave Bowman: I don't know what you're talking about, HAL?
HAL: I know you and Frank were planning to disconnect me, and I'm afraid that's something I cannot allow to happen.
Dave Bowman: Where the hell'd you get that idea, HAL?

HAL: Dave, although you took thorough precautions in the pod against my hearing you, I could see your lips move.

All in all this approach does not seem to be convincing, since it requires that computers have the active and passive communicative competence of a human. This theory is supported by Schukat-Talamazzini in [ST95] and it is also the message of Shneiderman in [Shn00], who states that although the recognition rate is increasingly accurate for dictation systems, the adaption outside the disabled-user community has been slow compared to visual interfaces.

In the past years people working in the area of Natural Language Processing [JM00, MS99, CMU+95] have made big steps in their research [Mic05, Gro05] towards this vision, but we are still a big step behind. Amy Neustein states in [Neu01] that this

> "... does not seem far fetched when we consider how the field of linguistics, with its wide spectrum of methods to study interactive speech, provides the building blocks for spoken language systems that simulate human dialog"

But she has to admit that these are only necessary first steps toward an open collaborative relationship between computational linguists and conversation analysts. As a consequence this leads to more interactive, conversational interfaces. But we need more of this sort of collaboration. Today this remains a vision. Otherwise the big advantage of audio, being more natural, would have long displaced the ubiquitous graphical user interface. In fact, banking companies who offer both web based customer self service and telephony based self service observe a trend in favor of the graphical oriented medium [Sch05].

Nevertheless the use of voice based user interfaces seem to be a promising alternative. Imagine a warehouse picker who needs to pick different items from different shelves. The worker's hands are busy, calling for the use of voice interaction, and the high mobility of the worker makes carrying additional equipment impractical.

The only infrastructure support we can assume is a wireless network and the information base. The worker, wearing a headset with local computation capabilities, receives instructions and confirms them. For example, the next task could be *"fetch 10 widgets from shelf 5 in aisle 7"*. When the worker has performed the task and has picked up the widgets, she would confirm this to the information base, which would then dispatch her onwards to the next pick-up.

In this scenario the headset provides two important functions. The first one is what is mentioned above, i.e., telling the worker what to do next and receiving confirmations from the worker that the task has been completed. The second function is providing the worker with help. For example, new workers might need instructions on what is the optimal route between two pick-ups or might need help finding the correct items. The information base might also deliver descriptions of items if needed. The main use cases that have been described so far are shown in Figure 1.1.

This simple scenario faces several challenges which we will explore in this thesis.

Speech recognition Due to the transient and one-dimensional nature of the medium, the design of voice based user interfaces is still an unsolved problem.

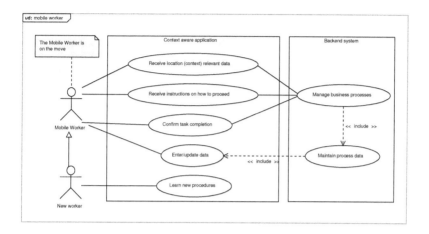

Figure 1.1: Main uses cases for a mobile worker

Computational limitations Mobile devices do not have the computational power, mainly speed and memory size, of desktop PC's. Since speech recognition
is computational intensive this becomes a challenging problem.

Context Awareness The use of contextual information, especially location, can
be used to aid the user in solving her current task.

Back-end system integration It is very common to use databases as back-end
systems for voice user interfaces. However, these systems are mostly proprietary implementations. One possible solution towards a more generic approach
is the use of workflow systems.

Task support Workflow engines can also be used as a runtime environment for
business processes. A businesses process contains a detailed description of the
task that have to be performed by the worker. This description can be used
as an additional source of context to aid the user in achieving her goal.

1.2 Organization of Thesis

This thesis will address all of the problems named in section 1.1 and offer a possible
solution for a combination of all of them by means of a framework. Figure 1.2 shows
a basic architecture of the target system. Within this thesis we have a closer look
at each of the components involved. Figure 1.3 shows the roadmap of this thesis.

Chapter 2 will give a short introduction to workflow systems. Workflow systems
also appear as part of *Business Process Management*. Business Process Management
enables companies to stay adaptable to environmental and internal changes as well as
realize that efficiency gains through exploiting cost-effective ways to produce goods

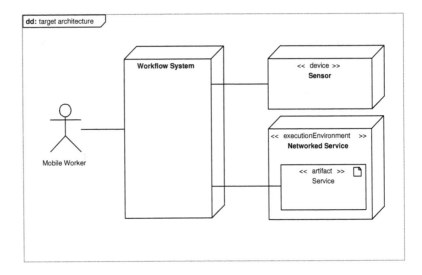

Figure 1.2: Target Architecture to support Mobile Workers

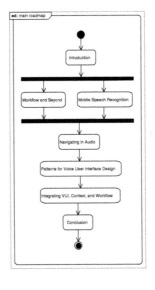

Figure 1.3: Roadmap of the thesis

and perform services [zM04]. Collecting information about an organization's business processes is complicated by absence of a common infrastructure. Frequently,

business processes cross organizational boundaries and they often involve a variety of information systems, frequently with heterogeneous data repositories. For the execution and monitoring of business processes, many organizations are increasingly using workflow management systems to improve the efficiency of their processes and reduce costs. During the execution of the business process, workflow management systems record many types of events, such as the start and completion time of each activity, the assigned resources and the outcome of the execution [MSzM05].

In the picker example from section 1.2 the business process encompasses the collection and update of the database, once the items are removed from the shelves. In addition, as an add-on to the business process integration, this might also trigger an ordering system to order more items if a lower bound has been reached. Workflow management systems presented so far concentrate mainly on office environments but leave out the increasing field of mobile workers. In recent years, computers have become smaller and mobile. This led to the invention of the wearable computer [Tho98]. Wearable computers are worn on the belt or carried in the pocket. The important difference is that the user is *on the move*. Context-awareness is an essential research area that facilitates and enhances the use of mobile IT systems. Context-awareness helps to provide information to the user relating to her location and the task that the user is currently executing [SSP98]. In the picking example, location information can be used to update the workflow management system with context data in order to monitor and improve the performance of the picking activities. Location is part of the context data of this scenario. An overview, what context-awareness means and a combination of the techniques, workflow systems and context-awareness, is also presented in chapter 2.

In the picker scenario we believe that audio information delivery is superior to traditional hands-and-eyes devices, such as a display, a PC, or a PDA. This is because workers typically have their hands busy with the task they are trying to perform. Hence they cannot easily use a keyboard or mouse because this will force them to stop working. The use of voice based interfaces is the most unobtrusive use of a mobile or wearable device [Bür02]. Some basics about speech recognition and text-to-speech technology with regard to usage in wearable devices are given in chapter 3.

In chapter 4 is shown that interaction with a voice based user-interface can be reduced to tree-like structures using the concepts of context-awareness, see section 2.2 and voice user interfaces, see section 2.6. This interaction is equivalent to the controlling functions of a web browser. The audio navigation document structures then borrow from hypertext the notion of enabling users to access information in an intuitive and associative way.

Navigation in the audio space is only one aspect within the design of voice user interfaces. While chapter 4 explores the limitations of this approach, we need concepts to apply the knowledge about voice user interface design and human cognitive limitations. Existing guidelines fail, since they are hard to select. Thus, the design of voice user interface became more an art than an engineering science. Chapter 5 shows how the interface design can be simplified and improved using patterns. Thus we are able to exploit the advantages of audio interfaces in an engineering manner.

In chapter 2 we introduce the requirements to enable context-awareness for workflow systems. In chapter 6 we show a reference implementation to meet these requirements, by extending the general purpose audio browser that was developed in chapter 4 using a business process oriented concept. In this way it is possible to support the integration of back-end systems needed, e.g. to automatically update the database when the items are removed from the shelves in the picking example. We use the results from chapters 3 and 4 to enable audio based interaction with the workflow system.

Chapter 7 concludes this thesis with a summary of the results and an outlook extending the presented concepts.

1.3   Contribution

The contributions of this thesis can be summarized as follows

- **Systematic analysis of current technologies to handle speech recognition running on wearable devices**
  There are several ways to handle speech recognition in distributed environments with wearable devices. This is often a key requirement for research using this technology. A general overview of the pros and cons of these architectures was not available so far. Moreover they are categorized into service-dependent and service-independent architectures, which is a basic requirement if they are used in smart environments.

- **New architecture to handle speech recognition running on wearable devices based on a publish/subscribe mechanism**
  The current architectures to support speech recognition and speech synthesis running on wearable devices have the disadvantage that they work either service-independent, consuming a lot of resources on the device and being inflexible if the device is used in another location, or service dependent, which also makes them highly dependent on the location. A new architecture is introduced, combining both worlds, with a general purpose basic command set for the service-independent recognizer running on the device that can be boosted by the environment.

- **Systematic analysis of the factors that make it difficult to develop voice based applications**
  The reasons why voice is difficult to handle are known. However we categorized them into problems that cannot be solved because they are inherent to the audio domain and problems, which diminish as technical progress is made.

- **Calculation of the limitations of audio browsers based on network topologies**
  The limitations of audio based interfaces and network topologies served as a basis for a thorough analysis to calculate the amount of information that can be delivered for an audio browser.

- **Introduction of a pattern language for Voice User Interface Design**
  The Human Computer Interaction community realized that patterns are superior to guidelines. Patterns exist for many user interfaces but were missing

for voice. In this thesis a pattern language is introduced that helps to handle the limitations of voice user interfaces.

- **Development of an MVC architecture that extends existing concepts of code generators to use a modality independent task model** Current approaches of code generators for user interfaces have modality dependencies in their task model. A disadvantage of this approach is that the task model cannot be reused to generate code for other user interfaces. In this thesis a new approach is introduced, applying the MVC pattern strictly, based on a workflow engine. The use of a workflow engine has the additional advantage of being based on processes that already exist in industrial settings.

- **Extension of existing concepts to handle context events in a workflow engine**
  Currently workflow engines are not ready to work in mobile settings. In this thesis the first approaches to fill the gap between workflow engines and mobile workers are extended, with a focus on data exchange with the environment. In addition, a concept was developed to control the environment by the workflow.

- **Development of a concept to handle resumption of tasks in audio-only environments to help the user to return to context**
  Graphical user interfaces can easily bring the user back into context, when she wants to resume an interrupted task. Currently there is no concept to handle this in audio-only environments. In this thesis, a general concept is developed to handle this issue, based on a psychological background, .

1.4 Publications

Parts of this thesis have been published in the proceedings of international conferences, workshops, and video tracks.

The pattern language for voice user interface design was published in [SLW05] and [SL06].

The generation of VoiceXML dialogs as a presentation layer for a workflow engine was described in [SK06].

The concept of task switching in audio-based systems was published in [HS06].

STAIRS, the prototype of an audio browser was described in [SJ05] and presented in [SAKM04] and [MSAK05].

Chapter 2

Workflow and Beyond

2.1 Motivation

The life-cycle of products is becoming shorter as a consequence of the ever increasing impact of technology on the production process. It is expected that this trend will continue over the next years [MSzM05]. If companies want to stay competitive and be successful in the long term they have to optimize their business processes.

Several approaches have been developed in this context and several technologies are actually being used. One promising approach to optimize business processes and to reduce costs is Business Process Management (BPM). BPM allows companies to model their business processes and the IT infrastructure with the goal to reveal weak points.

BPM is a newer term for the older term *Workflow Management System*. Neither theoretical nor practical comparisons were able to find a fundamental difference between these two terms. Strnadl states in [Str06] that workflow management systems tend to focus on the implementation in IT, especially automatization, rather than analysis, design, modelling and management. However, this has no relevance to applying the technology in a company. This thesis concentrates on the technical implementation in IT and we will use the term workflow in favour of the newer term BPM.

Companies have already adopted the idea of workflow systems. "Designed and implemented well, workflow systems provide a newfound order and simplicity. The results are higher productivity, smoother delivery of products and services and a better bottom line" [Ser06]. Existing implementations concentrate on office environments and are not automatically suited to be used in a mobile environment. The MOWAHS project [MOW04] started to fill this gap and to adapt existing workflow technology to handle the dynamics of a mobile user. Mobility introduces new challenges to workflow systems, like the modelling of resources and activities in a mobile setting.

This chapter explores the requirements to use context information, like sensor data, or services that are available via the network in a workflow system and how voice user interfaces can serve to interact with workflow systems. The target architecture in Figure 1.2 is therefore expanded to the components shown in Figure 2.1. The components and artifacts shown in Figure 2.1 will be discussed later in this chapter. One focus of this chapter is the *Context Integrator* and the requirements

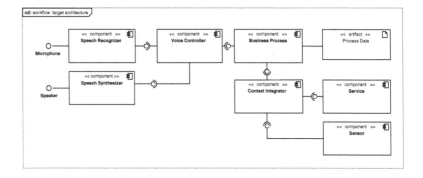

Figure 2.1: Target Architecture to support voice based interaction with a context-aware workflow

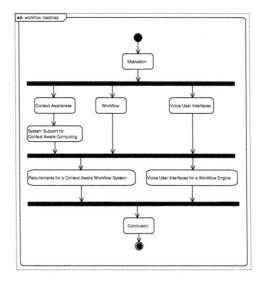

Figure 2.2: Roadmap to handle Context-aware Workflow Systems

for developing the interface between the *Business Process* component and the *Context Integrator* to make *Sensor Data* and *Services* available to the *Business Process* with a more general view on the topic.

Additionally, we look at the use of voice user interfaces and how they can be used through a *Voice Controller* as a front-end to enable voice based interaction with a workflow engine.

The organization of this chapter is shown in Figure 2.2. Following this motivation, section 2.2 introduces our understanding of context-awareness. Section 2.3 gives a short overview of tools that have been developed in the Telecooperation Group at Technical University of Darmstadt to support the development of context-aware applications. Next, a short introduction to workflow systems with a definition of the terminology is given in section 2.5.1, serving as a basis to discuss the requirements for context-aware workflow systems in section 2.5. Section 2.5.6 gives an overview of the work that has already been done in the area of context-aware workflow systems. Then we turn to voice user interfaces in section 2.6 and discuss approaches to a voice enabled workflow engine in section 2.7, before section 2.8 concludes this chapter with a short summary.

2.2 Context-Awareness

In order to use context effectively, we must understand what context is and how it can be used. This definition will be used in section 2.5 to define the requirements of a context-aware workflow system and will be explored in more detail in chapter 6. Moreover this understanding of context awareness serves as a basis for the exploration of audio browsing in chapter 4.

Our definition follows that of Dey [Dey00] and Schmidt [SG01] and is defined as

Definition 1 *Context describes the circumstances or events that form the environment within which something exists or takes place.*

This definition of context is very broad and allows nearly everything to be interpreted as context, which may be a reason, why there is no common understanding of context in the ubiquitous computing community. However, a common sense of people working in ubiquitous and pervasive computing is that context is a key in their efforts to disperse and enmesh computation in our lives. In order to be more useful for **u**biquitous computing (UC) we need a more precise definition. In [Sie01], Sieworek defines

Definition 2 *Context-aware computing describes the situation where a mobile computer is aware of its user's state and surroundings and modifies its behavior based on this information. [Sie01]*

Before discussing how context can support users in ubiquitous computing scenarios, it must be clear which aspects of the environment exist and which are of interest for our purpose. Gross and Specht summarize in [GS01] the efforts of Schilit, Dey and others to the following four main categories of context:

Location is specified in electronic and physical space. An artifact can have a physical or an electronic location described by URIs or URLs. Some authors make use of a cursor to indicate the electronic location, e.g. [BAM04]. Location based services can be based on mapping between the physical presence of the artifact and the presentation of the corresponding electronic artifact.

Identity is being used to hold highly sophisticated user models and to infer information about the user's interest, preferences, knowledge and detailed activity logs of physical space movements and electronic artifact manipulations. The identity can be defined by the group of people that shares a context.

Time is an important category to describe a context. Besides the pure specification of time it categorical scales as an overlay for other categories.

Environment or activity describes the artifacts and physical locations of the current situation. In several projects, approaches for modeling the artifacts and building taxonomies or ontologies about their relations are used for selecting and presenting information to a user.

Most applications focus on identity and location to present tailored information to the user. These are traditionally the most important categories for context-aware computing. A well known tool to support such application is the context toolkit from Dey [Dey00]. Dey differentiates between

- *presentation* of information and services to a user,

- automatic *execution* of a service for a user and

- *tagging* of context to information to support later retrieval.

These items become clearer in an example where a user moves through a building with her mobile computer and randomly starts some printing jobs. *Presentation* is done by her mobile computer that asks the user to select one of n nearby printers as she moves through the building. *Tagging* is done by an application that records the selected device in relation to the user's physical location *Automatic execution* is then using the last selected printer based upon the current physical location.

We will come back to these items, when we discuss the use of the contextual information according to the four main categories in section 4.9.

2.3   System Support for Context Aware Computing

2.3.1   The Talking Assistant

Mundo is the vision from the Telcooperation Group at Technical University of Darmstadt of a general infrastructure for Ubiquitous Computing. Mundo, Spanish for world, is an acronym for **M**obile and **u**biquitous **n**etworking via **d**istributed **o**verlay cells. The vision focuses on the network infrastructure, like global cooperation of services in peer-to-peer networks on the one hand and integration of different means of communication, like publish/subscribe, unicast/multicast and message/streams on the other hand. The user is wearing a device that is also called **m**inimal **e**ntity (ME).

The ME is used as a digital representative of the user, thus supporting identity. It satisfies several minimal constraints of communication, interaction, context-awareness and security. The *T*alking *A*ssistant (TA), shown in Figure 2.3 is a

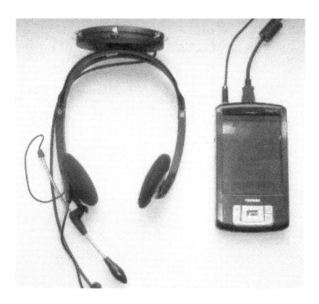

Figure 2.3: The Talking Assistant

prototype of such a ME. It features an audio based user interface, wireless network access (WLAN) and sensors to access context information. The most important contexts are the current location of the user and the user's line of sight.

The communication infrastructure is realized by MundoCore, which is introduced in the following section.

2.3.2 MundoCore

We use MundoCore [Ait06] to meet some of the requirements for context information representation and retrieval named in section 2.5.2. MundoCore is a communication middleware that is designed to work in smart environments. MundoCore uses a channel based publish-subscribe mechanism as illustrated in Figure 2.4. The *Publisher* uses a predefined *channel name* to publish messages to the network. The used network infrastructure is transparent. All receivers that subscribed to the channel name receive a notification when a message arrives over Mundo. The publish-subscribe mechanism makes it an ideal candidate to publish context events to their subscribers.

In the following, we do not differentiate between Mundo and MundoCore and use the terms interchangeably.

2.3.3 Context Server

As a further facility for development of software for smart environments a Context Server has been developed by Meyer [Mey05]. It is modelled after the context toolkit

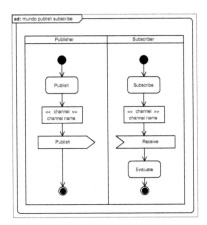

Figure 2.4: Simplified view on Mundo's publish subscribe mechanism via channels

of Dey [Dey00]. The Context Server has three basic goals

- Interpret data received from sensors and transform them into a common representation

- Maintain a geometric 3D world model of the smart environment

- Store histories of sensor data and generate high-level events and support queries and subscriptions in those histories.

How these issues are handled is shown in Figure 2.5. The sensor data is published over Mundo to a *Listener* in the Context Server. A *Listener* delivers the incoming message as input to a *ContextWidget*. The purpose of *Context Widgets* is to transform their input messages into another representation, for example, to translate an ID that has been received by an RFID tag into a human readable name. A *ContextWidget* may have multiple ingoing and multiple outgoing connections. It is up to the *ContextWidget* if it waits for all ingoing connections to deliver input or if one single input message is sufficient to perform its task. After the transformation, it delivers the transformed message to all outgoing connections. The possibility of chaining the Context Widgets allows for a high flexibility. The Context Widget may also store transformed data into a *Context Store* to be used as input of other Context Widgets or to be queried by a client. After the final transformation the data is published to all clients located on any server. Mundo has also the advantage that the real location of each component is transparent for the publisher and for the subscriber since the transport is transparent.

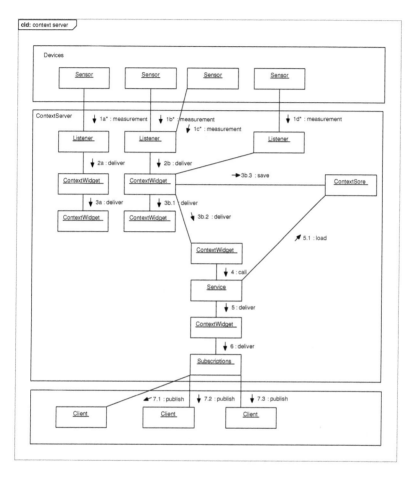

Figure 2.5: Functioning of the Context Server

2.4 Workflow

There is no generally and commonly used definition of workflows. In this section we provide some basic definitions about our understanding of workflow. The way we handle workflow is based on the specification of the WfMC, the **W**orkflow **M**anagement **C**oalition [TWMC99]. The following definitions are taken from this specification.

The WfMC defines workflow as follows.

Definition 3 *A **workflow** is the automation of a business process, in whole or part, during which documents, information or tasks are passed from one participant*

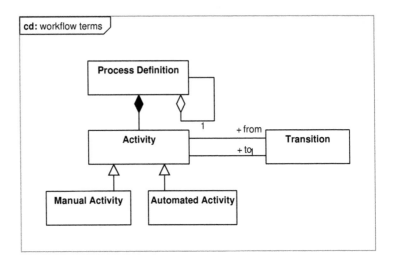

Figure 2.6: Workflow terms and their relationship according to [TWMC05]

to another for action, according to a set of procedural rules. [TWMC99]

Hence, the basic concept that appears in a workflow is the business process.

Definition 4 *A **business process** is a set of one or more linked procedures or activities, which collectively realise a business objective or policy goal. Normally it is made up of an organization structure defining functional roles and relationships. [TWMC99]*

The implementation of a business process in an IT infrastructure is called a process definition.

Definition 5 *A **process definition** is a representation of a business process in a computerized form. The representation supports automated manipulation, such as modelling, or enactment by a workflow management system. The process definition consists of a network of activities and their relationships, criteria to indicate the start and termination of the process, and information about the individual activities, such as participants, associated IT applications and data, etc. [TWMC99]*

A process definition again is a compound term made up of multiple activities as illustrated in Figure 2.6.

Definition 6 *An **activity** is a description of a piece of work that forms one logical step within a process. An activity may be a manual activity, which does not support computer automation, or a workflow (automated) activity. A workflow activity requires human and/or machine resource(s) to support process execution: where a human resource is required, an activity is allocated to a workflow participant. [TWMC99]*

This definition is not very precise, since *workflow activities* are defined to be automated. Hence it cannot be manual or requiring human resources as it is used in the rest of the definition. A more precise definition of activities is

Definition 7 *An **activity** is a description of a piece of work that forms one logical step within a process. An activity may be a manual activity, which does not support computer automation, or an automated activity. An activity requires human and/or machine resource(s) to support process execution: where a human resource is required, an activity is allocated to a workflow participant*

So an activity may be either an automated activity or a manual activity. The WfMC defines them as follows.

Definition 8 *An **automated activity** is an activity which is capable of computer automation using a workflow management system to manage the activity during execution of the business process, which it forms a part of. [TWMC99]*

Definition 9 *A **manual activity** is an activity within a business process, which is not capable of automation and hence lies outside the scope of a workflow management system. Such activities may be included within a process definition, for example to support the modelling of the process but do not form part of a resulting workflow. [TWMC99]*

Activities are connected by *Transitions*, thus forming a network which makes up the process.

Definition 10 *A **Transition** is a point of execution of a process instance where one activity completes and the thread of control passes to another, which starts. [TWMC99]*

A transition may have a *transition condition* which is evaluated by the workflow engine to decide the sequence of activity execution.

A workflow is created and managed in a *workflow management system* which is defined by WfMC in [TWMC99] as

Definition 11 *A system that defines, creates and manages the execution of workflows through the use of software, running on one or more workflow engines, which is able to interpret the process definition, interact with workflow participants and, where required, invokes the use of IT tools and applications is called a **workflow management system**. [TWMC99]*

There are several implementations available for such a workflow management system. One of them is WfMOpen [dan06] which is implemented as a J2EE component. It was chosen to support workflow implementations within this thesis. The main reason is that it is available as Open Source and that it follows the workflow reference model from WfMC shown in Figure 2.7.

The *workflow enactment service* is the execution environment for the the process definitions. Other components can interact with this component by a well defined set of interfaces. In the following, descriptions of these interfaces are given which will be used later i.e., in our architecture of a *Context Integrator*, see section 6.2, or the hook of the user interface, see section 6.3. These definitions are based on the ones given in [TWMC95].

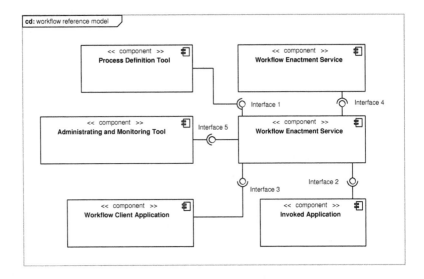

Figure 2.7: Workflow reference model according to [TWMC05]

Interface 1 The Workflow Definition Interchange Interface provides an interface for modelling and definition tools to support the exchange of process definition information over a variety of physical or electronic interchange media.

Interface 2 The Workflow Client Application interface provides the workflow participant with a front end, i.e. top make work lists available.

Interface 3 The Invoke Applications Interface provides direct interaction of applications which have been designed to be *workflow enabled* with a workflow engine.

Interface 4 The Interoperability Functions provide a means of information and control exchange between heterogeneous workflow systems (other Workflow Enactment Services).

Interface 5 The Administration and Monitoring Interface provides independent administration and monitoring tools with a means of interaction with the workflow engine.

The main reason to use workflow systems is to automate business processes. In [All01] Allen distinguishes the following types of workflow, according to how they are used and what features they have

Production workflow systems try to achieve the highest throughput possible. The human interaction with the system is minimized and as many as possible activities are automated. The tasks are usually very repetitive.

Administrative workflow systems focus on the definition of the process. The definition process is made as easy as possible. Many process definitions run concurrently, sacrificing throughput, but achieving flexibility.

Collaborative workflow systems concentrate on supporting groups working together. Process definitions can be changed often and they have a loose structure.

Ad hoc workflow systems feature easy process definitions and flexibility. This is done so that users can adapt easily to changing circumstances. Users own their own processes which separates this type of workflows from process workflows where the organisations own the processes.

2.4.1 XML Process Definition Language

The **XML Process Definition Language** (XPDL) is a format standardized by the WfMC [TWMC05]. It is designed as an interchange format between different workflow engines and is a standard for Interface 1, see section 2.4. The first definitions were in 1993. Until then the WfMC continued the development. The newer version 2.0, which was introduced in May 2005, has additional support for a graphical representation using the **Business Process Modelling Notation** [Whi04] (BPMN). BPMN was standardized by the **Business Management Initiative** [Bus06] to unify and ease the development of business processes. The main contribution of BPMN is the introduction of unified symbols for all components of business processes.

XPDL supports all artifacts of a workflow process, see Figure 2.7. For our purpose, the most interesting artifacts are activity and transition. Automated activities feature one ore more *implementations*. An implementation is an application that is called by the workflow engine using Interface 3 with a fixed number of parameters, the *formal parameters*. The formal parameters are used to exchange data between the participants of a workflow process.

WfMOpen [dan06] is an open source workflow management system developed by danet. It offers full support for XPDL and follows the guidelines of the WfMC and the **Object Management Group** [OMG06] (OMG). The OMG proposed an API for workflow management systems. The OMG API was enhanced by WfMOpen to achieve better scalability. Thus, WfMOpen offers an extensive API that allows for easy development of own applications and to control the workflow engine. In addition it features a web based demo application of an administration and monitoring tool using Interface 5. The implementations of automated activities are realized as so-called *ToolAgents*. ToolAgents simply receive activity definitions with the related data, update the data according to their purpose and return the activity to the workflow enactment service.

To author processes in XPDL we use JaWE [Enh]. The following listing in XPDL format shows the activity *Select Items* of the process shown in Fig. 2.8. The process is from a shopping scenario, where the user selects the items to buy.

```
<Activity Id="question" Name="SelectItems">
    <Implementation>
        <Tool Id="SelectItemsTool" Type="application">
            <ActualParameters>
```

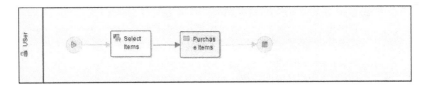

Figure 2.8: Shopping task: Select Items

```
            <ActualParameter>user</ActualParameter>
            <ActualParameter>booklist</ActualParameter>
            <ActualParameter>cart</ActualParameter>
         </ActualParameters>
      </Tool>
   </Implementation>
      ...
</Activity>
```

Once the activity becomes active, it calls the ToolAgent *SelectItemsTool*. Parameters of the task are *user* (the user's identification), *booklist* (a list of books, which has been obtained from a database) and *cart* (the items, which the user selected). This ToolAgent is used to exchange the data with the UI.

2.5 Requirements for Context-Aware Workflow Systems

In [NN04], Nøthvedth introduces several requirements for a context-aware workflow system. This section introduces the functional and non-functional requirements. We use actors based on the definitions which were given in section 2.4 and our definition of context-aware computing which was given in section 2.2. The requirements that are introduced in this section will be used to rate our proposed architecture in chapter 6.

2.5.1 Basic Workflow System

Before the requirements to mobile workflow systems are introduced, the requirements for a general workflow system must be clear.

The basic requirements adhere to the WfMC *Interface 1* specification in particular. It must be possible to interpret and enact multiple process definitions specified in the XPDL language [TWMC05] concurrently. The workflow enactment service must be able to communicate over a network to send and receive activities and evaluate the transitions. It must update the workflow relevant data based on completed activities from workflow participants, providing feedback on activity state. Figure 2.9 illustrates these requirements.

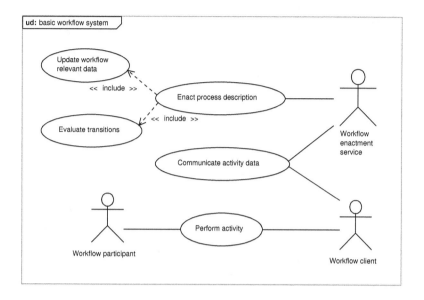

Figure 2.9: Use case diagram for a basic workflow system according to [NN04]

2.5.2 Context Information Representation, Interpretation and Retrieval

In order to make the workflow context-aware we need a context support system that provides an abstraction from low level sensor access. In section 2.3.3 we introduced the context server that is modelled after Dey's context toolkit. The context server is based on a widget abstraction for context sources from the main application code and provides limited context interpretation. Widgets are used to transform one context information item into another. Chaining of widgets can be used to transform low level context information, such as raw sensor data, into high level context information, such as the room coordinates of the user. Context sources reside as service in the environment. These services must be discovered to be used. Both types, polling and publish/subscribe mechanisms must be supported for context information retrieval. These requirements for the context framework and the context-aware application are illustrated in Figure 2.10

2.5.3 Functional Requirements for a Workflow Enactment Service

Based on the requirements for a basic workflow that were described in the previous sections, we now focus on the requirements for a context-aware workflow enactment service.

As a basic requirement, the context information must be usable in the workflow.

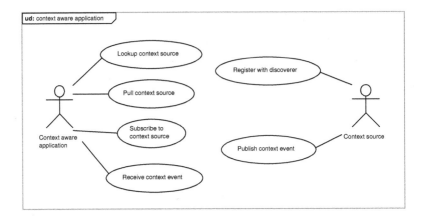

Figure 2.10: Use case diagram for a context framework and context-aware applications according to [NN04]

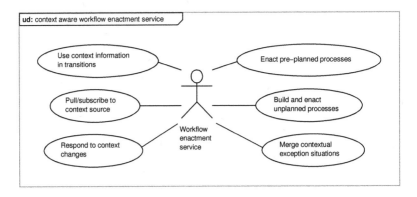

Figure 2.11: Use case diagram for workflow enactment service context-awareness according to [NN04]

This means at first place, that this information can be used in the evaluation of workflow transitions and for triggering of new processes. Secondly, the data, coming from the environment must be transformed to a workflow inherent representation, so that the data can be used by other participants.

This leads to the problems that context information might be not present if it is required to continue, or if it is present to open new paths to achieve the process goal. Therefore it must be possible to revalidate the path if the current path does not lead to the process goal. In addition, it raises the need for an exception handling of undefined contextual states. These requirements are illustrated in Figure 2.11

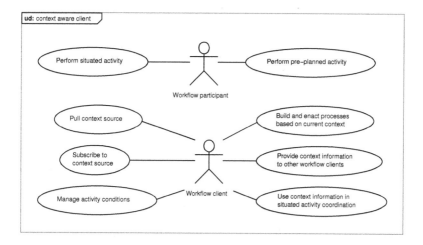

Figure 2.12: Use case diagram for workflow client based context-awareness according to [NN04]

2.5.4 Workflow Client Based Context-Awareness

Like context-aware applications we have similar issues for the applications that are implemented as workflow clients. The WfMC has defined a very simple interface for the clients as described in section 2.4.1.

In addition it might make sense to follow different strategies to achieve the process goal depending on the contextual conditions. Nøthvedth describes this in [NN04] as *situated activity*. Situated activity might also include coordination between multiple workflow participants, leaving also a context after the activity has been performed. These requirements are illustrated in Figure 2.12

2.5.5 Mobility Requirements

Besides the support of context processing the mobility of the user poses additional challenges related to the availability of used context sources in smart environments.

These issues are not covered by the research of Nøthvedth, but are addressed in this thesis.

Context information is being delivered using a mobile network connection. Mobile network connections are unreliable and so we need support for disconnected operation and asynchronous communication. Sessions should follow the user, independently of the used device. It should be possible, to pause a session and resume it later, maybe even in another environment. These requirements are illustrated in Figure 2.13

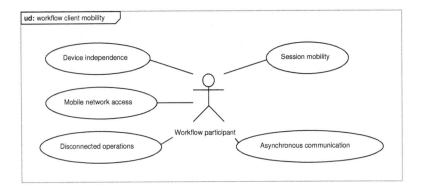

Figure 2.13: Use case diagram for workflow client mobility according to [NN04]

2.5.6   Related Work

There is not much work concentrating on the integration of context-awareness and workflow systems. Current approaches can be categorized into two main streams. The first one tries to enable context-aware computing for existing workflow engines, whereas the second category deals with distributed workflow systems. The focuses of this first category are *production workflow systems* and *administrative workflow systems*, after Allen's categorization of workflows which was introduced in section 2.4. The focuses of the second category are *Collaborative workflow systems* and *ad hoc workflow systems*. In the following we will name representative examples for both main streams.

HandyMan

HandyMan is a quite old application and a good example for a production workflow system. It was created in 1996 by the Norwegian company ePocket Solutions ASA and designed as a PocketPC application to support electricians in their work. The need for paper work was substituted with the capability of memo handling, time measurement for particular activities and material management. The most important fact, regarding workflow and context, is the task support based on workflow process management. The worker gets a list of all tasks to be carried out. The list shows the name and address of the customer, special messages from the office and priority of the task. When performing the task a checklist is displayed containing all predefined steps to ensure that they are all been carried out. The application had only a graphical interface and no automatism to communicate with the back-end system while the worker was on the move. After the worker returned to the office she had to use the synchronisation tool to upload the performed tasks to the system and return new tasks. The case study of Wang et al. [WSSF03] examined the experience of five Norwegian Companies with that tool. Their goal was

Analyse the usage of the tool HandyMan for the purpose of identifying requirements and problems for support systems for mobile work from the perspective of software developers in the context of the working environment of electricians.

The case study was carried out in the form of interviews of the companies.

The authors found five guidelines that must be considered when designing a system for mobile work

1. **The device must be suitable for the working environment**
   The working environment must be examined carefully, in order to find out, which device is suitable in the target environment, or if no device is suitable at all.

2. **The system must give the worker additional functionality**
   If the work is less efficient with the new solution, workers will refrain from using it. If the company sees a benefit, and thus enforces a use, but the worker does not benefit, it is not a good solution. Both, the company and the worker should benefit from the system.

3. **Usability must be top priority**
   Most workers are used to work with paper in the field. The usability of the tool must be very good to be used by the worker.

4. **A mobile work tool must be flexible**
   Since most mobile work is characterised by ad-hoc tasks, it is very important that the tools can cope with such tasks in an efficient manner. They should be treated as a normal case and not as an exceptional state. The tool must also be able to perform all tasks offline and online, e.g., when it is being used outside an area covered by mobile network.

5. **Organisational procedures must be in place**
   The workers need a proper education in using the tool. They are almost alone in the field, making it hard to ask a colleague for help. Further, the process of the workers should be adapted to the mobile work tool, requiring procedure rules to synchronise, recharging batteries, and for how to handle ad-hoc tasks.

The experience with this system makes clear that computer systems make sense to support a mobile workgroup participant. However, limitations in network connectivity and usability pose strong restrictions on those systems. Flexible computer systems are needed, providing added functionality. One possibility to add this functionality is the use of contextual information which is not exploited in HandyMan.

MOWAHS

Nødtvedt et al. introduce in [NN04] an architecture for the **Mo**bile **w**ork **a**cross **h**eterogeneous **s**ystems (MOWAHS) project to handle context information in a workflow system. They do not exclude distributed workflow systems explicitly but concentrate on centralized workflow systems. Their basic idea was to acquire and use context information while following the WfMC standards, see section 2.4. They achieve this by using an external component that is capable of receiving work-flow activities and updates of the necessary data by polling the components of an underlying context framework. This made it possible to achieve simple context re-sponsiveness by using the functionality of the WAPI (Interface 1) and that external component. The dynamic behaviour is limited to the methods defined in the WAPI, the requirement to make changes to processes while they run remains unsolved at the presented state of development. They propose to solve this issue by an extension to the defined set of interfaces. The proposed extension is *Interface 6* that enables the workflow enactment service to fulfill the need for situated actions.

Furthermore they enhance the types of activities defined by the WfMC of *Manual Activities* and *Automated Activities*, see figure 2.6, by a *Semi Automated Activity*. While manual activities are activities that cannot be run by calling applications, and automated activities are using applications, a semi-automated activity falls in between these two definitions. It is done manually by a human participant, but the way the activity is completed is controlled by automatic means. This requires another type of activities that were defined to be either work items or invoked applications to context sources.

However they do not look at communication related problems. The asynchronous nature of context information, see section 2.5.2, poses additional challenges which remain unsolved.

Micro-workflow

Another approach to have workflow in distributed environments with the goal to adapt the workflow depending on the worker's context is the use of distributed workflow engines. One implementation of a distributed workflow engine is micro workflow from Manolescu [Man01].

He realized that monolithic workflow systems are not well suited to address the problems of mobile computing. They lack flexibility for an easy integration into other environments. As a solution, he developed micro-workflow as a new generation of "lightweight workflow architectures that can be extended and tailored to particular problems and requirements" [Man01]. He claims that a lightweight architecture is also well suited to deal with unexpected situations and to change workflows at run-time, which targets mostly ad-hoc workflow systems.

Therefore, micro-workflows are ideal to build and enact unplanned processes, respond to context changes and to manage contextual exception situations, see sec-tion 2.5.3, but they can only be used in addition to monolithic workflow systems. Long lasting business processes are out of the scope of such workflow systems:

> The components at the core of the architecture provide basic workflow functionality. Other components implement advanced workflow features. Software developers select the features they need and add the corre-sponding components to the core through composition. [Man01]

The component centered architecture makes it possible to be very dynamic at the level of an activity or a sub-process, but the need for a workflow system running the whole process remains.

Moreover micro-workflow does not solve the issue to use context data in transitions or to use context data at all, see section 2.5.2.

2.6 Voice User Interfaces

The vision of ubiquitous computing will bring many challenges to the future workplace. Tasks get more and more complex which causes an ever increasing need to deliver information to workers. This can be e.g., information from a manual or instructions on how to proceed with the current task. One goal of ubiquitous computing is to deliver information to the worker while she is engaged in her task. Since workers typically have their hands busy while performing their tasks, the use of hands&eyes devices, e.g., mouse and keyboard, will force them to stop working. Use of the acoustic channel does not have this limitation. In addition, the acoustic channel is still functional under extreme cases, e.g., darkness and limited freedom of movement. A headset requires only limited space. Moreover the acoustic channel can be used in addition to other modalities, like conventional screens and buttons. A big drawback of voice is that it becomes unusable in noisy environments. Noise coming from the environment may cause the recognizer to detect unwanted commands and makes it harder for the user to listen to the system output. In this case, graphical interfaces are superior. Nevertheless, in many cases the use of audio has some advantages to be used exclusively or in addition to other interfaces in smart environments.

Interaction with voice user interfaces is different from interaction with graphical user interfaces. This section names the four main concepts of voice based interaction based on the major requirements for voice user interfaces.

These major requirements are specified by ETSI in [ETS00]. Voice based interaction must be

- Easy to learn,

- Easy to remember and

- Natural.

For the speech recognizer it is also important that the commands are acoustically different to reduce recognition errors.

There are four main approaches, also know as *dialog strategy* [CGB04], to use voice as an input medium:

Command & Control In Command & Control environments the application can handle a voice command menu that contains voice commands. This can be used to enable the user controlling the computer without the need of a mouse or keyboard. It also means that the user has to learn a special vocabulary. In general such a special vocabulary has to be developed for each application. Thus, this approach of developing special command sets does not scale. As a consequence companies and researchers started to find multi purpose command sets for several tasks to be solved with voice interfaces. Some command sets exist, like the ones from ETSI [ETS00], fulfilling all of the above mentioned requirements, for example a set of commands to control an audio player

Menu Hierarchy If the user has to provide data that can be gathered through a selection process and the options to be presented to the user are interrelated in a hierarchy, or can be made to appear that way, the application can prompt her with a set of options from which she may choose one.

Form Based This is the simplest and most common type. Form items are executed exactly once in sequential order to collect data from the user as if she was filling out a form. The computer directs the conversation, prompting the user for the next field to be filled.

Mixed Initiative In mixed initiative dialogs, both the computer and the human direct the conversation. The user can speak freely. Input items are set and the corresponding actions are taken in response. This dialog strategy requires natural language understanding (NLU) capabilities, confronting us again with the vision of the computer as a conversational counterpart.

In command & control environments, the user is the active part, controlling the computer by voice. This is why it is also called *user initiative*.

Applications that we find today are most of the kind of menu hierarchy and form based, or a combination of both. In these environments the computer directs the dialog while the user can only react. These dialog strategies are also called *system initiative*.

Some applications using *mixed initiative* exist, but since this requires a higher programming effort (having a direct relation to the money being paid for development) they are not very common. However, this dialog strategy is the most promising to be accepted by users. This is also the one that is the closest to the vision of the homunculus, see section 1.1.

All of these dialog strategies are relevant for smart environments. Especially mixed initiative dialogs can benefit from contextual data. Imagine a visitor of a museum, standing in front of an exhibit. If she wants to get more information about it, she can simply ask *what is this?* The unspecified term this can be filled from the knowledge about the contextual environment. This thesis will not explore the topic of multimodal and federated interaction, but concentrate on voice.

In this thesis you two fundamental terms are used to name user interfaces using the audio channel as their primary communication channel. These are

Definition 12 *Voice User Interfaces (VUI)s are user interfaces using speech input through a speech recognizer and speech output through speech synthesis.*

and

Definition 13 *Audio User Interfaces (AUI)s are an extension to VUIs, allowing also the use of sound as a means to communicate with the user.*

In the past years, the term VUI became more dominant and is also used to talk about AUI. In the rest of this thesis, we follow this trend and use the term VUI in the sense of the definition of AUI.

2.6.1 Limitations of Audio Based User Interfaces

VUIs are particularly difficult to build due to their transient and invisible nature. Unlike visual interfaces, once the commands and actions have been communicated to the user, they "are not there anymore". Another particular aspect of VUI is that the interaction with the user interface is not only affected by the objective limitations of a voice channel, but human factors play a decisive role: auditive and orientation capabilities, attention, clarity, diction, speed and ambient noise (noise coming from the environment).

These aspects can be grouped into the two categories named below. Each of them will be explained in more detail in the following sub sections. Some of them are named in [Mic98].

- Technical Challenges

- Audio inherent Challenges

It can be assumed that the technical problems can be as technical progress is being made. The problems inherent to audio will be impossible to solve completely, but it is important to know them and to find workarounds. A novel approach is introduced in chapter 3.

Technical Challenges

Synthesis quality   The quality of modern text-to-speech engines is still low, although a lot of progress as been made in speech synthesis during the past years. In general, people prefer to listen to pre-recorded audio because it sounds more natural. However, for this to work, the data to be delivered has to be known in advance and recorded as audio, which consumes additional memory. The effort to get pre-recorded audio is high and cost intensive. Too achieve a good quality, a professional speaker is needed and a studio environment to do the recording. For dynamic documents, where the content depends on the user's actions, text-to-speech may be the only feasible solution. As a trade-off it is possible to record only audio snippets and paste them together as needed. A professional speaker is able to produce voice with a similar pitch. Humans are very sensitive in listening and hear this difference in the pitch.

Recognition performance   Speech is not recognized with an accuracy of 100%. Even humans are not able to do that. There will always be some uncertainty in the recognized input which has to be handled somehow. This is different from the experience of developers of graphical user interfaces, where keyboard and mouse input are recognized without any doubts.

Flexibility vs. Accuracy   Speech can have many faces for the same issue and natural language user interfaces must serve many of them. This has a direct impact to recognition accuracy. To illustrate this trade off between flexibility of the interface and its accuracy, consider the following example for entering a date. A flexible interface would allow the user to speak the date in any format the user desires (e.g.,

"March 2nd", "yesterday", "2nd of March 2004", etc.). Another possibility would be to prompt the user individually for each of the components of the date (e.g., "Say the year", "Say the month", etc.). Obviously, the first method is much more flexible for the user but requires much more work from the recognition software (recall that computational power is limited on wearable devices). Additionally it is far more error-prone than the second approach.

Audio inherent Challenges

One-dimensionality The eye is active whereas the ear is passive, i.e. the ear cannot browse a set of recordings in the same way as the eye can scan a screen of text and figures. It has to wait until the information is available, and once received, it is not there anymore.

Transience Listening is controlled by the short term memory. Listening to long utterances has the effect that users forget most of the information that was given at the beginning. This means that speech is not an ideal medium for delivering large amounts of data. Transience has also the effect that users of VUIs often have the problem to stay oriented. They describe a phenomenon, which is called lost in space problem, which is also known in web based application. The lost in space problem will be explored in more detail in section 4.7.1.

Invisibility It is difficult to indicate to the user what actions she may perform and what words and phrases she must say to perform these actions. In contrast to graphical environments, where the means to enable user interaction are directly related to capturing the user input, the presentation of a voice user interface is completely independent to the evaluation of the entered data. Moreover, invisibility may also leave the user with the impression that she does not control the system. Note that there is a difference between *feeling to be* in control and actually *being* in control.

Asymmetry Asymmetry means, that people can speak faster than they type, but can listen much more slowly than they can read. This has a direct influence on the amount of audio data and the information being delivered. This property is extremely useful in the cases, where we have the possibility of using additional displays to supplement the basic audio interface. We can use the displays for delivering information, which is unsuitable for audio due to its length, and focus on using the audio device for interaction and delivering short pieces of information.

2.6.2   Additional Challenges from Smart Environments

The ubiquitous environment poses additional challenges to the voice user interface. Users calling voice applications in telephony environments or using them in a desktop environment have in their hands to look for a quiet place while they are using the interface in order to avoid as much ambient noise as possible. For instance, this is something that cannot be influenced by the system designer. Users on the move in contrast cannot deal like that. They have to use the voice interface in the place they are currently in. This has a direct impact on the performance of the speech recognizer, and vice-versa the user's ability to perceive all the auditory output of the system. In addition to the challenges named in the previous sections designers of voice based applications in ubiquitous environments have to master the following challenges:

Conversation If the user is speaking to another person, or if a person that passes by addresses the user by saying something, the recognizer has no clue to distinguish these utterances to other persons from commands to control the system. In contrast to noisy environments, which is part of the recognition performance challenge, the risk of unwanted triggering of the recognizer is higher, since the user may use words, which are valid input but have the same source.

Privacy Being on the move, other persons may be around the user while she is interaction with the system. Both, audio-input and -output, should be hidden from these persons. In practice this is a problem which is impossible to solve. The only workaround is, not to deliver critical information via mouth & ear devices.

Service availability While the user is walking around, some services may not be available, or even become no more available while they are used. The user has to be informed about the service she may use in a certain moment, since the current context may introduce a new vocabulary that is used to interact with the system. The user has to get notified about this change and about the commands that she may use to control the system.

2.7 Voice User Interfaces for a Workflow Engine

In section 2.2 we stated that *environment or activity* belongs to one of the four categories of context. Workflow engines as they were described in section 2.4 are an ideal execution environment for the tasks that a (mobile) worker has to perform. As pointed out in the previous sections, voice based interaction has significant advantages in mobile settings. In order to use this execution environment efficiently in mobile settings, we have to enable voice based interaction for workflow systems. Currently, there is not much research trying to combine workflow engines and voice user interfaces. Handcrafted solutions have the drawback, that they are labour intensive. A more generic approach can be found in the domain of code generators in smart environments. Generated user interfaces for multimodal applications are beyond the scope of this thesis. This thesis concentrates on the analysis of the challenges that come with the audio domain. Code generators are chosen because they offer a way to use voice based interfaces for a workflow engine, thus being a good candidate for the *Voice Controller* in Figure 2.1.

Code generators try to make use of input and output devices that are available in the environment or which the user carries with her. The interaction with the user has to be adapted to the current device. This implies also the use of different communication channels, or *modalities*, which are used to interact with the user [Bai01]. Voice based communication is also targeted, but more in terms of multimodal applications. Shneiderman names the example of a stock market where a survey result showed, that although trading is done by voice, the visual approach is 10 times more attractive to users [Shn00]. The limits of audio are not well understood and are therefore replaced by the approach to use audio as a complementary modality. Lingam [Lin01] also sees a solution in a complementary use of all available modalities, which is also the common tenor, that voice can only be used as a complementary modality, but not on its own. Because humans are more visually-oriented than aurally, there is much more research being done with a focus on graphical rendering, e.g. layout of forms, than on audio-based interfaces. However, under some circumstances audio is a first class medium, especially for visually impaired people or for workers who do not have their hands and eyes free to interact with the computer.

The community of authors and users of generated interfaces have already discovered the limits of their approach.

> "Using the same user interface for all devices means that the thinnest device will set the limits for the user interface, and unless the user interface is extremely simple, some device categories necessarily will be excluded" [Nyl03].

Gerd Herzog et al. [HKM+03] come to the same conclusion that "it is impossible to exclude all kinds of meaningless data from the language and the design of an interface specification will always be a sort of compromise" [HKM+03].

One of the modalities for which such a compromise has to be found is audio. Its unsolved technical and inherent challenges, as introduced in section 2.6.1. have to be mastered by the interface designer [Shn00]. Due to the fact, that multimodal applications are often considered to have both graphical and audio in- and output capabilities, it is astonishing, that audio-only applications seem to be considered with lower priority.

The development of multimodal applications is complex and time-consuming, since each modality has unique characteristics [May92]. Research and modern development approaches try to solve this by means of declarative markup languages, mostly XML-based. They promise that the same model can be reused for different modalities and output devices [Shu05]. The reusability concerns mainly the so called *business logic* of the application. We use workflow engines to handle the business logic in a reusable and device independent manner. Thus, they should be also ideal to be used with code generators to generate voice user interfaces.

Declarative markup languages typically use the **M**odel-**V**iew-**C**ontroller (MVC) pattern [GHJV92] to decouple model and business logic from representation and user interaction. An overview of the MVC pattern is shown in Figure 2.14. The MVC pattern is a classic design pattern to decouple data, the *model*, from the presentation, the *view*, using the *controller*.

The *model* represents the data and the business rules to access and updates this data. The *view* renders the contents of a model. It accesses the data through the model and specifies how that data should be presented. Since the view is responsible to maintain consistency in its presentation it needs to register for change notifications if the data changes. In addition the view can actively pull the model, when it needs to retrieve the most current data. The *controller* translates interactions with the view into actions to be performed by the model.

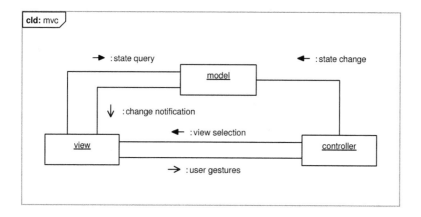

Figure 2.14: The Model-View-Controller pattern

Luyten [Luy04] transformed the MVC concept with his model-based approach to code generators. He distinguishes between *task model* $\mathcal{M}_{\mathcal{T}}$, *presentation model* $\mathcal{M}_{\mathcal{P}}$ and *dialog model* $\mathcal{M}_{\mathcal{D}}$.

Luyten defines task model as follows:

Definition 14 *A **task model** $\mathcal{M}_{\mathcal{T}}$ is a notation to describe the activities, tasks and subtasks that are performed to reach an arbitrary goal and the relations between them. A task model offers a way to structure and represent information about activities, tasks and subtasks and serves as a template for the result of task analysis: task specifications. A task specification $t_i \in \mathcal{M}_{\mathcal{T}}$ is the definition of a presentation using the structure and notation defined in $\mathcal{M}_{\mathcal{T}}$ [Luy04].*

This definition does not contain the business data that can belong to an activity. Relations among task specifications are not sufficient to represent the data flow which is important to give the execution of a task a meaning. Note that we regard only the data flow, not the modelling of data. The ignorance of the data flow may be a reason, why this technology has not been adopted by industry. Therefore we redefine a task model as

Definition 15 *A **task model** $\mathcal{M}_{\mathcal{T}}$ is a notation to describe the activities, tasks and subtasks that are performed to reach an arbitrary goal, the relations between them and the information flow that is needed to reach this goal. A task model offers a way to structure and represent information about activities, tasks, subtasks and their data. It serves as a template for the result of task analysis: task specifications. A task specification $t_i \in \mathcal{M}_{\mathcal{T}}$ is the definition of a presentation using the structure and notation defined in $\mathcal{M}_{\mathcal{T}}$*

In that sense, the definition of a workflow process is a task model.

A dialog model reflects the information flow and how navigation between the tasks is executed.

Definition 16 *A **dialog model** $\mathcal{M}_\mathcal{D}$ is a notation to describe the relations that exists between the set of tasks that are valid at one point in time and the presentation units that represent this set of tasks. A dialog specification $d_i \in \mathcal{D}_\mathcal{M}$ is the definition of a presentation using the structure and notation defined in $\mathcal{M}_\mathcal{D}$. [Luy04].*

A presentation model is the most concrete realization of a user interface.

Definition 17 *A **presentation model** $\mathcal{M}_\mathcal{P}$ is a notation to describe the set of presentation units that occur during the lifetime of a application. A presentation specification $p_i \in \mathcal{M}_\mathcal{P}$ is the definition of a presentation using the structure and notation defined in $\mathcal{M}_\mathcal{P}$. [Luy04].*

A presentation unit is defined as

Definition 18 *A **presentation unit** u groups the concrete realization of the interface(s)(or building blocks) that can be manipulated by the user(s) in a certain well-defined period of time. [Luy04].*

These models can be directly mapped to *model, view* and *controller* of the MVC pattern [GHJV92]. From the MVC perspective, controller and view are responsible for the presentation. The model can be reused for alternative representations. Some UI generators for declarative languages also reuse the controller. Since the controller is tightly coupled with the view, it is debatable if this approach can be successful for different modalities. Others try to generate the dialog model out of the task model [Luy04]. Luyten in fact tries to generate a mapping

$$\mathcal{M}_\mathcal{T} \to \mathcal{M}_\mathcal{D} \tag{2.1}$$

From the MVC point of view the controller serves as a mediator between task model and presentation model, but we doubt that it can be generated from the task model. Since the model contains no clues about the interface this attempt will result in basic interfaces that need further editing. An example for that is the form generator of Microsoft Access that creates a basic form UI from a table. However, the MVC approach seems to be promising, but we still need different dialog models for different modalities. These approaches, like the ones of Paterno and Luyten, are widespread in academic research but not in industry. One reason, besides the known limitations of generated interfaces, is that they primarily focus on the interaction with the user and only some even consider integration into back-end systems, which is a fundamental requirement for the business case. This is the second domain, where the use of workflow systems helps.

We have a closer look at the use of audio in generated interfaces in section 6.3. We investigate how generated user interfaces for audio can be used together with workflow engines as a handler for the task model. Our main focus is how the challenges with audio are reflected in the three models.

2.7.1   Related Work

Chug et al. have reviewed the influence and advantages of voice technologies on existing web and enterprise applications [CJ02]. They introduce an architecture built upon a centralized application server providing services through a CORBA API. One of the supported UIs is a phone-based access via a VoiceXML interpreter.

This architecture has the business logic in CORBA services which are more or less decoupled. The order in which they are used depends on the logic implemented on the client. This means, that parts of the business logic are shifted from the model to the controller. What is missing is a structured way to separate real business logic from presentation logic. Our approach uses a workflow engine to sequence service calls.

In [VR02] Vantroys et al. describe the architecture of a learning platform with a centralized workflow engine. The targeted platforms vary from desktop PCs to mobile phones. Their focus is to transform XML-formatted documents stored in the learning database into a suitable format for the current device, using XSL transformations. Since they use their own proprietary format for the documents this approach is strongly limited. They consider neither a general approach nor the way how users can access the documents. The main disadvantage is that they do not consider user input at all. In addition the approach takes no respect to special limitations of the used device. They stop at transforming into a format that is supported by the target device.

In [MPS04] Mori et al describe an approach called TERESA, where the *Task Model* is being used as a common basis for platform dependent *System Task Models*. In contrast to our approach their task model contains a mix of modality dependent and modality independent tasks. By filtering they then generate a *System Task Model* for each modality. Because of that, the main *Task Model* needs to be a compromise between different modalities. We believe that this approach does not support the design of efficient modality specific dialog models. Mori's Task Model allows the designer to specify targeted platforms and even allows storing dependencies among these platform descriptions. This becomes evident in their discussion of a demo implementation. The VoiceXML-enabled system plays a *grouping sound*, which makes only sense in visual environments. A grouping sound does not provide any information to the user of audio-only interfaces, but is transferred directly from the visual interface without questioning its sense. This is not compliant with our understanding of a model. We store only abstract task descriptions without any relation to possible implementations.

One of the main problems when dealing with (semi-)automatically generated user interfaces is the mapping problem defined by Puerta and Eisenstein [PE98]. The mapping problem is characterized as the problem of "linking the abstract and concrete elements in an interface model". Our goal does not deal with the mapping problem as the creation of modality dependent dialog models is left to the designer.

2.8 Conclusion

This chapter introduced our basic understanding of context-aware computing, workflows and voice user interfaces.

Context is used in the sense of context-aware computing, according to the definition of Dey and Schmidt, where a mobile computer alters its behaviour depending on the user's state and surrounding. Workflows are automations of business processes, which consist of a network of activities. Activities can be either automated or manual, requiring human interaction. Workflow engines which follow the WfMC standard feature several interfaces which can be used for supporting context-aware computing. In particular Interface 2 and Interface 3 are ideal candidates. Afterwards, we listed the requirements to support the mobile worker using a workflow engines that we consider to be important. These requirements enhance the basic functionality of workflow systems by several factors. One important requirement is to use context information in transitions of the workflow process. In the related work we named representatives for the two main streams for the integration of context-awareness and workflow systems. The most prominent example of a distributed workflow system is micro-workflow from Manolescu. His architecture is well suited to fulfill the requirements of a context-aware workflow enactment service, but still needs a workflow enactment service to keep track of long running processes. In this thesis we will concentrate on the second main stream to enable context-aware computing for existing workflow engines. Our focus is on the communication between the workflow engine and the environment, especially the use of context data in transitions, see section 6.2. This concept can also be transferred to micro-workflows, which can be plugged into monolithic workflow engines via Interface 4. The requirements of process adaption using context data remain unsolved in this thesis.

Another focus of this thesis is the design of voice user interfaces. In this chapter an overview is given of the problems that arise when using audio based user interfaces. These are categorized into three categories: audio inherent challenges, technical challenges and ubiquitous computing challenges. Depending on the category the way to master these challenges differs. While technical problems are less severe for higher quality speech recognizers and speech synthesizers, problems inherent to the domain cannot be solved completely. Ubiquitous computing problems are additional problems for the use of audio based interfaces in smart environments.

These challenges will be explored in more detail in the following chapters based on the four main concepts of interaction. Chapter 4 concentrates on command & control environments while chapter 5 focuses on a more general approach to solve these challenges.

After an introduction to speech input and output on mobile devices in chapter 3 we will investigate the use of context data in an audio browser in chapter 4. Workflow systems come back into play in chapter 6 where all aspects workflow systems, context-awareness and voice user interfaces are integrated into a single reference implementation.

Chapter 3

Mobile Speech Recognition

3.1 Motivation

If mobile workers need to access information, such as instructions on how to process a task, the use of audio has many advantages over traditional hands&eyes devices, especially if the user needs his hands to perform a task.

This chapter shows how voice user interfaces can be used in mobile environments. The corresponding part of this chapter is the interface between the mobile worker and the workflow system of the target architecture, introduced in section 1.2. It is shown in figure 3.1. Most theses using speech recognition in ubiquitous computing look at speech recognition as a black box, but this is not sufficient for the the use of speech recognition in enterprise applications. The difficulties that come with the attempt to implement speech recognition in mobile settings are mostly underestimated. In this chapter we look at it in a more general view, discovering that none of the architectures convince in all aspects. As a consequence, we developed our own, more flexible, architecture which is described in section 3.4.

The targeted scenario is as follows. The mobile worker uses a *Microphone* to enter commands while the output is given over a *Speaker*. Both may be part of a simple headset that can be connected over a wireless network to the *Speech Recognizer* and *Speech Synthesizer* on a remote server. Alternatively, the mobile worker is wearing a computer with a local *Speech Recognizer* and a local *Speech Synthesizer*, which are connected over a wireless network with the *Voice Enabled Service* on a remote server.

The organization of this chapter is shown in Figure 3.2. After this motivation section 3.2 gives an overview of the general architecture of a speech recognizer. This is the basis for discussing existing architectures which enable speech recognition for mobile workers in section 3.3. Since existing architectures are not flexible enough to all requirements for mobile worker support, we have developed our own architecture as described in section 3.4. Section 3.5 concludes this chapter with a short summary.

3.2 Speech Recognition

A speech recognizer has the task to transcribe spoken language into a text, see Figure 3.3. The input is the speech signal, human voice that is recorded e.g. with

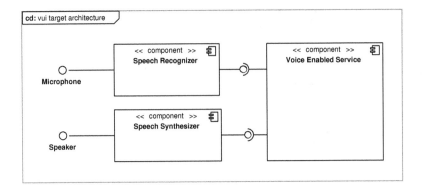

Figure 3.1: Target Architecture to support Voice User Interfaces for Mobile Workers

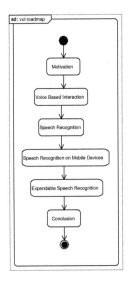

Figure 3.2: Road map to handle Voice User Interfaces

a microphone. The textual output, in this case *one two three*, is called *utterance*.

The architecture of a speech recognizer did not change over the past decades. An overview based on [Jel01] is illustrated in Figure 3.4. The figure shows the main components of recognizers as they are used today, independently of the used technology. They are available as pure software solutions or implemented in hardware to gain speed. Some recognizers may use additional components or components that are slightly different. In the following sections we focus only the main components

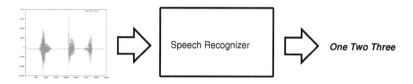

Figure 3.3: Principle of Speech Recognition

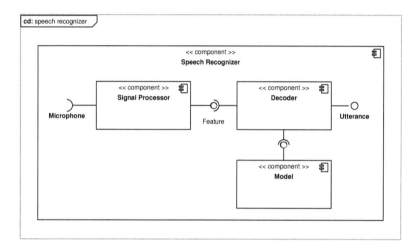

Figure 3.4: Architecture of a speech recognizer according to [Jel01] with own modifications

involved showing the main functionalities of each of them and discussing the main challenges that have to be faced, when it is applied to mobile devices.

The *Signal Processor* generates real valued vectors σ_i out of a speech signal, obtained i.e. from a microphone. These vectors are also called the *features* and represent the characteristics of a speech signal. Currently, most speech recognizers use at least 13 features in each vector. We will have a closer look at them in section 3.3.4. Normally computation of the features happens at regular intervals, e.g. every 10msec where the feature vectors are passed to the *Decoder* to convert it into the utterance. The *Decoder* uses the *Model* for decoding. In the simplest case, the *Model* contains a set of prototypes ρ_i, which are of the same kind as σ_i. Then, the *Decoder* finds the ρ_i closest to σ_i for a given distance function d.

$$a_i = min_{j=1}^k d(\sigma_i, \rho_j) \tag{3.1}$$

a_i is the acoustic symbol for σ_i, which is emitted to the rest of the recognizer for further processing.

For *word based speech recognizers* these acoustic symbols are the single words. For the example shown in Figure 1, this would be the concatenation of $\{a_1 = \text{one}, a_2 = \text{two}, a_3 = \text{three}\}$.

A *phoneme based speech recognizer* would output a concatenation of phonemes for each word. Phonemes are small sound units, e.g. the word *this* comprises the following phonemes $\{a_1 = \text{TH}, a_2 = \text{I}, a_3 = \text{S}\}$. Obviously this output requires some post processing to obtain an output comparable to word based recognizers that can be used by an application. The benefit of phoneme based speech recognizers is that they are generally more accurate, since they reduce the decoding problem to small sound units. Hence they are more flexible and can handle a larger vocabulary more easily. Remember the first attempts in writing, starting with symbols for each word over symbols for each syllable to the letters that we find today.

3.3   Speech Recognition on Mobile Devices

Speech recognition is computationally expensive. The advancements in computing power made speech recognition possible on off-the-shelf desktop PCs beginning in the early 90s. Mobile devices do not have that computing power and speech recognizers do not run in real time. There are even more limitations which will be discussed later in this section. Kathy Frostad writes in [Fro03] about this issue:

> "Most of what is written on speech is focused on server based speech processing. But there is another speech technology out there that's powerful enough to sit on a stamp-sized microchip. It's called "embedded speech". Advancements in computing power gave server side speech the power boost it needed in the early 90s. Now that same rocket fuel is launching embedded speech into the limelight."

Moore's law confirms this expectation stating that, memory size and computational performance increase by a factor of two every 18 months. Although computing power also increases on these smaller computers, making it possible to run small recognizer, performance is still not efficient enough to speech recognizers off-the-shelf on such devices. The attempt to use speech recognition on a mobile device, such as a computer of PDA size or a mobile phone, encounters the same problems, which have been faced on desktop PCs, years ago and which have been solved by the growth of computing power. The following section gives an overview of these limitations.

This leads to our understanding of a mobile device [Bai04].

Definition 19 *A **mobile device** is a device, that is specifically designed to be used while being carried.*

Note that Laptops or Tablet PCs do not belong to this category, since they require the user to sit down and use this device exclusively. Sometimes another term is used also in this context.

Definition 20 *An **embedded device** is part of another device with limited computational and interaction capabilities.*

The difference of mobile devices to embedded devices becomes more and more blurred, since these devices feature increasing computational power. We use these terms interchangeably.

3.3.1 Limitations of Embedded Devices

The development of all applications, especially speech recognition applications, for embedded devices has to tackle several problems, which deal with the computational limitations and hardware resources on the device. These limitations are:

Memory Memory Storage Capacity on embedded devices, such as a PDA or a cell phone, is very limited. This makes it impossible to have large *Models*.

Computational power Although the computational power of embedded devices has continuously grown over the last years, it is still far from that what is available at desktop size PCs. The *Signal Processor* and the *Decoder* perform computationally intense tasks.

Power consumption Battery lifetime is a scarce resource on embedded devices. The device will stop working, if the battery is empty. Since speech recognition is computationally intensively, the processing consumes a lot of energy.

Floating point Most processors for PDAs, like the Strong ARM or XScale processor, do not support floating-point arithmetic. It has to be emulated by fix point arithmetic, which is a lot slower than the direct support. The value vectors σ_i are real valued and most state-of-the-art recognizers work with statistical methods. Thus, support of floating point arithmetic is essential and emulation results in loss of speed. Moreover, this may lead to a loss of precision. Especially signal processing is a critical task, since the quality of the output has a direct impact on the preserved information. Jelinek states in [Jel01] that "bad processing means loss of information: There is less of it to extract".

In the following the approaches to work around these limitations will be discussed. A short overview of the used technology is given to understand how they cope with the challenges of embedded devices.

3.3.2 Main Architectures for Speech Recognition on Mobile Devices

Progress in speech recognition has made it possible to have it on embedded devices. Cohen states in [Coh04]:

> "Although we did not know in the 1990s all of the tricks we know today, we can use 1990s-like computing resources ... to good advantage to compute a task which would have been difficult in 1990, but is simpler today because of our technical advancements."

However, the limitations of mobile devices that were introduced in the previous section still pose a lot of challenges. There have been several attempts to deal with them and enable speech recognition on embedded devices. An overview of these approaches is given in the following sections. This list is not exclusive. We concentrate on the most common approaches that can be divided into two main categories:

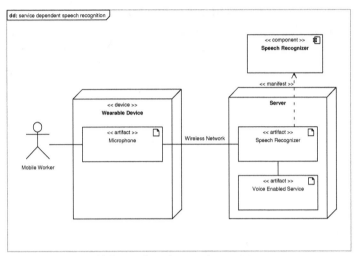

(a) Service dependent speech recognition

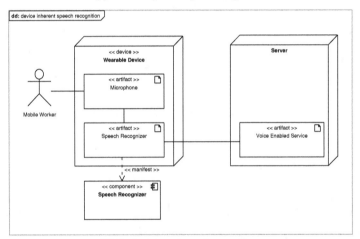

(b) Device inherent speech recognition

Figure 3.5: Deployment of voice enabled service usage with mobile devices

- service dependent speech recognition, figure 3.5(a)

- device inherent speech recognition, figure 3.5(b)

The main difference between these two architectures is the node, where the Speech Recognizer component is deployed. Architectures for service dependent speech recognition will be introduced in section 3.3.4 and those for device inherent speech recognition in section 3.3.5.

Zaykovskiy proposed another categorization [Zay06]. He distinguishes

- Client,

- Client-server, and

- Server-based architectures.

The main reason for his differentiation is the location of the *Signal Processor* and the *Decoder*. In the service oriented view of ubiquitous computing it makes more sense to emphasize the ability to have speech recognition as a network service or as an independent functionality of the device itself. This is a fundamental fact in smart environments, where services can be inaccessible while the user is on the move. Bailey [Bai04] requires that

> "...there need to be clear boundaries between the functionality of the device, and the functionality of the network".

The technological orientation of these approaches confirms this differentiation. Whereas service dependent speech recognition deal with APIs for remote access to a speech recognizer, device inherent speech recognition uses the techniques of desktop size speech recognition technology to enable speech recognition on the device itself.

3.3.3 Parameters of Speech Recognizers in UC

In order to rate the different architectures, we need an understanding about the core parameters. This section will give a short overview of these parameters.

Speaking Mode Word boundaries are not easy to detect. The presence of pauses is not enough, since they may not be present. Early speech recognizers forced the user to make a pause after each word. This is called isolated word recognition. If there are no such constraints, the speech recognizer is able to process continuous speech.

Speaking Style This parameter state, if a speech recognizer for continuous speech is able to process read speech, meaning a very precise and clear pronunciation, or if it is capable to process spontaneous speech, as we use it if we talk to each other.

Enrollment Some speech recognizers require an initial training before it can be used. This training is used to adapt to the speaker in order to achieve higher accuracy. Recognizers requiring an initial training are called speaker dependent. This concept is often used on desktop PCs, but is also possible in UC, where the device is personalized. The opposite case is speaker independent speech recognizers that are trained to work with multiple speakers. Thus they have a lower accuracy. This concept is used e.g., in telephony applications. There are only few scenarios that really require speaker independence with embedded devices. For these applications, speaker-independent systems do not have an advantage over speaker-dependent systems, but can benefit from a better accuracy.

Vocabulary The size of the vocabulary is one of the most important factors, since this strongly influences the way how users can interact with the application. A vocabulary is said to be small if it contains up to 20 words. A large vocabulary may contain over 20,000 words.

Perplexity Perplexity defines the number of words that can follow a word. This is an important factor if the recognizer has to decode an utterance consisting of multiple words and tries to find the path with the lowest error rate.

SNR SNR is the acronym of Signal-to-Noise-Ratio. It is defined as the ratio of a given transmitted signal to the background noise of the transmission medium. This typically happens where the microphone captures also some noise from the background which does not belong to the signal to decode.

Transducer A transducer is the device converting the speech into a digital representation. For speech recognition the transducer may be e.g. a noise-cancelling headset or telephone. Since each of them feature different characteristics, like the available bandwidth of the voice data or the ability to cut background noise like it is done with a noise cancelling headset. In UC environments noise-cancelling headsets are typically used.

In a UC world, there are some additional parameters, depending on the location, where recognition takes place. These parameters, as presented in [Bai04], are

Network dependency One major aspect is the dependency to a network resource. A recognizer located on the device will not need any network to be operated, while a recognizer streaming raw audio data to a server, see section Audio Streaming, will not work without a network. Apart from the technical aspect, the user expects the device to work and may not be able to distinguish between a non-functional recognizer and missing network connectivity if the device is *broken*.

Network bandwidth Available network bandwidth is a scarce resource. Architectures performing the recognition on the device have a more compact representation of the data that has to be transmitted than those architectures streaming pure audio data.

Transmission degradation With the need to transmit data from the mobile device to a server, the problem of transmission degradation arises. Failures, loss of packets or corrupted packets, while transmitting the data mean a loss of information. If the raw audio is transmitted to a server, recognition accuracy goes down.

Server load In a multi-user scenario it is important that the application scales with an increasing number of users.

Integration and Maintenance Embedded devices are hard to maintain, especially if parts of the functionality is implemented in hardware. A server, on the other hand, is easy to access and bug fixes are available for all clients at once. This issue goes into a similar direction as the discussion of centralized server architectures versus rich clients.

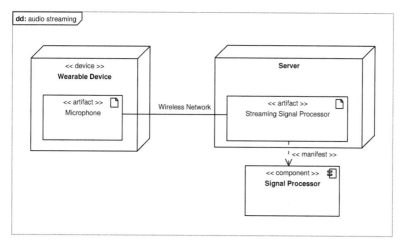

Figure 3.6: Architecture of an audio streaming speech recognizer

Responsiveness A must for speech recognition is, that the result is available in real-time. This means, that the result of the recognition process must be available as fast as possible.

In the following sections, the different architectures will be characterized according to these parameters.

3.3.4 Service Dependent Speech Recognition

The architectures presented in this section have in common, that they require network connectivity to work.

Audio Streaming

An immediate idea to solve the performance bottleneck on embedded devices is not to perform the recognition process on the device itself. A general model of the recognizer, shown in Figure 3.3.4, uses the audio recording capabilities of the embedded device as microphone replacement to record the raw audio as the input for the *Signal Processor*.

The audio is streamed over the Wireless Network, e.g. WLAN or Bluetooth, to the *Signal Processor* on a server. This allows using a full-featured recognizer with a large vocabulary running on the server. A disadvantage of this solution is that a stable wireless network connection is required. Another disadvantage is a possibly very large amount of data streamed over the network. Since recognition is not performed on the embedded device, we have all the benefits of a desktop-size speech recognizer at the cost of high network traffic.

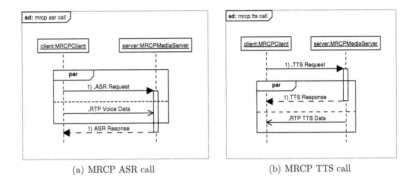

(a) MRCP ASR call   (b) MRCP TTS call

Figure 3.7: Simplified view on MRCP requests for ASR and TTS

MRCP

Since server side speech recognition is mainly an immediate idea, developers tend to implement this architecture on their own using a proprietary protocol, making it unusable with other applications that do not know anything about that proprietary protocol. In addition, real time issues are generally not considered which can result in misrecognition. A standard for server side speech recognition that has been adopted by industry is MRCP. MRCP is an acronym for **M**edia **R**esource **C**ontrol **P**rotocol. It was jointly developed by Cisco Systems, Nuance Communications and Speechworks and was published by IETF as a RFC [SME06].

MRCP is designed as an API to enable clients control media processing resources over a network to provide a standard for audio streaming. Media processing resources can be speech recognizers, text-to-speech engines, fax, signal detectors and more. This allows for a use in distributed environments, e.g. a small device that accesses a recognizer on the network. The specification is based on RTSP in Schulzrinne [SRL98], the **R**eal **T**ime **S**treaming **P**rotocol, as a MIME-type the **M**ultipurpose **I**nternet **M**ail **E**xtension. MIME is used to support e.g. no-text attachments in e-mail messages. RTSP defines requests, responses, and events needed to control the media processing resources. The protocol itself is text based. Mechanisms for the reliable exchange of binary data are left to protocols like SIP, the **S**ession **I**nitiation **P**rotocol, or RTSP. SIP enables control of sessions, like Internet telephone calls.

A media server that can be accessed by RTSP mechanisms controls all resources, in this case, recognizer and synthesizer. Figure 3.7(a) shows a simplified view on the messages that are exchanged in a **A**utomatic **S**peech **R**ecognition (ASR) request and Figure 3.7(b) a **T**ext **t**o **S**peech (TTS) request.

In an ASR request, the MRCP client initiates the request and delivers the voice data via RTP in parallel. The recognition process is executes on the MRCP Media Server and the result of the recognition is delivered to the client as the ASR Response. In a TTS request, the MRCP client initiates the request. The MRCP Media Server answers with a TTS response and delivers the synthesized voice data

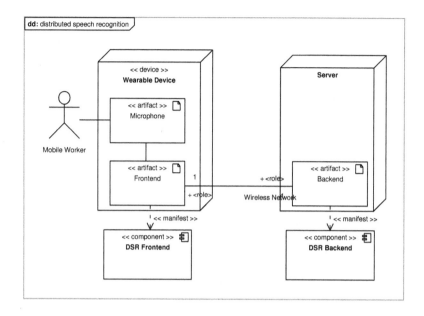

Figure 3.8: Architecture of a distributed speech recognizer

via RTP in parallel.

The architecture does not differ much from the one discussed in section 3.3.4, since the benefit from using MRCP is the use of a standardized protocol to use server side speech recognition and synthesis. This also means that it has the same features, but recognition can be used in other environments, if they use this standard. The protocol poses some minor additional computation requirements to the device and network resources. A further advantage of MRCP is that the offered service can be used by other applications, too (as long as they support the standard).

Distributed Speech Recognition

Another possibility to enable speech recognition on mobile devices deals with an architectural compromise. Since full-featured recognizers are hard to implement on embedded devices and streaming of raw audio data produces too much network traffic, ETSI [Pea00b], the European Telecommunication Standards Institute, introduced a solution to perform parts of the recognition process on the device and the rest is handled on a server. This architecture is called **D**istributed **S**peech **R**ecognition (DSR). Pearce named in [Pea00b] the component, which is deployed on the device the *DSR Frontend* and the component deployed on the server the *DSR Backend*. The concept of distributed speech recognition is shown in Figure 3.8.

An obvious point for such a splitting is the separation of *Signal Processor* and *Decoder*. Instead of sending the whole audio over the network, the feature vectors

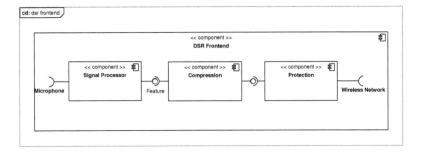

Figure 3.9: DSR Frontend

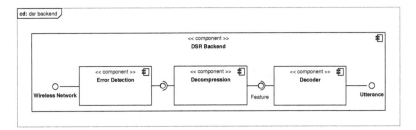

Figure 3.10: DSR Backend

are computed on the embedded device and sent to the Decoder on a server. In order to reduce the amount of data and to ensure a secure transmission, the data is compressed and a CRC value is added. The architecture of the DSR Frontend is shown in Figure 3.9.

The DSR Backend, shown in Figure 3.10, checks the CRC value and decompresses the data, before it is passed to the *Decoder*.

This way, the computational capabilities of the device are used for the tasks of the *Signal Processor* in the *DSR Frontend*, whereas the *Decoder* and the *Model* reside on the server in the *DSR Backend*. The architecture is a result of a discussion of multiple companies, i.e. Nokia and Motorola in the Aurora project. The data exchange of DSR Frontend and DSR Backend is standardized by ETSI. This specification includes the used features, CRC check and their compression. Compared to the pure audio streaming, the transmitted data is reduced without much loss of information. This also means that the error rates in transmission are reduced. As a positive consequence, DSR also works with lower signal strength, as shown in Figure 3.11. The experiment was conducted in the Aurora project and published in [Pea00a]. The figure shows the recognition performance of DSR compared to a mobile speech channel. The measurement was made in the Aurora project. It proves that recognition still works with lower signal quality. A great advantage of this technology over streaming solutions like Audio Streaming or MRCP is the

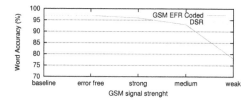

Figure 3.11: Performance of DSR with channel errors according to [Pea00a]

reduced network traffic. Like MRCP it defines a standard, but with fewer acceptances. Speech recognition can be used in various environments, as long as they are compliant to the DSR standard. Unlike MRCP it relies on the computation on the device, decreasing its chances to be established in a company network in contrast to a pure protocol. Again, the recognition has all features of a desktop size recognizer.

As a negative point, the set of feature vectors was a compromise. This means also, that other features, used in specific recognizers cannot be transmitted using this technology.

ETSI promises a better use of available resources and better transmission. The following section gives some insight into the computational requirements.

Evaluation on Sphinx 3.5 Sphinx is an open source speech recognizer from Carnegie Mellon University. It was DARPA funded and was used in many research projects around speech recognition. The anatomy of Sphinx can be divided into 3 phases:

1. Front-end processing,

2. Gaussian probability estimation, and

3. Hidden Markov evaluation.

The Gaussian phase and the HMM phase are part of the *Decoder*. A closer look at it is given in section 3.3.5. Mathew [MDF02] gives an overview of the time, which Sphinx 3.5 spends on each phase, see Figure 3.12. Obviously, the front-end processing constitutes the smallest part of the computation to be performed. This shows that this is an ideal candidate to be performed by smaller devices, as it is done with DSR. Consequently, Mathew consider it to be not worthy for further investigation, stopping their analysis at this point. He focuses more on the optimization of the latter two phases.

Front-end processing comprises usually the computational steps shown in figure 3.13. The following paragraphs show how these steps are handled in Sphinx. A more general view can be found in the literature e.g., in [ST95].

Processing starts with a speech signal, as it is captured e.g. from a microphone. An example of such a speech signal is shown as the input to the speech recognizer in Figure 3.3. The transformation into a digital representation, also called *quantization*, means also a loss of information, but which can not be avoided.

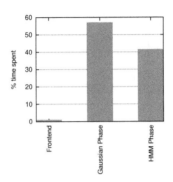

Figure 3.12: Profile information of Sphinx 3.5 phases according to [MDF02]

Figure 3.13: Front-end processing

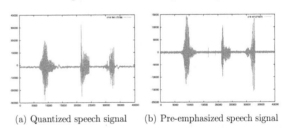

(a) Quantized speech signal   (b) Pre-emphasized speech signal

Figure 3.14: Pre-emphasis of the speech signal

Pre-Emphasis In this step the quantized signal is filtered. This step becomes necessary from the observation, that the signal is weaker in higher frequencies, which can be solved using a digital high-pass filter:

$$f'_n = f_n - \alpha f_{n-1} \tag{3.2}$$

Values for α are in the range of $[0.80, \ldots, 0.95]$. Figure 3.14(b) shows an example of the speech signal and the effect of this filtering step.

Framing The input signal is divided into overlapping frames of N samples. The

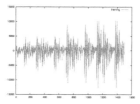

Figure 3.15: Framing of the speech signal

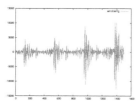

Figure 3.16: Hamming window

frame shift interval, i.e. the difference between the starting points of consecutive frames, is M samples.

Windowing The **F**ast **F**ourier **T**ransformation (FFT) is known from the domain of signal processing to compute the spectrum of a signal. FFT requires a periodical signal, it is assumed that the time segment continues periodical. Since speech is changing over time, we try to get segments of the signal f_n, where it can consider being constant. These time segments last 5-30 ms. With

$$f_n'' = f_n' * w(n) \tag{3.3}$$

the signal apart from the current window is faded out and f_n'' is a weighted modification of f_n'. An example for such a windowing function w is the *Hamming Window*

$$w_n = 0.54 - 0.46 \cos(\frac{2\pi n}{N-1}) \tag{3.4}$$

The following figure shows four of such time segments of the utterance. It is noticeable, that the signal is smoothed to the borders of the time segments.

Power Spectrum For speech recognition, the discrete case of the FFT, the *Discrete Fourier Transformation* (DFT) is used. The spectrum at time m is computed via a DFT:

$$F_n = \sum_{n=0}^{N-1} f_n e^{\frac{-2\pi i M n}{N}} \tag{3.5}$$

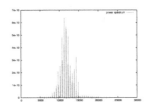

Figure 3.17: Power spectrum

We assume that the window continues periodically, which means $f_n = f_{n+jN}$. Regions with a positive energy can be found at $f_A \frac{k}{N}, k = 0, \pm 1, \pm 2, \ldots$.

The output of the DFT consists of, usually a power of 2, complex numbers. The power spectrum is computed by its squared magnitude of these complex numbers.

$$S_n = (\text{real}(F_n))^2 + (\text{imag}(F_n))^2 \tag{3.6}$$

The following figure shows the power spectrum for the word one of the utterances.

Mel Spectrum The next step is a filtering step to filter the input spectrum through individual filters. One of these filters is the Mel filter.

$$\text{mel}_l(\nu) = 2595 \log(1 + \frac{\nu}{700}) \tag{3.7}$$

An idea of this filter is shown in the following figure.

The Mel spectrum of the power spectrum is computed by multiplying the power spectrum by each of the L triangular Mel weighting filters and integrating the result

$$\tilde{S}_n = \sum_{k=0}^{\frac{N}{2}} S_n mel_l(k) \tag{3.8}$$

The output is an array of filtered values, typically called Mel-spectrum, each corresponding to the result of filtering the input spectrum through an individual filter. Therefore, the length of the output array is equal to the number of filters created.

Mel Cepstrum Davis (1980) showed that Mel-frequency cepstral coefficients present robust characteristics that are good for speech recognition. The artificial word cepstrum is obtained by reversing the letter order in spectrum to emphasize that this is an inverse transformation. These cepstral coefficients are computed via a discrete cosine transform.

A discrete cosine transform is used to obtain the Mel cepstrum

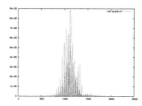

Figure 3.18: Mel spectrum

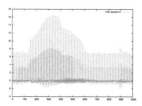

Figure 3.19: Mel cepstrum

$$c_n = \sum_{i=0}^{L-1} \ln(\tilde{S}(i)) \cos(\frac{\pi n}{2L}(2i + 1)) \qquad (3.9)$$

Sphinx uses 16bit raw audio data as input and produces 13 cepstral parameters as output for each time segment. In order to determine the execution time consumption by individual parts of Sphinx, we used a profiling tool to get detailed information on functions and routines on a Sparc processor based platform. The profiling was done with three audio files of different lengths as input:

1. Short (2.05 sec),

2. Medium (6.02 sec), and

3. Long (30.04 sec).

The profiling result is shown in Figure 3.20.

Obviously, the computation of the power spectrum, which comprises the methods *fft*, and *spec magnitude*, consume most of the time. Both are part of the power spectrum computation. Tuning this method can speed up the computation a lot. Alternatively, it can be replaced by a hardware solution, like a **D**igital **S**ignal **P**rocessor (DSP). This issue will also be addressed in section 3.3.5.

The process becomes more complicated if the device does not support floating-point operations. Junqua mentions, "While most automatic speech recognition systems for PC use are based on floating-point algorithms, most of the processors used in embedded systems are fixed-point processors. With fixed-point processors there

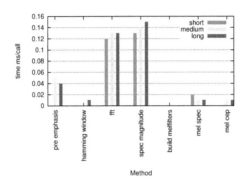

Figure 3.20: Profile information of sphinx 3.5 front-end

is only a finite amount of arithmetic precision available, causing an inevitable deviation from the original design" [Jun00]. A study by Delaney [DJH+02] showed that for Sphinx 2 a Strong ARM simulator spent over 90% of the time on the floating-point emulation. These results can be transferred to Sphinx 3.5, since they use the same code base for front-end processing.

A way to solve these issues is to substitute floating-point arithmetic by fixed-point arithmetic. This is done using scaled integers to perform basic math functions. The scaling factor, i.e. the location of the decimal point, must be known in advance and requires careful decision. For adding two numbers, the number n of bits after the decimal point must line up. A multiplication of two numbers yields a number with $2n$ bits after the decimal point.

Unfortunately, this also means a loss of information and the risk to overflow the register size of 32 bits. This is especially important for the computation of the power spectrum (3.6) and the Mel spectrum. Delaney suggests in [DJH+02] changing the computation for the Mel spectrum (3.8) using a square root to compute the Mel coefficients.

$$\tilde{S}_n = \sum_{k=0}^{\frac{N}{2}} (S_n \sqrt{\text{mel}_l(k)})^2 \tag{3.10}$$

It is guaranteed, that the square root $\sqrt{\text{mel}_l(k)} \ll 1$ results in small values that means that the result of multiplication is small. They also suggest storing the Mel coefficients in a lookup table to avoid the computationally complex calculations of the square root. An experiment conducted in Huggins [HDKC+05] showed that feature extraction on a Sharp Zaurus had a 2.7-fold gain in speed using this method. The loss in precision for the result in computing the Mel Cepstrum increased from 9.73% to 10.06%.

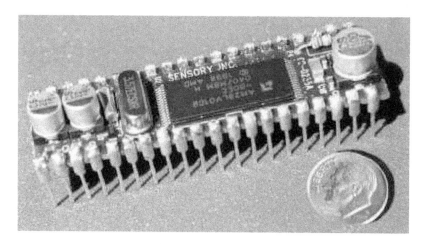

Figure 3.21: Sensory voice recognition module

3.3.5 Device Inherent Speech Recognition

In contrast to the architectures described above, those described in this section are handled on the device only, without the need for a server or service from the network. These architectures are also often referred to as *software-only* and *embedded architectures* [Eag99, Fro03]. Embedded architectures are requiring the existence of a dedicated DSP. They reside as hardware based speech recognition, since the term embedded is totally overloaded with the meanings of a DSP, an embedded device or embedded into an application. So this architecture does not deal only with software-based architectures, but also include partial or full support with hardware.

Hardware based Speech Recognition

Some manufacturers offer designated chips for mobile devices. An example of such a chip is shown in Figure 3.21. The technology that is used in these chips differs. All software based speech technologies for device inherent speech recognition, as described in the following sections, can be found implemented as a port to a DSP. It is even possible to replace just certain parts of the recognizer, e.g. the FFT computation for the feature extraction in DSR, with a hardware solution. The main advantage is that a hardware-based solution does not have the runtime problems of software-based approaches, since the hardware is designed to address this specific problem. This is gained at the cost of less flexibility. The range of hardware implementations is as broad as the underlying technology. It starts from a fixed vocabulary used in toys over Dynamic Time Warping, the technology used in most mobile phones, up to programmable DSPs like the Sensory chip shown in Figure 3.21.

Advantages and drawbacks of these solutions are not discussed in this section, since they are inherited from the used technology. Benefits and drawbacks of the architectures are discussed in the corresponding sections.

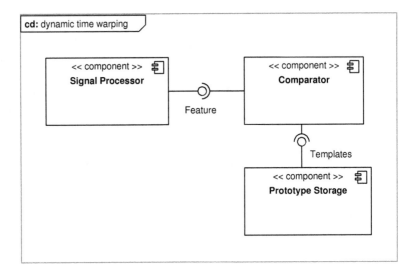

Figure 3.22: Architecture of a DTW speech recognizer.

Dynamic Type Warping

One of the earliest approaches to enable speech recognition is the **D**ynamic **T**ime **W**arping (DTW). The architecture is shown in Figure 3.22.

The *Signal Processor* is responsible for the feature analysis of the raw speech signal. The computational steps are the same as the front-end processing of DSR refer to Figure 3.13. An output of the feature analysis component is a feature vector of a test utterance $\sigma = (\sigma_1, \ldots \sigma_n)^T$ which is compared in the *Comparator*, which replaces the *Decoder*, with all reference feature vectors $\rho_i = (\rho_{i,1}, \ldots, \rho_{i,m})^T$ stored in the *Prototype Storage*, replacing the *Model*, of the utterances in the set of trained utterances with the help of a distance function that was already mentioned in section 3.2. Usually the prototypes are gained in a single recording. The features of this recording are computed, stored in the *Prototype Storage* and associated with the output. If the distance of the currently spoken word to the template is too big $d(t, r_i) > \theta$, it is likely, that no prototype matches the utterance. In this case, the comparator rejects the input.

The problem of calculating the distance from σ to ρ_i with the help of a distance function $d(\sigma, \rho_i)$ consists of two parts:

- Definition of a distance function to calculate the distance of two related feature vectors

- Definition of a time warping function to define a relationship between the elements of ρ and σ_i

Multiple distance functions exist and are used. For a Gaussian distribution the Mahalanobis distance is used.

Multiple distance functions exist and are used. For a Gaussian distribution the Mahalanobis distance is used

$$d = \sum_{i=1}^{n} (\rho - \sigma)^T K^{-1} (\rho - \sigma) \qquad (3.11)$$

with K being an estimate for the covariance matrix of a feature vector.

Since this one is complex and we do not have much computational resources on the device, the Euklidean distance is more common.

$$d = \sum_{i=1}^{n} (\rho_i - \sigma_i)^2 = (\rho - \sigma)^T (\rho - \sigma) \qquad (3.12)$$

This requires that the features are normed to unity variance.

The problem with a pair wise distance calculation is that it is unlikely that the lengths of the template and of the input are the same, e.g. the length of the o in *word* may vary. DTW uses **D**ynamic **P**rogramming (DP) to find an optimal match between two sequences of feature vectors allowing for stretching and compression of sections, see [SC90].

The minimal warping cost can be found by

$$d(i, j) = d + \min(d_{i-1,j-1}, d_{i-1,j}, d_{i,j-1}) \qquad (3.13)$$

The template word having the least distance, satisfying equation (3.1), is taken as a correct match, if it's value is smaller than a predetermined threshold value θ.

The technique of comparison with a template word makes this an ideal candidate for isolated word recognition with a small vocabulary, but unsuitable for continuous speech. Since the templates are generally taken on a single recording, DTW is also speaker dependent with small computational effort. The computational requirements are slightly above those for DSR, see section 3.3.4, but smaller than Hidden Markov Models, next section, or Artificial Neural Networks, section 3.3.5.

Hidden Markov Models

Most modern speech recognizers are based on **H**idden **M**arkov **M**odels (HMM). An overview of the architecture of a HMM based recognizer is shown in Figure 3.23, which is in fact a phoneme-based recognizer. It is also possible to use HMM based recognition for word-based models. In this case, the architecture is slightly different as Schukat-Talamazzini [ST95] points out. More about the basics of Markov chains and their use can be obtained from the literature e.g., Rabiner [Rab89]. Although this approach is very old, it is still the most successful approach for speech recognition.

Instead of using the computed features as a seed for the states, most recognizers use **V**ector **Q**uantization (VQ) to reduce the data rate. Since speech recognition deals with a continuous signal, a certain amount of data arrives periodically. This is called the data rate. Since HMM decoding is time consuming, a lower data rate promises real time performance. Furthermore, the storage size is reduced, since only

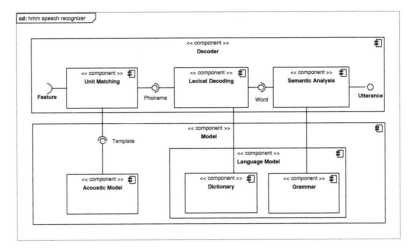

Figure 3.23: Architecture of a HMM based recognizer

the codebook is stored instead of the cepstral parameters. A codebook stores the mapping of the feature vectors as they are computed from the speech signal to a discrete label. Thus the codebook is a discrete representation of the continuous speech data.

The most common one is the K-means clustering algorithm [RJ93]. VQ calculates the distance between each vector of the codebook $C = \{c_1, c_2, \ldots, c_m\}$ and each input vector f_i using

$$d(f_i, c_j) = \sum_{k=1}^{K} (f_{ik} - c_{jk})^2 \tag{3.14}$$

where f_{ik} is the k-th element of the input vector of size K and c_{jk} is the j-th element of the codebook vector.

Unit Matching HMMs are the core of the Unit Matching component. They are described as a tuple $\lambda = (S, A, B, \pi, V)$ with

- $S = s_1, \ldots, s_n$ representing a set of states,

- $A = a_{ij}$ representing a matrix of transition probabilities, where a_{ij} denotes the probability $p(s_j, s_i)$ for the transition from state s_i to s_j,

- $B = b_1, \ldots, b_n$ representing a set of output probabilities, where $b_i(x)$ denotes the probability $q(x|s_i)$ to observe x in state s_i, and

- O as a set of observations, which means the domain of b_i.

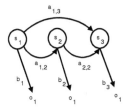

Figure 3.24: Schematic overview of a Hidden Markov Model

A schematic view on a HMM is given in Figure 3.24.
The probability of observing an output sequence $O = O_1 O_2 \ldots O_T$ is given by

$$P(O_1, O_2, \ldots, O_T) = \sum_{s_1, s_2, \ldots, s_T} \prod_{i=1}^{T} p(s_i | s_{i-1}) q(x_i | s_{i-1}) \tag{3.15}$$

Rabiner poses three basic questions in [Rab89], which are to be solved for speech recognition with HMMs.

1. Given the observation sequence $O = O_1 O_2 \ldots O_T$ and a model λ, how do we efficiently compute $P(O|\lambda)$, the probability of the observation sequence, given the model?

2. For decoding, the question to solve is given the observation sequence $O = O_1 O_2 \ldots O_T$ and the model λ how we choose a corresponding state sequence $Q = s_1, s_2 \ldots s_T$ which is optimal in some meaningful sense (i.e. best 'explains' the observations)?

3. How do we adjust the model parameters λ to maximize $P(O|\lambda)$?

The first problem is also known as the evaluation problem, but it can also be treated as a scoring problem. In that case, the solution to this problem allows choosing the model which best explains the observations.
The third problem tries to optimize the model parameters to describe a given observation sequence as good as possible. This optimization can be used to train the model. Training means to adapt the model parameters to observed training data.
The most important one for speech recognition is the second problem, since it tries to find the "correct" state sequence.
A well-known approach to this is the Viterbi Algorithm, based on DP to find the most likely sequence of hidden states. A more detailed description, related to speech recognition, can be found in the literature, e.g. [Jel01, RJ93], The Viterbi Algorithm tries to find the best score, which means the highest probability, along a single path at time t, also known as *trellis*.

$$\delta_t(i) = \max_{q_1, q_2, \ldots, q_{t-1}} P(q_1, q_2, \ldots, q_t = i, O_1 O_2 \ldots O_t | \lambda) \tag{3.16}$$

The algorithm is initialized with

$$\delta_1(j) = \pi_i b_i(O_1) \tag{3.17a}$$

$$\Psi_1(i) = 0 \tag{3.17b}$$

and uses recursion to find a solution for equation (3.16).

$$\delta_t(j) = \max_{1 \le i \le n} (\delta_{t-1}(i)a_{ij})b_j(o_t) \tag{3.18a}$$

$$\Psi_t(j) = \operatorname*{argmax}_{1 \le i \le n} (\delta_{t-1}(i)a_{ij} \tag{3.18b}$$

Recursion stops if

$$\hat{P} = \max_{1 \le i \le n} \delta_T(i) \tag{3.19a}$$

$$\hat{q}_T = \operatorname*{argmax}_{1 \le i \le n} \delta_T(i) \tag{3.19b}$$

The path can be determined by backtracking

$$\hat{q}_t = \Psi_{t+1}(\hat{q}_{t+1}), t = T - 1, T - 2, \dots, 1 \tag{3.20}$$

Then, the optimal sequence is $\hat{Q} := \hat{q}_T, \hat{q}_{T-1}, \dots, \hat{q}_1$ with the probability given in equation (3.19a).

Computational Optimizations   The Viterbi algorithm is computationally intensive, especially for larger vocabularies. It requires roughly $\|A_u\|n$ multiplications and additions, where $\|A_u\|$ is the number of transitions in the model [BGGM93]. In order not to search the entire Viterbi trellis, the number of branch-out search candidates can be limited using beam-search as Lowerre [Low76] points out.

The idea is to eliminate all states s_k from the trellis that have a probability above a certain threshold, which depends on the maximum probability of the states at this stage.

$$\delta_{i-1}(s_k) < \frac{\max_s \delta_{i-1}(s)}{K} \tag{3.21}$$

$\max_s \delta_{i-1}(s)$ is the maximum probability of the states at stage $i - 1$.

This reduces the number of states without affecting the values $\delta_i(s)$, if the threshold is appropriately chosen. Novak suggest in [NHK$^+$03] an even more aggressive pruning with their two-pass strategy. Instead of using the probabilities directly, they convert them to probabilities based on their rank. Thus, the probability space is bounded and the values of the best and worst state output probabilities remain the same for each time frame. Instead of computing the output probabilities, they simply take a single value from the tail of the ranked probability distribution. This is based on the approach described in [BGGM93] where the authors claim a speedup by a factor of 100.

There are many more attempts to simplify the computational effort of the Viterbi search. Most of them try to replace multiplications by additions, which are faster to compute Ming [Min03]. Usually these attempts gain speed at the cost of accuracy and/or memory demands.

Lexical Decoding and Semantic Analysis The result of the unit matching is a scoring for the different recognition hypotheses. The next two steps help to determine the word chain with the highest probability with respect to the constraints from the language model. For word-based recognition with HMMs, the recognition process is finished at this point.

In the *Lexical Decoding* phase those paths are eliminated that do not have an existing word in the dictionary. In an alternative approach, the so-called *statistical grammar*, the sequences are reduced a couple of phonemes in a row, e.g. trigrams. The output of the latter case is a list of trigrams, ordered according to their probability. This is not suitable for isolated word recognition. The next step is the *Syntactic Analyses*, where those paths are eliminated that do not match an allowed sequence of words from the dictionary.

These steps do not require intensive computation except for a fast memory access to the dictionary and the grammar. Again, smaller vocabularies offer a faster result and require less memory.

The word or utterance with the highest probability in the remaining list of possible utterances is taken as the recognition output.

HMM-based recognition is computationally intensive, but shows good results in isolated word recognition as well as continuous speech. If the HMM is trained well, it is also a suitable technology for speaker independent recognition,

Artificial Neural Networks

Artificial **N**eural **N**etworks (ANN) is a method in computer science that is derived from the way the human brain works. The goal is to create a system that is able to learn and that can be used for pattern classification. More detailed information about the use of ANN for classification and their use in speech recognition can be found in the literature, e.g. [Cho99].

The expectations were very high when ANNs were discovered as a means for speech recognition. Modelling of speech recognition by artificial neural networks does not require a priori knowledge of the speech process and this technique quickly became an attractive alternative to HMM [AR06]. Neural nets tend to be better than HMMs for picking out discrete words, but they require extensive training up front, see [Kum02].

ANNs are in principle implemented as **M**ulti **L**ayer **P**erceptron (MLP) networks as shown in Figure 3.25. An output of a neuron in is computed via

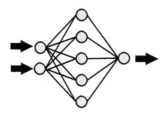

Figure 3.25: Schematic overview of an Artificial Neural Network

$$f_z = \sum_{i=1}^{N} w_i x_i \qquad (3.22)$$

There is nearly no optimization to reduce the large amount of calculation that have to be done to compute the output of a complex multilayer perceptron. The good point is that there are only additions and multiplications. The bad point is that there are too many of them, which makes it unusable on devices with a lower CPU frequency. A way out of this dilemma is the use of proprietary hardware, as it is used in hardware based speech recognition, ref. section 3.3.5.

Nowadays ANNs play a minor role in continuous speech recognition, but are still used in hybrid architectures with HMM-based recognition. In contrast to HMMs, trying to achieve their goal based on statistical and probability models, ANNs deal with classification. They are able to classify a given pattern into phonemes, but are not ideal to process continuous speech. This means that Neural Networks are used as a replacement of various pieces of a HMM based recognizer. This is more a philosophical difference with little relevance to the use in embedded environments.

As an example of such a network, we look at the multilayer perceptron developed by Bourlard et at. [BMWr92]. This network has nine 26-dimensional feature vectors to compute 61 phonemes with 500-4000 neurons in a hidden layer. It allows computing the a posteriori probability $p(q_k|x_i)$. The Viterbi algorithm requires $p(x_i|q_k)$ which can can be guessed using the Bayes Theorems via

$$p(x_i|q_k) = \frac{p(q_k|o_T)p(o_T)}{p(q_k)} \qquad (3.23)$$

where $p(o_T)$ can be treated as a constant for all classes and $p(q_k)$ is the frequency distribution of all phonemes which is known in advance.

3.4   Expandable Mobile Speech Recognition

The previous section gave an overview of current architectures to enable speech recognition on embedded devices. The best architectures are not depending on network resources. The input device should be always accessible, independent of network services. This requirement is solved best by service independent architectures. As pointed out, service independent architectures, like DTW, will work for a limited command set with a reasonable amount of required resources. However, the limitations inherent to the medium pose strong limitations to the usability of such a system, see section 2.6.1. Improvement of the mathematical model were able to workaround the limited resources at the cost of recognition accuracy, resulting in lower usability, refer to section 2.6.1. A higher usability is only available with a better speech recognizer, enabling all the other techniques that improve the quality of the interface. This is only available with service dependant speech recognition, since we need more computational power.

This section introduces a new architecture, combining both worlds: service dependent speech recognition and device inherent speech recognition. An overview of the architecture is given in figure 3.26. The basic idea is, to have a low end speech recognizer on the device, enabling us to handle all kinds of applications with a basic

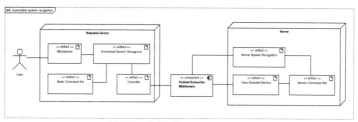

(a) Expandable Speech Recognizer

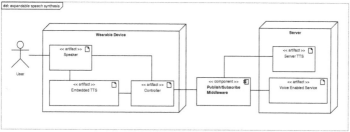

(b) Expandable Speech Synthesizer

Figure 3.26: Architecture of an expandable audio interface for wearable devices

command set. There is a service independent audio interface satisfying the basic needs without requiring many resources on the device. The limited audio interface can be replaced by the environment with a service dependent audio interface if a better quality is needed. This means also, that the required infrastructure to use the device and its audio interface is low. It is possible, to have support at those points, where services are available.

3.4.1 Channel based Audio

We use a channel-based publish subscribe mechanism to implement this idea, using Mundo as the underlying communication infrastructure as shown in figure 3.27(a) for text-to-speech, and in figure 3.27(b) for speech recognition.

Voice enabled services use the channel `speech.tts` to send the texts to be synthesized and subscribe to `speech.utterance` to receive the input from the recognizer. This way, it is transparent for them, where the synthesizer and the speech recognizer are located.

Channel based TTS

Text to be synthesized is published to all subscribers to the `speech.tts` channel. The synthesized text may be either markup text, e.g. JSML, or plain text. In addition to the markup, we enhanced our port of JSML to support the `audio` tag, which is in the SSML specification [Spe04]. The synthesizer must support, besides synthe-

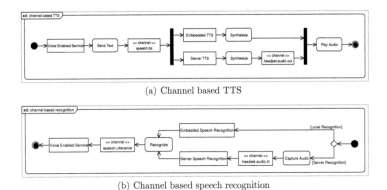

(a) Channel based TTS

(b) Channel based speech recognition

Figure 3.27: Data flow of an expandable mobile speech recognizer

sizing text, the streaming, or playback in the local case, of audio. The synthesizer that subscribed to the `speech.tts` channel evaluates the text and synthesizes the text and plays the audio files, if requested.

The TTS engine on the device uses the speaker of the device for the output. For synthesisers that are located on a server, the controller subscribes to the channel `headset.audio.out` to retrieve audio data that has to be played back. The audio data is delivered to the device using audio streaming as it is described in section 3.3.4. The audio data was packeted in so-called chunks The audio format was attached to each audio chunk, to support different audio formats of different synthesizers.

The presence of a TTS engine was detected by the *Controller* on the device. The MUNDO framework allows to automatically detecting the number of subscribers to the channel. This was used on the controller to automatically toggle the state of the local synthesizer. The state of the local synthesizer was visualized by the state of a check-box on the device.

A problem arises, if there are multiple TTS engines available in the environment. The synthesizers S_i are not aware of the presence of the other synthesizers S_k and will convert a synthesize request for an utterance, e.g., *Take seven items from shelf four* into a sequence of audio chunks $(s_{i,1}, s_{i,2}, \ldots, s_{i_n})$ while S_k sequences the utterance into $s_{k,1}, s_{k,2}, \ldots, s_{k_m}$). Both sequences will be published to the same channel at the same time. As a consequence, a random sequence of audio chunks will arrive at the controller, e.g., $(s_{i,1}, s_{i,2}, s_{k,1}, s_{i,3}, \ldots)$, resulting in a non understandable output. A solution for this problem could be to mark the audio chunks with a synthesizer specific stamp that allows for filtering in the controller. For now, we disabled the input over audio streams, if more than one synthesizer is detected.

Channel based Speech Recognition

Channel based speech recognition works similar to channel based speech synthesis. The principle is shown in figure 3.27(b). In contrast to the synthesizer, the recognizer is turned off by default to reduce false alarms. The user can turn on the recognizer, using a push-to-talk mechanism, by clicking a button on the device, or by uttering a special command. Services that are available in the environment can also enable the recognizer, e.g. after the service received the event, that the user is standing at a certain location. The local recognizer captures the audio directly from the microphone and publishes the recognized utterance as plain text over the `speech.utterance` channel.

We used HandHeld speech [Spe06] for our prototype. It turned out, that this recognizer uses a small footprint and had a high recognition rate. The audio from the microphone is also streamed via the `headset.audio.in` channel. MUNDO is able to detect, if there are any subscribers for the channel. This way, the audio data is only published, if there is a subscriber. The published audio data can be used to feed a speech recognizer that is located on a server. The recognized utterance is again published over the `speech.utterance` channel. In contrast to the output of synthesized text, the effect of having multiple recognizers running at the same time is not that disruptive. If there are multiple subscribers, the utterance is published by all publishers. The service that subscribed to that channel receives multiple events. This may cause an unwanted behaviour and has to be filtered by the applications.

3.4.2 Consequences

The main advantage of a distributed recognizer, based on publish-subscribe mechanisms is, that a basic audio interface is available which can be boosted by the environment. The applications, using the voice based service need not to care about the location of each part of the audio interface.

The protocol is proprietary, but we are able to support nearly any audio format for input and output and if the applications are MUNDO enabled, it is easy to make use of the audio interface. However, a certain overhead is needed to ensure that there is only one instance of a synthesizer and a recognizer running. Currently we did not investigate the behaviour, if there are services that have contradictory requirements. In this case, we have a design problem that the audio channel is overloaded. Here we need other mechanisms, like priorities, to schedule the use of the channel.

As mentioned above, this method is not a standard that is accepted by a big community. We made the first steps towards an audio interface that is based on publish-subscribe mechanisms. The first experiences that we made using the system are convincing: Flexibility in the quality of the audio interface on the one hand and ease of use for voice enabled services on the other hand.

3.5 Conclusion

There are multiple architectures and technologies to implement speech recognition on mobile devices. They can be divided into service dependent speech recognition and device inherent speech recognition. Service dependent architectures require a service running on the network to shift the computational burden from the client. These architectures offer the same potential of desktop size speech recognition at the cost of environmental dependencies. Speech recognition on the device is independent of services running on the network but pose high computational effort for the mobile

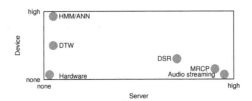

Figure 3.28: Distribution of computational resources

device.

This is also the main reason why the speech recognition parameters of service dependent speech recognition cannot be determined exactly. They depend on the technology used on the server side. This results in full network dependency and high server load. The ratings of the additional parameters for UC are generally worse than those for device inherent speech recognition. The required network bandwidth is better for DSR than for the streaming architectures since it aims to reduce the transmitted data. As a consequence, transmission degradation and server load is slightly better.

HMM and ANN based recognizers offer the greatest flexibility and have the best scoring for the parameters of speech recognition systems. This is the main reason why service dependent speech recognition performs better in this area. The transducer is, in all cases, a noise-canceling microphone. Thus SNR is no crucial factor.

Implemented on the device, these technologies require too many resources to achieve the same performance as their counterparts on the server. This results in smaller vocabularies, smaller models and lower complexity. They have generally a lower recognition rate than server implementations. In addition, implementations may not have real time capabilities, resulting a a low scoring for responsiveness. The decisive factor is the use of computational resources.

Figure 3.28 shows a graphical representation indicating how the type of architecture influences the distributed use of computational resources on the device and on the server. Hardware based speech recognition seems to be an appropriate candidate to enable speech recognition on mobile devices, but its rigidity makes it impossible to address multiple application scenarios. Thus it has the worst rating for integration and maintenance. DTW requires less resources on the device than HMM or ANN, but is highly speaker dependent. It requires enrollment and supports only isolated word based recognition which makes it unusable for certain scenarios.

This can serve as a decision criterion for the architecture to implement or to use. The careful analysis of attempts to enable speech recognition with the help of improved algorithms showed that they gain speed at the cost of accuracy. None of the architectures is ideal in all contexts. Especially the use in enterprise applications refrain from the investment dictated by server dependent architectures. We used this as a basis to develop a more flexible architecture, combining the concepts of device inherent and service dependent speech recognition.

As regards our targeted architecture, introduced in section 1.2, we can expand

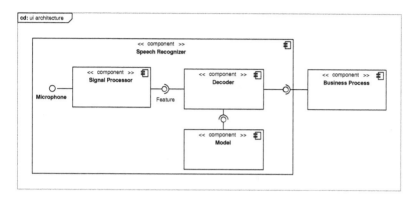

Figure 3.29: Architecture to support Voice User Interfaces for Mobile Workers

the *UI* interface of figure 3.1 with the general architecture of a recognizer, shown in figure 2.1 resulting in the architecture shown in figure 3.29. At this point, we make no statement about the node where each component of the recognizer resides. Also not considered is the audio output.

Chapter 4

Navigating in Audio

4.1 Motivation

Ubiquitous computing enables the user to access information from her current location. Being able to deliver this information to the worker while she is engaged in her task will also enable us to offer *training at work*. That is, teaching the workers how to perform their tasks while they are doing them. This requires a careful exploration of the mechanisms for delivering information to the workers.

In office environments, workers typically use their web browsers to access the information. Web browsers have the task to graphically render HTML pages. As pointed out in section 3.1 the use of audio has in many cases some advantages to be used exclusively or in addition to other interfaces in smart environments. Audio renderers for HTML exist, but are not designed for the worker on the move. The information which the workers access is stored in an information base in the network of the organization. This information is structured to allow for easy delivery over audio and also contains information on how to navigate through the information base. The workers can navigate through this information base and access the information they need at any given time. Voice interaction, however, requires a new type of interaction device and information access paradigms, refer to section 2.6.

Browsing in audio is different to browsing with a graphical browser in hypertext. However, the functional requirements are comparable. These are, on the one hand, requirements to control the browser, on the other hand requirements for representation of the content.

Controlling the browser Besides the tasks of rendering a web page in audio, the user must be able to control the browser, to navigate to the pages of interest. The main functions for controlling a typical web browser is shown in figure 4.1. For visually impaired users or users of a purely audio browser these functionalities are invoked by a special command to call the corresponding method. As an example, the opera browser uses the command *opera reload page* to reload the current page.

Document representation The main task of a browser is to *display* the contents of a document. Hypertext documents are generally written in HTML which is not designed to work with audio. Nevertheless, there is a need to transform

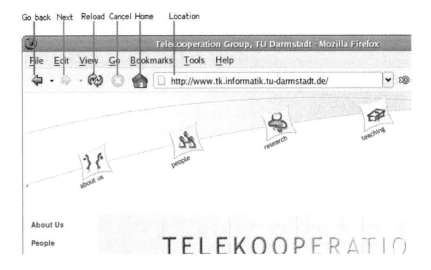

Figure 4.1: Analogy to a web browser

documents into audible information. One of the triggers is web accessibility. This issue has had increasing importance within the past years, especially
for people with visual disabilities. In 1997 the Web Accessibility Initiative
(WAI) [KsTML97] was launched to promote the development of browser standards and guidelines to improve the accessibility for individuals with visual
disabilities. Microsoft's accessibility initiative [Mic06], IBM's Special Needs
program [IBM06] and Sun Microsystem's Java accessibility API are similar
initiatives that are driven by industry.

This chapter focuses on the usage of audio documents in smart environments.
It focuses on two components for realizing the target architecture introduced in
section 1.2. The relevant components are shown in figure 4.2. One component is
the control of the UI interface, see chapter 3. The other component is responsible
for the integration of context information, as shown in chapter 2.

The organization of this chapter is shown in figure 4.3. Following this motivation, section 4.2 introduces some existing applications for audio browsers in smart
environments. Then three aspects of audio browsers are investigated.

The first aspect deals with controlling the browser. Section 4.3 describes a survey
that has been conducted to find a minimal command set to control an audio browser.
This command set is also suitable to serve as a basic command set for use in smart
environments.

The second aspect deals with document representation. Section 4.4 describes
concepts for treating audio as a hypertext. Our study is based on a topological
analysis. How topology influences browsing is handled in section 4.5. In section 4.6.1
we show some use cases, where the concept of an audio browser can be used and

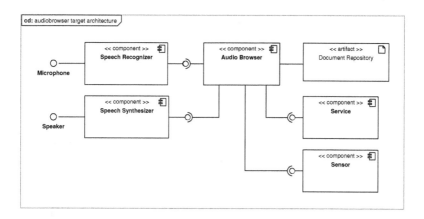

Figure 4.2: Target Architecture to support Audio Browsing for Mobile Workers

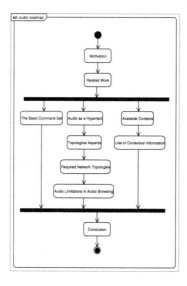

Figure 4.3: Road map to handle Audio Browsing

map those to the relevant topologies in section 4.6.2. In section 4.7 we point out the limitations of voice based user interfaces, through a careful examination of the challenges that were named in section 2.6.1.

The third aspect deals with the integration of contextual information into the audio browser. Our understanding of context-aware computing was introduced in section 2.2, which serves as a basis for the analysis in section 4.8 showing which data should be taken into account.

Section 4.10 concludes this chapter.

4.2   Related Work

There are already existing solutions for navigating within audio based information coming from different application scenarios.

4.2.1   Audio Rendering from HTML

Coming from the world of HTML browsers, the first approaches to get an aural representation of HTML documents were *screen readers*. They transform visual information into sound using a process called *sonification*. Screen readers use a purely spoken output of the information which is quite unsatisfying to aurally render HTML, since the additional information, inherent to the structure gets lost [EL99, GM97].

Audio renderers use both the structure and the content, which are transformed differently into hearable information. For audio rendering of HTML, the structure of the HTML document must be analyzed. This structure information is used to create a virtual tree, which the user can navigate. The leaves of this tree are the contents being read to the user. Content comprises also all of the structural elements, obtained from the nodes that are on the path from the root to the leave. That is, e.g. a text block in a frame aligned using `div`-block-elements in a nested list. This means, that the text block is at the end of a hierarchy of structural elements. The location of the user in the document is represented by an auditory icon or an earcon that has been associated to the current structural element. Each of the structural elements to represent arrangement of contents, the so-called macro-structure, has an associated auditory icon, if the association is intuitive or an earcon otherwise. To be not too intrusive, it is necessary to select the earcons properly.

It is possible to deliver further information using parametrization, e.g. to control the amount of information of a container element or the number of items of a list element. Distinct items of a list element can be emphasized by the use of an earcon.

Scrollbars are not needed in audio and can be ignored since the spatial restriction does not exist in the acoustic representation [ME92]. Images do not have a representation in audio. The only statement that can be made is the existence of an image and, if available, the contents of the `alt` attribute. Some approaches, like the *image-to-sound-mapping* from Hans Petter Selasky [Sel06] or the image restitution by sonorous signals from Frederic Paquay [Paq05] exist, but are more or less academic approaches without any impact on the audio renderers that are currently available.

Not all macro-structure elements feature a unique meaning. Examples are containers to group multiple text elements, links to other documents or targets within the same documents. Some elements were meant to be used for a certain purpose, but were used by designers different to their original intent. One of them is the table. Its intention is to structure content, but it is also used for positioning of images or other elements. This is a serious problem for audio rendering from HTML, since this happens in the first phase of the transformation of the HTML document into audio. The creation of the tree to represent the structure is fully depending on the arrangement of the elements. If their semantic is not clear without ambiguity, a unique transformation is not possible. Another example of an element with an ambiguous semantic is the hr-tag to create a horizontal line. In general lines are used to separate two sections of a document. In this sense a horizontal line is an identifier for another section, but it can also be used to underline text or to emphasize images. The use of an auditory icon, heading for a certain meaning may thus lead to confusion. It suggests a sense that is not explicitly said by the author of the HTML document.

It is common sense to render such elements by a neutral sound effect or a change in the speaker's voice, without insisting on a certain interpretation of the element [Jam96].

Micro structures are structural elements for text formatting, like bold or underlined and elements to mark headlines. Micro structures can be also expressed using earcons or auditory icons or by modifications of the speaker's voice. An example would be to change the pitch according to the size of the headline.

Besides sound effects, it is possible to use different speakers, or changes of the speaker's voice to represent structure. This can be used to represent formatting of continuous text. An example can be found at news broadcasting. Different topics, like sports or weather is being read by different speakers. A study [Jam96] showed, that this technique is not adequate to be used to render micro structures in audio interfaces. A possible reason for this is that the new speaker will present different thoughts than her predecessor. Thus, the use of different speakers for the rendering of micro structures hinders the users in combining their output to a single statement. In order to represent micro structures the change of a single speaker's voice is more adequate. Different speakers are better to be used to render macro structures. In this case, the speaker change has the desired effect.

In order to make rendering for audio easier aural style sheets were defined. They are part of the W3C's CSS 2 recommendation [Cas98] and are designed for defining the style of Web content. The style sheets are intended to give auditory clues for people accessing the Web with audio renderers. Style sheets do not define any navigation but leave it up to the audio renderer. Authors using them may associate different voices with HTML elements. They may also define a sound file as auditory cues to be played before or after any element and can define the length of a pause after an element.

Both technologies, screen reader and and audio renderer, show that HTML is not an ideal format, if audio output should be supported. However, the strategies of representing structural information are adopted. This is explored in section 4.7.

4.2.2   HearSay

With their Voice Browser Activity [Voi04], W3C is working to expand access to the web to allow people to interact with the voice browser via key pads, spoken commands, listening to prerecorded speech, synthetic speech and music. Their goal is to use any telephone to access appropriately designed web-based services, focusing people with visual impairments or people needing web access while keeping their hands and eyes free for other things.

An interesting approach in this direction is HearSay [RSY04] which is based on a novel approach to automatically create audio browsable content from hypertext web documents in VoiceXML. It combines two key technologies: HearSay uses the technology of audio rendering for automatically partitioning of web documents through tightly coupled structural and passes this through a semantic analysis, which transforms raw HTML documents into semantic structures so as to facilitate audio browsing.

HearSay is just the tool to browse HTML web pages. The user's cognitive limitations navigating in the rendered pages remain unexplored.

4.2.3 HyperSpeech

B. Arons' HyperSpeech system [Aro91] is inspired by both graphical hypertext systems and phone based menu systems. It presents a selection of interviews to its users. These interviews form a strongly connected graph where users are free to browse in. When browsing, the system discriminates between several types of links between nodes; as almost every node has a link of each type to another node this leads to a unified command set for navigating between elements. Users navigate by uttering the type of link they want to follow. The system does not use confirmations, but directly goes to the node recognized. In case of misrecognition it is up to the user to initiate an undo command. Arons identified that both sparse graphs and overly smart systems may contribute to the lost in space problem. Sparse graphs, because the users are missing landmarks for navigation which causes the system to fall apart. Smart navigation was tried by automatically transporting the user back from a node with no links originating from, as this lead to confusion about the node the user was currently in.

The main reason for this is the fact, that Aron did not take respect the challenges inherent to audio, which were described in section 2.6.1. A detailed analysis is described in sections 4.7.1 to 4.7.4.

4.2.4 EmacsSpeak

The roots of EmacsSpeak [Ram98] are screen-readers which are designed to help visually impaired users. Usually, such software only reads the screen content aloud while leaving it up to the user to build a mental model of the data presented. EmacsSpeak, however, augments the API of Emacs such that speech is a first class interface element. That way, each element of Emacs visible user interface may have associated spoken text which may be read before or after the element. In addition, the system is able to do audio formatting using different voices for different elements. Users navigate within EmacsSpeak by positioning the editor's cursor. Positioning may be done by each input device supported by the system, but typically uses the keyboard. Once positioned, the system reads the current line to the user. In different edit modes, the system may utilize audio formatting for designating hyperlinks, misspelled words, etc.

The principle of editing showed, that navigating within a document is a complex task. EmacsSpeak is, like HearSay, only the tool supporting audio based interaction, without exploring the effect on audio browsing to the the user. Navigation in the audio space is explored in section 4.7.4. EmacsSpeak is a desktop application and does not care about use of context information.

4.2.5 GuidePort

One application scenario is to revamp existing audio guides for museums with an interactive component such that visitors are not limited to a preset tour but can move around freely within an exhibition. Sennheiser's guidePORT [gui] is an example for such a system. guidePORT-users carry a set consisting of a wireless receiver and earphones, exhibits are associated with triggers that send out a near-range signal containing an ID for the exhibit. Once a visitor enters the range of the trigger, her wireless receiver fetches the audio file associated with the ID from a wireless network and plays it back. Navigation within the knowledge base of the guidePORT system is limited. Wireless receivers also have a unique ID. As the decision which audio file to fetch is based upon both exhibit ID and receiver ID it is possible to have several programmed theme sets or languages based on the receiver the visitor carries. Apart from that, selection of content is solely based on the location of the visitor.

GuidePort uses context information as an additional source of input. Users control the device by buttons leaving audio as an output modality without caring about the special characteristics of the medium.

4.2.6 HIPPIE

HIPPIE [GS01] is a context-aware nomadic information system that supports users with location aware information services. The used context is defined by the physical environment, the geographical position, social partners, user tasks and personal characteristics. Context is used to adapt the multimodal information presentation. The default information presentation is multimodal, containing written text, graphics and animations on the screen and spoken language via headphones. Focus of project is a the realisation of a visitor walking in the physical space while getting access to contextualized information space tailored to the individual needs and the current environment. Not treated is the movement of the visitor in the electronic space, see section 2.2.

4.2.7 SmartWeb

SmartWeb [Smab] is the follow-up project to SmartKom [Smaa]. SmartWeb goes beyond SmartKom in supporting open-domain question answering using the entire Web as its knowledge base. It provides a context-aware user interface, so that it can support the user in different roles, e.g. as a car driver, a motor biker, a pedestrian or a sports spectator. One of the planned demonstrators of SmartWeb is a personal guide for the 2006 FIFA world cup in Germany providing mobile infotainment services to soccer fans, anywhere and anytime. Another SmartWeb demonstrator is based on P2P communication between a car and a motor bike. When the car's sensors detect aquaplaning, a succeeding motor biker is warned by SmartWeb "Aqua-planing danger in 200 meters!". The biker can interact with

SmartWeb through speech and heptic feedback. The car driver can input speech and gestures.

SmartWeb is based on two new W3C standards for the semantic Web, the **R**esource **D**escription **F**ramework (RDF) and the **W**eb **O**ntology Language (OWL) for representing machine interpretable content on the Web. OWL ontologies support semantic service descriptions, focusing primarily on the formal specification of inputs, outputs, preconditions, and effects of Web services. In SmartWeb, multimodal user requests will not only lead to automatic Web service discovery and invocation, but also to the automatic composition, inter operation and execution monitoring of Web services. This is an interesting aspect of the project to use context information. However there is no differentiation between movements in physical and electronic space and the navigational challenges are not covered.

4.3 The Basic Command Set

In order to use speech as an input medium it is common practice to build a grammar that matches exactly the input requirements of the application to implement. These applications are generally carefully crafted menu hierarchies, see section 2.6, using short spoken utterances or touch tones. Menu driven application are easy to build and are thus attractive for the orderer of the application. However, they are generally too rigid and require big learning efforts from the user. These systems will be explored in more detail in section 5.5.3.

Another possibility is the use of **N**atural **L**anguage **I**nterfaces (NLI) which are very successful in narrow domains. NLI applications are crafted by experts which is data and labor intensive. We will have a closer look at these applications in section 5.5.3.

Both approaches are extremes as they are common today, but which are not satisfying either on the user side or on the orderer side. An optimal solution is expected in between.

A promising approach is *Speech Graffiti* from the **U**niversal **S**peech **I**nterface (USI) project of Carnegie Mellon University. An overview of this project can be found in [CMU+]. The project tries to find a standard that is already present in the GUI world and which was successfully ported to handwriting recognition through *graffiti* by Palm OS [Pal06]. The target is to transfer the idea of *look & feel* from the world of graphical user interfaces to audio based user interfaces. This conflicts with the efforts being made to reproduce a natural language like human-computer-dialog. The USI project describes their efforts like this:

> Yet another interface alternative is specialized Command-and-Control languages. While these are viable for expert users who can invest hours in learning their chosen application, they do not scale dozens of applications used by millions of occasional users. Our system, on the other hand is universal – that is, application independent. After spending 5 minutes learning the interface, a typical user should be able to communicate with applications as diverse information servers, schedulers, contact managers, message services, cars and home appliances. *In essence, we*

> *try to do for speech, what the Macintosh universal "look and feel" has*
> *done for the GUI world.*

This is the main reason of a small command set: Being simple and easy to learn.

Due to the nature of an embedded device a recognizer which runs on such a small device has strong limitations in memory and computing power, see chapter 3. This is a further advantage of a small command set.

Our approach is minimalistic. The goal is to deliver audio documents to the user, comparable to a web browser which can be used to retrieve textual documents or to start applications. Although the documents or applications can be complex, the basic functionality of such a browser is not that complicated. A browser can be controlled by only few commands. The basic command set can be boosted by the environment if the user enters an application that needs more complex interaction mechanisms, as it was described in section 3.4. However, the command set should satisfy the basic needs to navigate to those applications and access audio based information.

This section discusses a survey that we conducted to find a minimal command set to handle the functionalities named in section 4.1 to control an audio browser.

4.3.1 Existing Command Sets

The efforts being made in the USI project are not new. They are based on the ETSI standard defined in [ETS00] which is targeted at application developers for telephony based environment and comprises several fields of application. Table 4.1 shows those fields that are of potential interest for navigating in structured audio based information.

The ETSI standard assumes that the choice for a command set depends on the environment and proposes only a few commands that are context independent. In addition, they propose different, context dependent commands for different environments. The commands should meet the requirements that were introduced in section 2.6.

Table 4.1 shows the words from ETSI for English and German words. The original standard considers furthermore French, Italian and Spanish. ETSI has paid particular attention to the words being acoustically different. As our study shows, sometimes these words are counter-intuitive to users.

One of the contexts that they define is a navigation context, which consists of five commands to browse lists. Web browser however use only these five basic commands to handle the whole application, see figure 4.1, motivating us for a survey to find a command set, that can be used accordingly and which is self-contained.

The USI command set is built upon the ETSI command set. The ETSI command set provided the basis for a survey for the acceptance of the USI commands. The survey and its result is described in [SR02]. They identified several contexts besides a core of eight commands. The commands are not terminated. If the user wants to ask for details about something that was mentioned in the system output, she may use words that are not part of the command set.

It becomes clearer with the help of an example that was given in [CMU+03].

System: ...movie is Titanic ...theatre is the Manor ...day is Tuesday ...

Table 4.1: ETSI Generic spoken command vocabulary

Area	Function	German	English
Context independent	List commands and/or functions	Menü	Options
	Terminate service	Beenden	Goodbye
	Go to top level of service	Hauptmenü	Main Menu
	Enter idle mode	Stand-by	standby
	Transfer to human operator	Hotline, Service	Operator
	Go back to previous node or menu	Zurück	Go back
Context dependent	Help	Hilfe	Help
	Read prompt again	Wiederholen	Repeat
Core	Confirm operation	Ja, OK	Yes
	Read prompt again	Wiederholen	Repeat
	Reject operation	Nein	No
	Cancel current operation	Stopp, Abbruch	Stop
Media Control	Play a recording	Wiedergabe	Play
	Stop temporarily	Pause	Pause
	Resume interrupted playback	Weiter	Continue, Play
	Stop playing a recording	Stopp	Stop
	Move forward faster than play	Vorspulen	Fast forward
	Move backward	Zurückspulen	Rewind
Browsable list for navigation	Go to next item	Weiter	Next
	Go to previous item	Zurück	Previous
	Provide more information about selected item	Details	Details

User: What are the show times?

The phrase *what are* is standardized in USI, but the concretion *show times* is domain specific. This is a drawback with respect to an enclosed command set and a tribute to a more comfortable interface.

4.3.2   Requirements

Figure 4.4 shows the basic requirements for an audio browser.

Besides the five basic commands that are already known from graphical web browsers, see figure 4.1,

1. Home,

2. Go Back,

3. Next,

4. Reload and

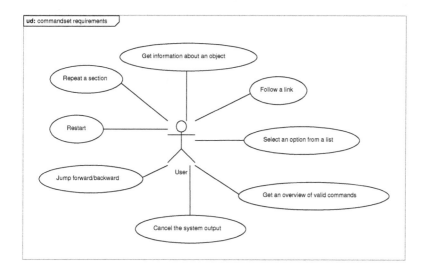

Figure 4.4: Commandset requirements for an audio based browser

5. Cancel

there are some more commands needed which will be discussed in the following.

Entering of a location URL does not exist in that sense. It is replaced by a trigger, coming from the environment, which the user can use as a starting point to *get information about an object.*

Besides the global navigation that is handled by the browser buttons, the document may offer further navigation options. In that case the user must be able to *follow a link.*

Some of the actions will require to *select an option from a list.* The intuitive way to deal with lists would be to use the name of the list item. This strategy has a few drawbacks:

- If the list has many items the user can lose track of the available options.

- All list items must be in the dictionary of the recognizer. This is contrary to our requirement to be minimal.

In a menu driven dialog, it is common practice to use a number or keyword to select an item. The more general way using numbers would increase the command set by 10 new commands, which are the numbers 0,...9. A better approach would be to have some time after the item has been played to utter a selective keyword. F. James describes SCRIPTED INTERACTION in [Jam98] another advantage as

> This means that, at every possible interaction point (such as a link), the user will have an opportunity to decide whether to follow the link or continue on in the current document.

This concept will be explored in section 5.5.6.

If the user needs help, it must be possible to *get an overview of valid commands*.

Not considered are requirements, like modifying the speed of the audio output, as is the case for systems like SpeechSkimmer [Aro93]. The advantage of these systems is that the user can easily skip section of low interest without losing context. This can happen if a user simply jumps forward or backward in the document. When the audio output starts after the jump, the user has to reorient about the actual context.

4.3.3   Survey to Find the Command Set

A survey was conducted to find out which commands users would prefer in the scenarios describes in section 4.3.2. The users were asked to name the command that they would use to make the system behave as described in the scenarios. Commands should be named for English and German. We got responses from 16 persons (12 male and 4 female, aged from 26 to 46). Their experience with voice based user interfaces was generally low. The respondents had neither very good nor very bad experiences with such systems in general. Overall, their expectation of voice based systems was neutral.

There were more answers for English than in German. Unfortunately we got only few answers from native English speakers. Since there were many native German speakers, the answers to the German command set can be considered more reliable. Our survey results may be less accurate for English than for German, since non-native speakers may lack the *feel* for the language that is helpful for determining these kinds of answers.

It is obvious that this survey is not representative of the whole field of users, since there are too few answers. However, one of the goals with the survey was to find out how closely the answers would correspond to the words proposed by ETSI. The users answering the survey were unaware of the ETSI words. In addition, ETSI does not provide words for all the scenarios needed for our prototype. The survey was a source for the missing words.

4.3.4   General Commands

The result of our survey showed, that many of the answers are in accordance with the ETSI command set. This is even the case for the same scenarios independent of the language. In some scenarios, like the English *forward* for the function *Go to next node or item* got more votes, but the ETSI command (*next*) has a count that is very close to it. In cases like this both words are possible. Even if one of the words will not be used as a valid command, it can be a good fall-back solution if the users are in trouble with the chosen command. In contrast, the word *skip* has a count far away from the ETSI command. Hence, it will not be considered. Generally, for our minimal command set, the ETSI command was chosen over the results of the survey, in cases where there is significant doubt.

For some scenarios ETSI does not have a suggested command. This concerns the following functionalities, which are part of the *Jump forward/backward* requirement.

- get table of contents

- get the index

- go to last node or item

The answers of the survey are quite reasonable and have a non-ambiguous most preferred answer. Due to the lack of an ETSI command the answer from the survey will be in the minimal command set.

There remain only some scenarios which need a more detailed discussion:

1. provide more information about selected item

2. go to top level of service

The requirement *provide more information about selected item* has been used in two ways:

- start the dialog

- follow a link

The difference between these two functionalities is that the first one is based upon a context outside the dialog, whereas the second one concerns a link within the system's context. In general there is no real difference between them. The answers may me influenced by the word *information* in the scenario. This scenario was defined as *Get more information about the object*. We chose the ETSI word in this case.

The function *go to top level of service* has a different ETSI command because ETSI is based on a menu like dialog. This will not be the case for our prototype and hence the ETSI command is not useful. It is difficult to find a command that fits the desired purpose because there is no clear tendency and no clear favorite in the users responses. The word *repeat* and *Wiederholen* may not be used because they conflict with the command for *read prompt again*. The next suggested command is *start*. This is a better choice than *up* which may be confused with the users aim to *cancel the current operation* and go one level up. The corresponding German command will be *Anfang*. Here the alternative *Zurück* conflicts with the command to *go to previous node or item*. The other suggested command *nochmal* may be be confused by the user if he wants to *read the prompt again*.

In the end, the words *start* for English and *Anfang* for German were chosen.

People were asked in the survey to name a command to *select an option from a list* using numbers or SCRIPTED INTERACTION. The answers to the latter option show that people are not familiar with that approach. The range of answers was very broad. As a consequence the answers to the list preference tend to number dialing. The result is shown if figure 4.5.

Target of our audio browser are systems which will not have menu based navigation. The user wants to access information that is unknown to her. For that reason this disadvantage will have no influence. Large lists will be divided into smaller parts so that the user can easily skip parts of the list of no interest. The user has to understand intuitively how the list is sorted so that he is able to navigate quickly to the desired item.

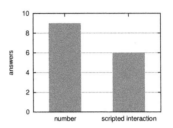

Figure 4.5: List preference

Table 4.2: Interrogative list selection

Function	English	German
Confirm operation	Yes	Ja, OK
Reject operation	No	Nein

The selection of a list item will depend how the list is presented to the user. The easiest way will be to present lists like a question. In the use case of a museum guide a list may look like this:

> You are looking at the painting Mona Lisa. I can tell you more about it. What do you want to know more about? *pause...*
> the painting? *pause...*
> the painter? *pause...*
> ...

The user simply answers to the questions with *Yes*. In this manner the problem of selecting a list item reduces to answering a question and we assume that all lists can be mapped to this question-answer format. The commands for the list selection are shown in table 4.2. An alternative to say nothing in an interrogative list selection is to utter a reject command. Since there was a broad area of answers the ETSI command is taken for this.

Table 4.3 summarizes the commands we have chosen for each action. We show words for both German and English. This is the command set which will be implemented and used in the later stages of this project. In case it turns out that this set is incomplete, we will add new words to it, but only when it is absolutely necessary.

This concludes the aspect of controlling the browser by voice. In the following section, we focus on the document representation.

Table 4.3: The minimal command set

Function	Command
Provide more information about selected item	Details
Get table of contents	Contents
Get the index	Index
Help	Help
Cancel current operation	Stop
Stop temporarily	Pause
Resume interrupted playback	Continue
Read prompt again	Repeat
Go to next node or item	Next
Go to previous node or item	Go back
Go to top level of service	Start
Go to last node or item	Last
Confirm operation	Yes
Reject operation	No

4.4 Audio as a Hypertext

Nowadays the term *hypermedia* emphasizes the integration of graphics, video and audio into traditional hypertext systems. Does this mean that hypertext systems can contain only pure text? In this section a definition of all these terms is given and the impact on voice based applications is discussed. It follows the discussion of Dagmar Unz in [Unz00], in which she focuses on hypermedia, whereas this discussion has its focus on applications that use audio only.

For a better understanding of the terminology a short introduction of hypertext and hypermedia is given. A more detailed historical introduction is given by Nielsen [Nie93] and Schulmeister [Sch96].

The term hypertext has been introduced by Ted Nelson [Nel65]. His idea was based on an architecture which combined server and client based storage of information. This did not include the linked document bases which allowed jumping between documents. This feature was introduced by Andries van Dam [vDea69] when he developed his *Hypertext Editing System*. The break-through came with Apple's *HyperCard* system [Goo87] for the Macintosh computer. From Jacob Nielson's point of view, HyperCard was no more than a hypermedia program, since links started from regions on a card rather than text objects. Nevertheless HyperCard lost its popularity with the growth of the *world wide web*, starting from the first ACM conference on hypertext *Hypertext '87* at the University of Carolina in 1987.

Hofmann et al. [HS95] identified four aspects for hypertext:

1. Structure: Hypertext consists of information nodes and links among them.

2. Operations: Authoring and reading of hypertext is not sequential.

3. Medium: Hypertext is only usable with computers. Content is expressed by means of static media using text, images or symbols.

4. Interaction: Hypertext is accessed by a graphical interactive user interface.

In [Unz00] Unz defines Hypertext covering some of the features named so far as

Definition 21 **Hypertext** *denotes the computer aided integration of data in a network of information nodes and links. Hypertext is used as a generic name for nonlinear information systems, even if the system includes non textual information. This accentuates the structural aspects, the construction principle.*

This definition is based on the ones given by Nielsen [Nie93] and Schulmeister [Sch96]. Unz also gives a definition for hypermedia based on this definition

Definition 22 **Hypermedia** *is a special kind of hypertext, a multimedial hypertext.*

She concludes this definition with an outline to hypermedia systems, which are not required to own an informational network with nodes and links. Multimedia and hypertext name two independent entities with the intersection multimedia. This is also the statement of Nielsen [Nie93]:

> The fact that a system is multimedia based, does not make it hypertext
> ... Only when users interactively take control of a set of dynamic links
> among units of information does a system get to be hypertext.

Different authors have different opinions about the terminology hypertext, hypermedia and multimedia. Some authors define hypermedia as a multimedia extension to hypertext [FC95], others as a special hypertext [Jef95]: "Hypermedia [is] a term used to describe hypertext which contains a large proportion of non-text information...". Duchastel [Duc90] sees hypertext as a special kind of hypermedia limited to textual representation. This means that hypertext is a first generation hypermedia. Nielsen [Nie95] and Hofmann [HS95] use these terms synonym.

Most of the confusion is caused by the word fragment *text* in hypertext, which can only be understood in a historical context [Kuh91].

Audio only hypertext systems seem to be not covered by both terms. Several authors tried to find their own terminology, starting from *HyperSpeech* [Aro91] over *HyperPhone* [MD90] to *hypermedia*. The above mentioned common understanding of hypermedia shows, that this seems to be still an unsolved question.

Arons himself describes his system as HyperSpeech. The fact that his system deals with "speech only hypermedia" [Aro91] and the analogy to hypermedia made him choose this name. This is also in the tradition of Duchastel [Duc90]. He discovered that speech-only applications are different to other hypermedia applications, since "speech exists only temporally".

To get a proper understanding about the terminology, the term hypertext is substituted with the more mathematical term *hyperbase*.

Definition 23 *A* **hyperbase** *H is an ordered pair $H = (\mathbf{N}, \mathbf{L})$ where $\mathbf{N}$ is a finite set of information nodes and $\mathbf{L}$ is a set of directed links between pairs of nodes, defined in turn as ordered pairs (m, n) of elements of $\mathbf{N}$.*

In the hypermedia world, each information node is being presented in one or more media, i.e. text, audio, graphics, animation, video, and interactivity. This means, a multimedia hyperbase is defined as

$$\mathbf{H_M} = (\mathbf{N_M}, \mathbf{L}) \tag{4.1}$$

A multimedial information node is defined as

$$\mathbf{N_M} = \{n_{m_0, \dots, m_i} | m_k \in \mathbf{M}\} \tag{4.2}$$

The relationship between hyperspeech, hypertext and hypermedia then can be reduced to $\mathbf{M}$. Audio only hyperbases fulfill all aspects of Hofmann et al, with the only exception of the interaction since we do not need a graphical interface. But it satisfies our definition of hypertext, which we gave in the beginning of this section. Consequences are, that

- audio only hyperbases exist and can be used for browsing

- audio only hyperbases are a special kind of hypermedia

- audio only hyperbases are different to hypertext

- the mathematics, known from hypermedia can be used in audio only applications

In the following sections of this chapter, this is explored in smart environments, based on existing experience of audio rendering from HTML.

4.5 Topological Aspects

Besides the pure rendering of a web page, the user must be able to navigate multiple documents. Some common navigation strategies for hypertext are discussed by Parunak in [Par89]. Parunak discusses the problem of navigation, based on several network topologies which are shown in Figure 4.6(a) to Figure 4.6(d). In addition, there is the arbitrary graph which is any connected graph.

Intuitively, a user can move directly from one node m to another node n only when there is a link $(m, n) \in \mathbf{L}$ between them. In addition the directionality of a link must reflect the *normal* direction of traversal, which is assumed to be accessed differently by the user than the reverse direction. For example, one may be able to traverse a link in reverse only if one has first traversed it in the forward direction. This means in the terminology of a web browser, that a user can navigate only to those links that appear in the current document. After she followed a link, it is possible to navigate back using the browser back button. Every hyper-base is thus trivially isomorphic to a finite directed graph $\mathbf{G} = (\mathbf{V}, \mathbf{E})$, by identifying the nodes $\mathbf{N}$ of $\mathbf{H}$ with the points $\mathbf{V}$ of $\mathbf{G}$ and the links $\mathbf{L}$ of $\mathbf{H}$ with the edges $\mathbf{E}$ of $\mathbf{G}$.

For the following some relationships are needed to express the navigation possibilities in the different network topologies which are shown in Figure 4.6.

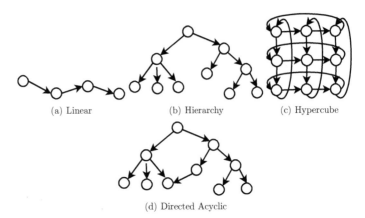

(a) Linear   (b) Hierarchy   (c) Hypercube

(d) Directed Acyclic

Figure 4.6: Network topologies according to Parunak [Par89]

Let n_1 and n_2 be two nodes. n_1 *is a parent of* n_2 if

$$P(n_1, n_2) = \begin{cases} \text{true} & \text{if } (n_1, n_2) \in \mathbf{L} \\ \text{false} & \text{otherwise} \end{cases} \tag{4.3}$$

In turn n_1 *is a child of* n_2 if the following equation holds

$$C(n_1, n_2) = P(n_2, n_1) \tag{4.4}$$

n_1 *is an ancestor of* n_i if the following equation holds

$$A(n_1, n_i) = \begin{cases} \text{true} & \text{if } P(n_1, n_i) \vee (\exists n_2 \ldots, n_{i-1} \in \mathbf{N} : \\ & \quad P(n_1, n_2) \wedge \ldots \wedge P(n_{i-1}, n_i)) \\ \text{false} & \text{otherwise} \end{cases} \tag{4.5}$$

and n_1 *is a descendant of* n_2 if the following equation holds

$$D(n_1, n_2) = A(n_2, n_1) \tag{4.6}$$

Based on these functions we define sets P, C, A, D to represent the nodes defined above:

$$S(n_i) = \{n_i | n \in N \wedge \exists n_k \in N : S(n_i, n_k) = true\} \quad , S = P, C, A, D \tag{4.7}$$

For any set $\mathbf{S}$, $|\mathbf{S}|$ is the cardinality of $\mathbf{S}$. With the help of these definitions the topologies shown in Figure 4.6 can be described as follows:

Linear $H_L : (\exists n_i \in \mathbf{N} : |P(n_i)| = 0 \wedge |C(n_i)| = 1) \wedge (\forall n_k \in \mathbf{N}, k \neq i : (|P(n_i)| = 1) \wedge (|C(n_i)| \leq 1))$ In other words, each node has exactly one parent and one child (with the exception of the first and last nodes).

Hierarchy $H_H : (\exists n_i \in \mathbf{N} : |P(n_i)| = 0) \wedge (\forall n_k \in \mathbf{N}, k \neq i : |P(n_k)| = 1)$ There is a root of the hierarchy and each node has only one parent.

Directed acyclic graph $H_{DAG} : (\exists n_i \in \mathbf{N} : |P(n_i)| = 0) \wedge (\forall n_k \in \mathbf{N}, k \neq i : A(n_k) \cap D(n_k) = \emptyset)$ There is a root of the DAG and the second condition ensures that there are no cycles in the graph.

Hypercube Hypercube is not used in this document and is left undefined because it has no practical relevance. The only viable structure to apply the structure of a hypercube is a table. Tables, however, are better to be implemented using a DAG structure, where the user can either navigate along the columns or the rows of the table. The additional feature of the hypercube to navigate from the last element of a row or a column to the first field can be replaced by navigating back to the top element. Thus hypercubes do not offer features that are expected to be exploited.

Arbitrary $\exists n_i \in \mathbf{N} : \forall n_k \in \mathbf{N}, k \neq i : A(n_i, n_k)$ For the arbitrary graph we assume that there is a starting node (i.e., the entry point) and that each other node is reachable from the starting node.

4.6 Required Network Topologies

4.6.1 Use Cases

For a more concrete discussion, we have a look at some usage scenarios. This list is by no means exhaustive, but serves as an example of the different kinds of scenarios where the results are applicable. We will show, which features of the audio browser are needed in industrial size applications. However, the main focus is on determining the relevant network topologies for those scenarios.

Laboratory Worker

One application scenario is delivering information to workers in laboratories, such as chemical or pharmaceutical laboratories. In this scenario, the workers need their hands to perform their tasks, leaving voice as the logical interaction modality.

The information base contains information about all the different processes and the worker can access the parts relevant to her current task using the Talking Assistant (TA) headset. She will receive instructions on how to proceed and can ask for more details or help, when needed.

Workers in a laboratory are typically stationary when performing their tasks. They have all their instruments on their desks and perform their tasks at their desks. This offers us also the possibility of augmenting the information delivery by exploiting any displays on the desk. Note that such displays, if used, are only for displaying information. Interaction would still happen using voice commands issued to the headset. Mechanisms for using additional displays are beyond the current scope of this thesis and may be explored in a subsequent research.

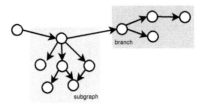

Figure 4.7: Linear graph with a hierarchic sub-graph

In this scenario, the worker receives only one instruction after the other to achieve her goal. The topology for this case is linear in most cases. Dependent on intermediate results the remaining steps may not be applicable any more. In that case, there is a branch and the DAG topology applies. Branching of a linear graph is illustrated in Figure 4.7.

Mobile Inspection

Another interesting field of application is mobile inspection. Possible examples include automotive and aerospace industries, but also inspections of ships and trains. In these scenarios the hands and eyes are busy performing the task.

In contrast to the laboratory, we cannot assume that there is any computer infrastructure for supporting the worker, except for a wireless network. In a laboratory it is possible to install displays at the desks, but in a mobile inspection scenario, e.g., inspecting an airplane, the worker must carry all the equipment with her in addition to any tools she might need to accomplish her task. This implies that the device used to access information should be as light-weighted as possible, yet provide a useful service to the worker.

The information base in this case contains information needed by the worker, such as how the inspections are to be performed, what things need to be verified, etc. It also contains solutions for common problems, as shown by the following example: Consider a worker inspecting a car who sees fluid leaking from a valve. Using the information base she can get information about possible causes of the leakage and solutions for these.

A possible extension to this scenario would be adding a head-mounted display onto the headset. This would allow us to deliver low quality graphical images, such as schematics or blueprints, to the worker to aid complex tasks. The details of this are not covered in this discussion and are left for future work.

The organization of documents is comparable to the one which was presented for the mobile worker. The instructions for the inspections to perform are linear at their core. Depending on the inspection result the worker leaves the linear main path and can browse for additional information. The information to look for is organized in a hierarchical structure where the DAG topology applies. A linear graph with a DAG sub-graph is illustrated in Figure 4.7.

Warehouse Pick list

A similar scenario to the previous one is a warehouse worker who needs to pick different items from different shelves. Again, the worker's hands are busy, calling for the use of voice interaction, and the high mobility of the worker makes carrying additional equipment impractical.

As in the mobile inspection scenario, the only infrastructure support we can assume is a wireless network and the information base. The difference between the mobile inspection and warehouse pick list scenarios are that in the former the worker is accessing information and in the latter she receives instructions and confirms them. For example, the next task could be "fetch 10 widgets from shelf 5 on aisle 7". When the worker has performed the task and has picked up the widgets, she would confirm this to the information base which would then dispatch her onwards to the next pick-up.

In this scenario the headset provides two important functions. The first one is what we mentioned above, i.e., instructing the worker what to do next and receiving confirmations from the worker that the task has been completed. The second function is providing help. For example, new workers might need instructions finding the optimal route between two pick-ups or help finding the correct items. The information base might also deliver descriptions of items if needed.

Again, the list of items to pick from the shelves is organized linearly. There is only one optimal route which will be presented to to the picker. Even, asking for help by novices do not alter this structure. As a result, the graph will have more nodes but remain linear.

Training at Work

Although all of the previous application scenarios are of great interest and usefulness in themselves, the results of this analysis can help augment them further. A major issue in modern world is training workers to perform new tasks. Many industries attempt to shorten production cycles in order to bring products to the market faster. This desire to speed up production is often hampered by the need to train the workers to follow new procedures which accompany the manufacturing of new products.

The browser can help shorten the training periods by providing training at work. In other words, it helps teaching the new procedures to the workers while they are actually performing them. We can deliver information from the information base directly to the worker and, more importantly, we can tailor this information to be relevant to the task she is currently learning. If the worker needs more information concerning a particular task, she can easily access it via the headset and have it delivered to her instantly. This does not not only shorten learning time but also includes quality as workers experience "learning by doing". This is also known as *Training@Work*.

Another major benefit in training scenarios is the ability to talk directly to other people. This can be used to provide a help-desk for individual workers without requiring them to interrupt their tasks or requiring a large number of help-desk attendants.

This scenario is comparable to the inspection scenario. The worker has to follow a given list of steps to assemble the product. If something unusual happens, she can

Table 4.4: Mapping of audio browsing use case scenarios to network topologies

scenario	topology
Laboratory Worker	Linear with branches
Mobile Inspection	Linear with sub-graphs
Warehouse Pick List	Linear
Training At Work	Linear with sub-graphs
Better Museum Guide	Directed Acyclic Graph

browse for help in a sub-graph (or talk with a colleague for clarification).

Better Museum Guide

Currently many museums offer visitors the possibility to borrow audio guides which explain many details about the exhibits in the museum. Also, museum guides have traditionally been among the first application scenarios for ubiquitous and pervasive computing research.

The main problem with the current audio guides is that they distract the visitor's attention. The visitor is expected to look at the exhibits while listening to a usually quite lengthy explanation of it. Such audio guides allow the visitor to listen to only parts of the information; either the visitor does not listen at all, thus negating the usefulness of the guide, or the visitor listens to all of it and has to divide her attention between the exhibit and the explanation.

A museum guide based on the Talking Assistant and a structured audio information base can help alleviate this problem. By default, the visitor gets only a brief description of the exhibit, e.g., title and painter for a painting. The visitor would then have the option to query for more details about the painting or the painter, depending on her interests. This eliminates the binary nature of modern audio guides and introduces many intermediate levels of detail between no information and all of the information.

In contrast to the previous scenarios, the user of a museum does not need to follow a predefined route but can walk around and browse for information at any exhibit. This is comparable to the browsing for information in the inspection or mobile work scenario. The topology for this scenario is a DAG topology.

4.6.2   Mapping of Use Cases to Network Topologies

Table 4.4 summarizes the mapping of the scenarios to the network topologies. Obviously, only the linear (Figure 4.6(a)) and the directed acyclic network (DAG) topology (Figure 4.6(d)) are of interest. The hierarchic topology is a special case of the DAG and is therefore included. The arbitrary graph does not have a concrete structure and should therefore be avoided. The main reason for this is that it can contain cycles. Cyclic references should be avoided to reduce the lost in space problem (see Section 4.7.1).

It is noticeable that most use cases rely on a linear structure whereas only one

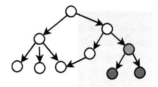

Figure 4.8: Iterative resolution method

scenario is built upon a hierarchic topology. The main difference between those two is that the scenarios for the linear have a clear defined goal which is very similar to following a work flow. With the museum guide the user does not have a predefined goal. She stops using the system if the abstract goal *I want to get all information I need* is satisfied. There will be no main path to achieve this. Hence the scenarios can be classified into two main classes:

- goal oriented scenarios and

- inquisitiveness oriented scenarios.

In goal oriented scenarios the user has a clearly defined goal (e.g., fetch a list of items from a warehouse) and the user is aware of that goal. Hence, they are easier to handle for users. In inquisitiveness oriented scenarios the user is browsing the graph to satisfy her need for information. In most cases it is impossible to define a clear "goal"; the user knows when she has found the information she seeks, but may not be able to formulate properly what she needs. Inquisitiveness oriented scenarios result in more general graphs in which it is easy to get lost.

The borders for these two classes are not sharp. Goal oriented scenarios may have hierarchic sub-graphs for some nodes as shown in Figure 4.7. Especially the Training@Work scenario, see section 4.6.1, should provide some more detailed information on demand. The more often a user walks along the main path the less will she be interested in visiting the sub-graphs. In addition, following a linear graph may be interactive; hence, branches are also possible. Imagine a laboratory assistant who has to continue in different ways depending on the state of the mixture.

From the mathematical point of view there is now no difference between the linear and the hierarchical topology. This will be used to find a solution for the challenges of an audio only application.

4.6.3 Iterative Resolution Method

The approach for determining how to handle complex document structures is iterative. We call this approach *Iterative Resolution Method*. This approach concentrates on the navigation possibilities in a single node as a first step. If this can be solved, it can be extended to a global navigation. It should be noted that this approach does not address the lost in space problem; this will be discussed in Section 4.7.1.

An example of this resolution method is shown in figure 4.8. The user comes from a document, listens to the current document and has to decide where to go next.

This is the basic situation which appears in any of the topologies from section 4.5. In other words, it is assumed that the user is aware of the preceding node, the current node and the possibilities for choosing the next node.

If it is possible to perform this for an arbitrary node, then this can iteratively be applied to cover the whole document graph. This method applies to all the scenarios in section 4.5. In fact, it further applies that

$$H_L \subset H_H \subset H_{DAG}. \tag{4.8}$$

Hence, if it is possible to solve a DAG, it is also possible to handle hierarchical and linear graphs, since they are both special cases of a DAG.

It can be easily seen that a DAG satisfies the conditions above. The user starts from the root and navigates through a path in the DAG. Even though a node in the DAG may have multiple parents, the user's navigation path determines which of the parents the user came through. Hence the condition for a node having a unique parent (from the user's point of view) is satisfied and the iterative resolution method applies.

4.7　Audio Limitations in Audio Browsing

This section discusses the impact of the limitation of audio based user interfaces for audio browsing that were introduced in section 2.6.1. We conducted two user studies to explore the corresponding parameters.

In the first setting, the participants had to browse a web page by audio, which was implemented in VoiceXML. The principal object was to determine the factors influencing the user while she is navigating a set of documents via a telephone, using only audio for input and output. The application was quite inhomogeneous, since it was designed to observe how the participants dealt with different arrangements. There were 29 participants, aged from 17 to 53 with an average age of 30. The average experience with computers was high, but the experience with audio based interfaces was neither good nor bad.

In the second setting, the users had to browse a list of documents that were displayed on a screen using audio commands and gestures. Object of this test was to compare visual and gesture interaction. There were 16 participants. Their experience with computers and audio based user interfaces was similar to the other test.

4.7.1　Transience

The main problem is that the user must remember all possible actions. The psychological background is stated in [Nor88]:

> Short-term memory is the memory of the just present. Information is retained in it automatically and retrieved without effort; but the amount of information that can be retained is severely limited. Something like five to seven items is the limit of STM, with the number going to ten or twelve if a person also rehearses, mentally repeating the items to be retained.

The items do not include only plain information I but will also take respect to the navigation possibilities in the current node.

This leads to the very hard requirement

$$\delta_c|C(n_i)| + \delta_h n_{i-1} + \delta_i|I(n_i)| \leq \max(STM) \tag{4.9}$$

where δ_c, δ_h and δ_i are weighting factors to be determined through our user study and $\max(STM)$ denotes the maximum capacity of the short term memory. In other words, the sum of the number of possibilities where the user can go ($|C(n_i)|$), where the user came from (n_{i-1}) and the information in the current node ($|I(n_i)|$) must not be greater than 7, with respect to the limit of the short term memory.

The amount of information is hard to determine. We will take this as a black box for now and explore this later. The weighting factors take care of the different requirements for remembering the different items and need to be determined experimentally.

The value of δ_c depends on the locations of the links within the voice stream. There are two classes of links:

- detail links and

- choice links

Detail links are comparable to hyperlinks in graphical web browsers and occur somewhere within the voice stream. If the user knows about the marked area she will just ignore it and forget about it and δ_c will be small. If the user wants to get detailed information she follows the link and we have the same situation as in the current node. This corresponds to links within hypertext. Users simply over read them. Just in case she is interested in more details she follows the link. An example is shown in Figure 4.10.

Choice denote the case that the user actively selects an options. Here the user has to remember the named items to be able to make her choice. Hence for choice links the value of δ_c will be high.

In practice, choice links being different to detail links means, that a node that has many children (e.g., possible choices to proceed) can only contain little information in the node.

Hence, linear topologies will be able to provide more information in a single node than DAG. Furthermore, it will not be possible to handle lists with more than seven items. Section 5.5.6 and section 5.5.8 will introduce possible solutions for this problem. For now, the goal is to achieve an easy handling for lists with a small vocabulary.

A solution to handle lists with a small vocabulary is SCRIPTED INTERACTION which was described in our survey for a small command set, see section 4.3.4. SCRIPTED INTERACTION enables the user to select an option from a list using a single command. Although users are not familiar with this approach, we expect that this way to handle lists is intuitive enough, since it reduced the selection process to a short question answering.

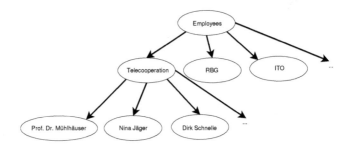

Figure 4.9: Structure of the employee search task

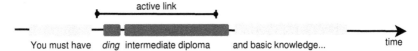

Figure 4.10: Activable link in a voice stream

User Study

This user study used the first setting. The tests related to transience are described below.

Number of choice links A first test in our study aimed at determining the rules for choice links, the participants were asked to retrieve the telephone number of a certain person. The persons that could be looked up were employees of TU Darmstadt and members of a group within TU Darmstadt. The structure is shown in Figure 4.9. Each group had a different number of members: Six, eight and ten. The names of the groups and their members were read to the participants as lists. They had to say *yes* or *OK* to select the item, group or person for selection. Having selected the person, the participants got some information about the selected person.

After each run the participants were asked to rate the number of options on a scale from 1 (too short) to 10 (too many).

Number of detail links In another study, we tried to find the rules for detail links. The users were asked to browse for information in the tree. The links to child documents were within the spoken text, comparable to a hyperlink in HTML documents. The users could activate the link by saying *details*. An example is shown in Figure 4.10. When the link starts, a short sound *ding* was played to indicate the start of the link. The link text was followed by a short pause to leave some more time to activate the link. The participants listened to different documents with one, three and five links

After each run the participants were asked if there were too many links in the document.

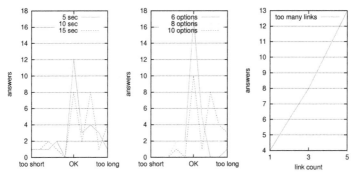

(a) Length of information (b) Number of children in a (c) Number of detail links
node   choice node

Figure 4.11: User study to determine amount of information per node

Hierarchy level Another test case of our user study aimed at determining the impact of the hierarchy level in inquisitiveness oriented scenarios onto the user's navigation capabilities. In a test with the same settings as the previous test, the users were asked to activate the links and to search a piece of information that was given in the document itself, like the previous test, after activating three detail links and after four detail links. Thus the users had to navigate down the tree to find the information.

Length of information A fourth test was designed to determine the amount of information in a single node. The users were asked to listen to a longer passage of text and answer a question regarding the content. The text was split into multiple information nodes in a linear graph structure. The users were able to navigate back and forth the information nodes n_i. Since it is hard to quantify $I(n_i)$, we cut the text at the length of 5, 10 and 15 sec as a measurement for the amount of information per node.

After each run the participants were asked to rate their impression, scaled from 1 to 10, about the amount of information that was being delivered.

User Study Evaluation

The result of the choice link test is shown in Figure 4.11(b). The amount of information corresponds to the number k of members in each group. In this case we have simply $|I(n_i)| = k$. The result proves the assumption that more than seven information items are hard to handle for users. For equation (4.9) this means: If we measure $|I(n_i)|$ in seconds in DAG topologies, the following condition must hold

$$|I_{DAG}(n_i)| \leq 7 \qquad (4.10)$$

The result of the node length test is shown in Figure 4.11(a). The optimal length is 10 seconds. A length of 5 seconds is considered to be worse but still OK, whereas a length of 15 seconds is too long for most participants.

The expected result was that the length of the nodes $t_{n,i}$ is directly proportional to the impression to get too many information and accepted for $t_{n,i} < 10s$. This was not the case. The impression was also high for the shortest length. A reason might have been, that this was the first task and the participants needed to learn how to deal with the test application. This effect would vanish, if the participants were divided into several groups. Unfortunately this was not possible, since there were too few participants. However our expectation $t_{n,i} < 10s$ was validated.

Reasons for our observation are given in [AS68]. Atkinson et al. state that the lifespan of the short term memory is only 10 seconds. Information gets lost if there is more information to process. For equation (4.9) this means, if we measure $|I(n_i)|$ in seconds in linear topologies, the following condition must hold

$$|I_L(n_i)| = t_{n_i}\frac{1}{s} \leq 10 \tag{4.11}$$

If we take the *phonological loop*, which is described e.g. in the psychological studies of Baddely et al. [BH74], we can assume that length is an alternative measurement for the number of items. The phonological loop is part of Baddely's model of working memory that rehearses audio information. It is a phonological memory store that can hold traces of audio based information. They found that durations of approximately 1.5 sec match the information of a single item. Assuming a direct proportionality of the length and the humans ability to remember, we have a simple formula to determine $|I(n_I)|$ from $t_{n,i}$:

$$|I_L(n_i)| = \frac{3}{2s}t_{n,i} \tag{4.12}$$

This matches also the result of our user study.

The result of these tests can be used to determine the weighting factor δ_i. From the observations of equation (4.8) and equation (4.9), we can assume that

$$\delta_i \approx 1 \tag{4.13}$$

The concrete value of δ_i is user dependent.

For choice links, we can assume from the above discussion, that the number of child nodes $|C(n_i)|$ is limited to seven. Thus we need no special test for this.

The hierarchy level test helps to determine the weighting factor δ_c for detail links. In contrast to the previous tests, this test posed a heavier load onto the user's short term memory. The result is shown in Figure 4.11(c). It is obvious, that the rejection of the interface increases with the number of links. Five links were rejected by half of the participants, whereas up to three links were accepted by most. From our observation we have to require for detail links

$$|C(n_i)| \leq 3 \tag{4.14}$$

Another lesson from Figure 4.11(c) is, that the the more links exist the more the users reject the interface. In the regarded interval, we can assume that the reaction rate scale linear with a factor of 10. Scaled to the magical number of seven, we can approximate δ_c in for detail links to a value of 2.

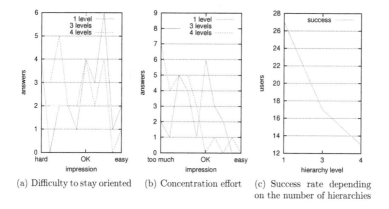

(a) Difficulty to stay oriented   (b) Concentration effort   (c) Success rate depending on the number of hierarchies

Figure 4.12: User study to determine hierarchy level

Summing up both results, we get the following approximation for δ_c:

$$\delta_c \approx \begin{cases} 1 & \text{for choice links} \\ 2 & \text{for detail links} \end{cases} \quad (4.15)$$

Again, the concrete value is user dependent.

Detail links seem to be more difficult to handle than choice links. Therefore, we asked the participants for the the reasons. Figure 4.12(a) shows their answers to the question, if it was hard to stay oriented. In most cases it was no problem to stay oriented if the information was given in the document itself. It got worse when the level increased. A level of four seemed to be too hard for most users. Figure 4.12(b) shows that already a level of three required full concentration from the users. Consequently, not all participants were able to find the information with increasing levels, as shown in figure 4.12(c). This makes it unusable, in smart environments, where information from the environment poses additional load onto the user's memory.

As a result, we found, that detail links should be avoided, since they pose too much load onto the user's memory. However, a level of one should be acceptable. If there is no additional load, users can also cope with three levels, but in that case, they need their full concentration onto this task. Choice links were not tested explicitly, but the users had no problems to navigate the tree using choice links. For example, most telephony applications work menu based and feature more than one hierarchy level.

Another problem in the context of transience of speech is the handling for nodes without children, i.e., nodes for which $|C(n)| = 0$. This problem typically occurs in inquisitiveness oriented scenarios. In goal oriented scenarios, when we reach the last node, we are finished and the user has to start again manually. In inquisitiveness oriented scenarios the user has the following options:

- The user wants to return to the parent node.

- The user wants to hear the information again.

- The user is satisfied and wants to stop.

- The user is lost and unsure what to do next.

The system knows nothing about the user's goals. A clue that *the user is satisfied or is lost* maybe if there is a long pause after the document stops. The problem of being lost will be addresses in section 4.7.1. It is not advisable to end the document and wait for a response from the user. This may cause the user to feel that she is not in control of what is going on. The better choice would be to add a *final leaf node* to each leaf of the graph containing the list shown above. This also matches the observation from HyperSpeech, refer to section 4.2.3, where we pointed out that an automatism confused the user.

In general long pauses should be avoided. People do not like dead air in a conversation. Pauses may also occur at the end of a document if the system is awaiting the next command or answer to a choice link. If such a long pause is detected the system must take control and ask if the user needs help. In a telephone environment, applications wait a certain time for input from the user and then reprompt. The user has no chance to escape from it. Hence there should be a choice left to the user, what to do next. She may want to

- hear the prompt again because she cannot remember it,

- hear the information again,

- proceed with the next document,

- stop because she is satisfied, or

- need more help and connect to an operator.

Having detected a long pause the system should present these choices to the user.

Lost in Space

A well known phenomenon that is also known in the domain of graphical web browsers is the *lost in space problem*. It can be defined as follows:

Definition 24 *A user gets **lost in space** if she does not know where in the graph she is.*

This is also part of the work of some artists to express the feeling of being lost, as Wolfgang Glass expressed it in his picture *Lost in Teleportation* 4.13. The grade of this phenomenon depends on knowledge of the user about the graph. If the user listens to the documents for the first time, she has no clue about the structure that will be presented. In a training environment, users will in time learn this structure. This is typically the case for most goal oriented scenarios. Inquisitiveness oriented scenarios have an abstract goal and lack a targeted structure that can be learned. As a consequence the probability to get lost is always higher for inquisitiveness oriented scenarios than for goal oriented scenarios.

Barras names in [Bar97] the following solutions for this in the context of navigating in a 3D visualization of geological structures.

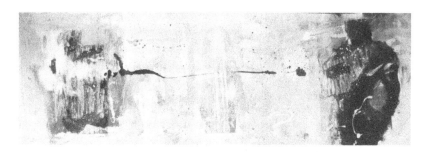

Figure 4.13: Lost in Teleportation courtesy of Wolfgang Glass

Calling Someone calls to you from somewhere and you can head in that direction to find them.

Telling Someone sitting next to you gives you directions, as in driving a car.

Landmarks You hear a familiar sound, such as the clock chiming in the village and you can use it to orient yourself and work out where to head.

Implementation of calling does not apply to the domain of browsing. In UC an calling could be applied in the way that smart items make noises to help the user finding them. This principle can not be transferred to audio documents. For our purposes only *telling* and *landmarks* are relevant.

In order to apply telling, a representation of a path is needed that is told to the user upon request. Furthermore, we suggest that all documents must have a title or a primary headline. This is part of the document that is played to the user. She will recognize it and will help her in locating her current position within the graph. Another advantage is that this helps the user to remember most of the information that is delivered within a single node. Users tend to rely more on information being delivered at the beginning, as if it is burned into the user's brain. Magicians, for example, know about this and present their best tricks at the beginning and at the end of their show. This way, the spectators remember mainly their best tricks. In psychology this effect is also know as the *start-end model*. The STM codes the positions of items in a sequence relative to the start and end of that sequence.

However, another command to get this path information is needed, extending our basic command set, see section 4.3, by the command *path*. A more concrete discussion about the creation of paths is in section 4.8.1.

Another possibility is to use landmarking. Different auditory icons can be used to indicate grouping of related documents. In addition they can be used as a possible clue for indicating the current depth. Distinct auditory icons for different depth can easily be confused but playing two tones with different pitch with a short delay can help to get an idea about the current depth. This can be done automatically before playing a document. It has to be evaluated how much this can help prevent the user getting lost.

4.7.2　Invisibility

One aspect of speech being invisible is that a user does not know what action she may perform and what phrases she must say to perform these actions. Since we are working with a reduced command set this problem should be less severe. Nevertheless, it is important to aid the user when this problem occurs. This can be done with the possibility to list the valid commands and to be able to talk to an operator. Since the problem may occur while the system tells something, e.g. "I didn't want that. How can I stop it?", it must be possible to stop the current output using barge-in.

This leads to another problem that occurs because speech is invisible. Users may feel that they are not in control. We have to give the user the impression that she is in control. As already mentioned in section 2.6 there is a difference between *feeling to be* in control and actually *being* in control.

Therefore, interaction with the systems needs to be predictable. It should behave in a manner such that users can accurately predict what will happen next. In case the content is not predictable, this leads to an exceptional situation. Because of the limitations of the human memory such exceptional situations are difficult to cope with and should be avoided. In order to achieve predictability, the user's mental model must match the conceptual model. In addition, the system should be able to monitor user behavior and make a reasonable guess as to the action or speech the user is trying to apply. A misinterpretation of the user's intentions can lead to challenging problems. Context can help with this. We discuss contextual information in more detail in section 4.9.

In order for the user to feel to be in control, she needs feedback from the computer. When she issues a command, the system should acknowledge that the user has been heard. Users also want feedback when the system is busy. This can be achieved with auditory icons.

Another form of feedback is required to signal the user that the recognizer is turned on and she may utter a command. In order to reduce the recognition of unwanted commands, it makes sense to enable the recognizer just when it is necessary.

User Study

Feedback The participants had to browse a set of documents using voice commands. The documents were displayed on a screen. The participants were asked to search a certain piece of information. They started with a deactivated recognizer which had to be turned on by the participants. We tested three kinds of feedback about the recognizer's state:

1. an auditory icon

2. an icon on the screen

3. no feedback

Having finished their task, the participants were asked

- how their impression of being in control of the system was,
- if they were able to know the system state and

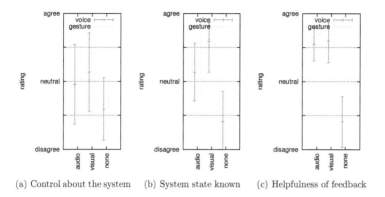

(a) Control about the system   (b) System state known   (c) Helpfulness of feedback

Figure 4.14: User study about feedback on recognizer status

- if the current kind of feedback was considered to be helpful.

User Study Evaluation

The result of the feedback test is shown in figure 4.14(a).

The difference between gestures and audio are not significant, see Figure 4.14(b). Gestures seem to be slightly better in all cases, but it was very much depending on the kind of feedback the users got. The best feedback is visual. It is always there, since the participants were able to read the recognizer's state on the screen and most participants felt being in control of the system. An audio feedback is slightly worse, rated neutral.

With audio, the participants got a confirmation about the activation and deactivation of the recognizer. As long as they were interacting with the system, there was no additional mental load to remember the state. This became worse when there was no feedback at all. The participants had no idea if their command was recognized and they were not sure about the recognizer's state. This is confirmed by the responses to the question, if the participants were always sure about the recognizer's state. Their rating is shown in figure 4.14(b).

This means that a strong relationship between the presence of a feedback and the user's feeling of being in control of the system exists. Permanent markers are preferred, transient markers are accepted, but no feedback was rejected, see figure 4.14(c).

Another aspect that may make the user feel not being in control is insufficient trust in recognition performance, which was discussed in Section 2.6.1. The user may also be afraid to get lost in the audio space, which is discussed in Section 4.7.1.

4.7.3 Asymmetry

The fact that users read faster than they type, but can listen much more slowly than they can read is more important for multimodal scenarios. In these scenarios,

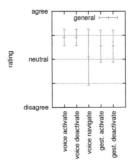

Figure 4.15: General comments on the system

the user can use speech to enter date and use graphical output devices to retrieve data. We are mainly targeting audio only environments where no visual feedback exists. The influence on the amount of data being delivered has been discussed in Section 4.7.1.

As mentioned in Section 2.6.1, in some cases we may have support for displays in the user's environment. In such cases we should decide what information to show on the display and what to deliver to the headset. We can leverage the asymmetry, by showing long passages of text on the display and use the headset for navigation and delivering short messages as well as audio cues or icons to the user.

4.7.4 One-dimensionality

One of the main disadvantages of audio is the linearity of the medium. Once the user navigated to a certain document it has to be presented to the user. Most screen readers read the document to the user, thus condemning the user to a patient listener. As we showed in section 4.7.2 this leads to the user's impression of not being in control. Raman states in [Ram98]:

> When perusing printed text, a reader can quickly skip portions of the document, reading only those sections that are of interest. ...The passive information in a printed document is accessed by an active reader capable of selectively perusing the text. Hence, visual documents themselves need not to be interactive. Things are different with audio. This passive-active relationship is reversed in traditional oral communication; the information flows past a passive listener who has little control on what is heard.

The main difference between the navigation within a document comes from the eye, which is active, and the ear, which is passive. Raman summarizes this to the requirement:

> Therefore, to be effective, audio documents need to be interactive.

This is the reason why navigation in the audio space makes no difference between the navigation between documents and the navigation within a document. Reading a footnote, for example, comprises the following steps:

1. Mark current position

2. Go to upper document level

3. Search footnote

4. Read footnote

5. Go back to marked position

This means, that each documents forms an own navigation space with a DAG topology. This nested structure will be present in most documents.

4.7.5 Speech Synthesis Quality

The quality of speech synthesis is still very poor but offers a high grade of flexibility. People have more trouble remembering messages spoken in synthetic speech versus natural speech, unless trained to do so. For novice users, slow speech should be used to increase the comprehension of messages. The efforts needed to get pre-recorded audio are too high for our purposes. Hence we will use speech synthesis hoping that it can be replaced by a better one some day. If a production version would be built for a particular use case, it would certainly be possible to pre-record all the necessary segments of audio to improve the user experience.

4.7.6 Speech Recognition Performance

In contrast to visual user interfaces speech recognition as an input medium is still error prone. Errors can be reduced by improving the technology but they can not totally be eliminated. Consequently an application that uses speech recognition has to make to think about error handling.

Junqua says in [Jun00]:

> The cost of an error is application dependent, and so is the error correction technology used. Errors have serious consequences because they can destroy the user's mental model.

This is especially true regarding our purposes. Consequences of an error are that the user navigates somewhere where she didn't want to go. This increases the lost in space problem and the feeling of not being in control as well.

Handling Detected Errors

We will be able to detect an error only on those cases where a word is detected that is not allowed in the current context. These cases are

- the user wants to start the dialog, e.g., start the system

- the user wants to follow a link

- the user wants to choose something from a list

In all of these cases only a few, known commands are possible, hence any other command we detect implies an error. However, this error could of course be caused by the user uttering an incorrect command which was correctly recognized. This situation can be handled by requesting the user to repeat the command; if it is a recognition error, it is unlikely to be repeated, while a user error will be repeated. In the second case we are in a situation where we do not know the source of the error.

Possible causes for the second type of error are:

- an out-of-vocabulary word

- a word that cannot be used in this context

- recognition error

- background noise

- incorrect pronunciation (e.g. non-native speaker)

Note that in all of these cases, we know that an error has occurred, but do not know the source. Asking the user to repeat the command once may help us solve problems with recognition errors, incorrect pronunciation, or noise. However, if the error persists, it is likely that the user is trying to use a wrong command. In this case we should prompt the user again, with an indication that the command is not appropriate in the current situation.

Junqua suggests in [Jun00] the following possibilities to deal with a detected error:

- do nothing and let the user find out and correct the error

- prevent the user from continuing

- complain and warn the user using a feedback mechanism

- correct it automatically without user intervention

- initiate a procedure to correct the error with the user's help through

Unfortunately, all of the above mentioned strategies, especially the first one, have the drawback that users may refrain to work with the application, because dialogs become too long and they do not want to confirm everything. A better solution is to prevent errors.

Error Prevention

In most cases we are unable to detect an error. In return, we should find solutions to prevent evaluation of unwanted commands.

To reduce the probability of misrecognized words we have to

- limit background noise and

- enable the user to turn off the input device.

This is also the main item where high-performance speech recognizers would help. In [DH04], overcoming the challenge of making speech recognition systems robust in noisy acoustic environments is classified as a fundamental challenge. It has been one of the most popular problems addressed by both academic and industrial researchers of speech recognition.

In addition, it is common practice to have the user confirm the speech recognition result. As already mentioned above, this technique is not always advisable to use. If the user wants to step quickly through some points, she will not be pleased if the application always demands a confirmation. There needs to be a trade-off between the user's wishes and the confirmations.

Since the costs of an error are relatively low in our environment, there is no confirmation needed. In case of an error, the user can simply go back.

User Study

Error Handling In our audio navigation scenario, the participants were asked to find a certain piece of information. We gave no clues about the accepted commands, telling the participants, the application is self explanatory and they would find their way. However, the application accepted only a limited set of commands to browse for the information, which was not mentioned in the first prompt. We did this to enforce error situations, no input on the one hand and wrong commands on the other hand. The different kinds of errors called, *noinput* if the user did not say anything and *nomatch* if she used a word that could not be recognized successfully, led to different levels of help, increasing with it's occurrence in a row.

After the participants experienced the error they were asked

- if the given help was adequate to achieve their goal and

- how many error levels should be provided.

User Study Evaluation

The answers to the helpfulness are shown in figure 4.16(b). The answers to the number of error levels show, see figure 4.16(a), that something between two and four appear to be adequate.

In our limited environment, it is relatively easy to find out the user's intention. Using the source of the error, the user did not say anything (noinput) or she used a word that was not recognized successfully (nomatch), the escalation of the detail messages was considered to be helpful for most users. The shorter error messages

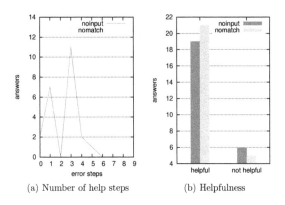

(a) Number of help steps   (b) Helpfulness

Figure 4.16: User study about error handling

at the first level are no additional burden for experienced users, because they had not to listen to long explanations of the one-dimensional medium.

Since we want to help the user but cannot make really good guesses, we need the user's help to correct an error. Our observation showed also, that errors detected by the users themselves were easy to undo by navigating back to the previous location.

4.7.7   Recognition: Flexibility vs. Accuracy

As mentioned in Section 2.6.1, we have decided to set this trade-off in favor of accuracy. This is because we are using a simple command-and-control interface, which naturally provides an easy way to get accurately recognized speech, but may lack flexibility in some use cases. However, given the low resources for speech recognition of embedded devices, it is natural to restrict the flexibility in favor of accuracy. Furthermore, the goal is to provide a means of *navigating* through an audio information base, not to provide a generic audio interface. Such navigation can be easily achieved with a small number of distinct commands, hence our decision to favor accuracy.

4.7.8   Conversation

User Study

Activation The participants had to browse a set of documents using voice commands. The documents were displayed on a screen. The participants were asked to search a certain piece of information. They started with a deactivated recognizer. The recognizer could be turned on and off with the voice in the one group and with gestures in the other group. The voice group used the command *computer on* to activate the recognizer and *computer off* to deactivate it. The gesture group used a short and fast turn of the right hand, as if they had to open a bottle to activate the recognizer and a left turn, as if a bottle had to be closed to deactivate the recognizer. As a side effect we could test the activation of a recognizer by voice. We achieved this by a simple one-command-grammar that contained only the command to activate the recognizer. If the command was detected, the active grammar was substituted with the grammar for browsing.

Evaluation

During our activation tests we observed no false alarms. The recognizer was never activated if the user did not utter the specific command, although there was a lot of talk between the participants and the testers and the recognizer was turned on all the time.

This proves that this simple strategy is suitable to be used in mobile settings.

4.7.9 Privacy

Privacy is a complex topic that must be addresses by our mobile audio browser. Critical information must be hidden from others. Since the users are wearing a headset, problems with privacy are not applicable for the system output. User input is the critical factor. Others may hear what a user says. This is unwanted in certain scenarios.

We did not investigate this topic in this thesis, but focus on the analysis of navigation in the audio domain.

4.7.10 Service availability

Services may become not accessible, if the user moves around. This issue was also addressed for workflows in section 2.5.5.

This issue will be addressed in section 6.3. We did not investigate it for the audio browser prototype.

Another point that comes with this challenge is the possibility to expand the current grammar depending on the context. This issue will be addressed in section 3.4 and was also not investigated for the audio browser prototype.

4.8 Available Contexts

The previous sections showed how the audio browser can be controlled using voice commands and we analyzed the limits of browsing in audio using voice commands. The audio browser is designed to work in smart environments. This section addresses what context information needs to be taken into account based on our understanding of context-awareness which was introduced in section 2.2. The analysis serves as a basis to discuss how these contexts will be combined afterwards in section 4.9.

4.8.1 Location

As mentioned in section 2.2 location is considered as a parameter specified in electronic and physical space. Our prototype uses both. The physical location is deter-

Figure 4.17: Relative Positioning

mined by the positioning model whereas the electronic location is specified by the path to the current audio document.

Physical Location

Multiple location systems exist. An overview is given by Hightower in [HB01]. He distinguishes three different location sensing techniques:

Triangulation can be done via using multiple distance measurements between known points, or by measuring angle or bearing relative to points with known separation.

Scene analysis examines a view from a particular vantage point.

Proximity measures nearness to a known set of points.

Triangulation and scene analysis have in common that they determine the exact location in although they achieve this by different techniques. Proximity is different since it does not need the exact location. This allows us to classify the relevant positioning systems into

- relative positioning and

- absolute positioning.

The physical location is obtained from a positioning system. The prototype of the audio browser uses the TA, see section 2.3.1, which features both positioning models. Determining the physical location is part of the TA concept, see [AM02].

In the following both concepts are described using the TA as an example implementation. However, the core concept can be transferred to any other implementation. The museum guide guidePORT [gui] is another example for a system that uses relative positioning.

Relative Positioning   Relative positioning uses tags to get an idea of the user's location. When the TA *sees* a tag, the TA sends a location enter event, whereas it sends a location leave event when it gets out of the range of it. Tags are only visible to the TA if the user approaches close enough and is within a certain angle as it shown in Figure 4.17.

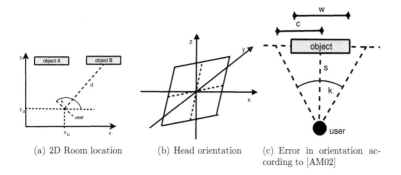

(a) 2D Room location   (b) Head orientation   (c) Error in orientation according to [AM02]

Figure 4.18: Absolute positioning

A tag is visible, if the user's receiver is somewhere in the area that is covered by the tag. Thus visibility $v\mathrm{TA}_{\mathrm{tag}}$ of an object is expressed by

$$v\mathrm{TA}_{\mathrm{tag}}(d, s) = \begin{cases} 1 & \text{if } d < d_\theta \wedge k < k_\theta \\ 0 & \text{otherwise} \end{cases} \qquad (4.16)$$

where k is the angle to the center of the tag and k_θ is the maximum angle where a user is in the range of the tag. This has already been used by our previous prototype that we described in section 4.6.2.

Absolute Positioning Absolute positioning, as described in [AM03], offers a more concrete idea of of the user's location. The Talking Assistant features an infrared-based local positioning system. The positioning system delivers the values to determine the users position (x_u, y_u) in the room, see figure 4.18(a), head orientation k and tilt, as shown in figure 4.18(b).

With these values it is easy to determine the user's line of sight. But this will not be enough to determine the object of interest for sure. Imagining a user looking at a match box at a distance of 10 meters it becomes clear that there must be a relationship between the distance d and the visible surface s of the object.

According to [AM02] an object of size w must be completely covered by $2c$, see Figure 4.18(c). In case the user is looking straight ahead, the visibility of an object is expressed by

$$v\mathrm{TA}_{\mathrm{iris}} = \frac{w}{2c} \qquad (4.17)$$

With $\tan(k) = \frac{c}{s}$ and solving for c equation(4.17) can be rewritten as

$$v\mathrm{TA}_{\mathrm{iris}} = \frac{s}{2d\tan(k)} \qquad (4.18)$$

where k is the measurement error of the TA's internal compass.

Both systems deliver an ID of the object of interest that can be linked against documents. Furthermore the absolute positioning is able to evaluate a *near* relationship between objects of the real world. The use of the Context Server, refer to section 2.3.3, allows us to map the location to a single ID. This way, the transition in the workflow can be checked against this ID.

This is also our representation of a mapping between the physical presence and a corresponding electronic artifact. A location can have a related node that can be either the starting point of a whole graph or a node with the graph.

Electronic Location

The electronic location is represented by the user's position within a graph. In section 4.7.1 we stated that telling can be used to inform the user about that position.

In order to apply telling a representation of a path is needed. Following the definition of Fronk in [Fro02] and using the relations that were introduced in section 4.5 a path from node n_i to node n_k is recursively defined as

$$\text{path}(n_i, n_k) = \begin{cases} \emptyset & \text{if } n_i \equiv n_k \\ n_i \frown \text{path}(n_{i+1}, k) & \text{if } n_{i+1} \in C(n_i) \\ \perp & \text{else} \end{cases} \qquad (4.19)$$

The operator $\frown$ denotes the composition of path elements. Then a path $path(n_1, n_i)$ from the root node n_1 to a node n_i can be expressed as $\vec{n}_i$. The concrete representation of a path depends on the topology. This will be explored in the following sections.

Path in a Linear Topology   Goal oriented scenarios feature a mostly linear topology. Linear topologies can be compared to the wizards in a GUI. To inform the user about the progress there is always a line telling *Step 4 of 12* in a graphical wizard.

The size of the current step can be easily determined by $|\vec{n}_i|$. However, there may be branches $|\vec{n}_i|$ that might not be unique. In this case the size of the current step depends on the current branch, which means that the length of the main graph may be changed by each choice node within the graph. In addition each choice node must have knowledge which of it's children is the main trunk. The length can then be expressed by

$$|\vec{n}_i| = \begin{cases} 1 & \text{if } |C(n_i)] = 0 \\ 1 + |\vec{n}_c| & \text{if } |C(n_i)| = 1 \wedge C(n_c, n_i) \\ 1 + |\vec{n}_{\hat{c}}| & \text{if } |C(n_{\hat{c}})| > 1 \wedge C(n_{\hat{c}}, n_i) \end{cases} \qquad (4.20)$$

where $n_{\hat{c}}$ is the first child node of the main branch. Knowledge about a main child is only required in linear topologies. In a hierarchical topology there is no main child.

$$\vec{n}_i = (n_1, n_2, \ldots, n_i) \quad , \quad n_k \in N_{DAG} \wedge P(n_1) = \emptyset \wedge \\ (\forall k : 2 \leq k \leq i \wedge n_k \in C(n_{k-1})) \qquad (4.21)$$

For the announcement of the progress we have two possibilities:

- always tell the progress in the beginning of a document

- tell the progress on demand

In section 2.6.1 we discussed that the number of items we can present is limited. In addition, it will be annoying to the user if she goes through the graph multiple times and always hears the progress and can't skip this. It would be better to tell the progress on demand, but this requires another word in the minimal command set, because this function is not readily covered by any of the existing commands. Furthermore, if the linear graph has any branches, the concept of progress may not be unique and it may add to the user's cognitive load.

Path in a DAG Topology   Inquisitiveness oriented scenarios feature a hierarchical topology. Things are different with DAGs. Here, the metric is not progress in the graph but how deep the user descended into it. In the visual world, users have the same problem when they navigate in a web site. With the age of dynamically created pages, the URL does not always give enough hints to let the user know how she navigated there. Web designers help users by following a style guide that displays the path in a predefined area (e.g., a navigation frame). We will need an equivalent mechanism for expressing the document name or the path in audio. Therefore some information is needed to build the path. Two possible sources of information we consider are:

- the graph and

- the documents in the graph

For the graph, we only know the distance to the root node and the visited nodes. Telling this to the user means to say something like *"You are on level five"*, which means nothing to the user. This is in contrast to the linear case, where such numbers are useful.

We can consider only those nodes that the user recently visited. With this, determining the path can be reduced to a simple stack problem. If the user traverses to a child node, the document is pushed onto the stack, and if she navigates back, the latest document is popped from the stack. Thus, the stack is an equivalent representation for the path from the root node to the current document.

Another situation where this title path can be helpful is in linear topologies, when, for example a described procedure requires an interruption for 30 minutes. The title path can be used to aid the user in getting back into the context when resuming.

General Path Constraints   Following the requirement in section 4.7.1 the length of the path is limited because it can't be remembered by the user. The limitation of STM requires

$$|\vec{n}_i| \leq 7 \tag{4.22}$$

For DAG topologies this will limit the maximum of information to

$$|H_{DAG}| \leq 7^7 \tag{4.23}$$

In other words, the maximum depth of a DAG is 7 levels and each level can have a maximum of 7 items. Although this seems to be a lot at first sight, it requires the author to find a clever solution to spread the deliverable information over the whole graph.

Linear topologies do not have a comparable limitation, since the user does not need to remember the steps that she performed to stay oriented.

The above discussion leads to the following value for δ_h of equation 4.9:

$$\delta_h \approx \begin{cases} 1 & \text{for inquisitiveness oriented scenarios} \\ 0 & \text{for goal oriented scenarios} \end{cases} \tag{4.24}$$

Again, the concrete values are user dependent.

4.8.2 Identity

The TA is a personalized device representing the user's identity. Identification of the user is considered to be a basic feature of the TA and is not included in this thesis.

However, we can exploit this identity feature to maintain a profile for the user. The profile is a set of preferences that have a direct impact on the representation of audio documents and navigational help. It is even possible to relate other contexts to the profile [GS01]. Since the TA is a personalized device there is no need to share profiles among multiple TAs.

The profile of the user delivers some common attributes of the user like *Id*, *name*, and *address*, These common attributes are useful in identifying the user for the computer, by her ID, or for a human, by name, address, ... For our audio browser the only relevant piece of data is the ID.

Furthermore a profile can contain two categories of data:

1. attributes that affect alternative representation and

2. attributes that affect navigation within the graph.

Alternative Representation

Alternative representation means that there are either multiple audio documents for the same node or that we use the DECORATION pattern that is also known from [GHJV92].

Support of multiple languages is an example for having multiple audio documents for the same node. Language is the most important attribute that has an influence to the representation. We choose English as our default language. Other languages, German at first place, can be supported at a later development stage. If the documents are not generated the only option is to translate each document into the language to support. A similar technique is used in the Apache web server, where the `.htaccess` file can be used to forward a request to a page in the language that is set in the user's browser. If an English speaking user request a page `index.html` she would be forwarded e.g. to the page `index.html.en` while a German user would be forwarded e.g. to the page `index.html.de`. Each of these pages is written in the user's language. For the audio browser, this means that the whole graph has to be cloned for each supported language. Users with different languages will use different graphs.

Things are slightly different if documents are generated. The skeletal structure of the document is known in advance. Depending on the user's profile the system selects the appropriate decorator and transforms it into the final document at runtime. This can be achieved via a template mechanism. In order to support multiple languages, users with different languages use the same graph. Those parts requiring translation will be replaced by the corresponding part in the user's language at run time.

In addition some data for the social background and knowledge of the user can be used to offer different representations for people at different ages and different educational level.

Navigational Support

Navigational support means that the system offers some aid when the user traverses through the graph. Help can be offered via

1. evaluation of context data for better guesses about the user's aim and

2. tailoring the graph.

Both imply that the actions the user has taken so far are tracked. Depending on the task it may also make sense to track the actions of a co-worker. The prototype did not support group awareness.

In order to track the user's actions we need to know the context where the action takes place. This context is formed by the task context and the location context. Location context means only the representation in the physical space. The location in the electronic space can be restored by evaluating the history. System messages do not appear in the history. The user's action is expressed by her utterance. We are interested in how often each command was taken during the past and when it was made. Furthermore we are interested in the link that the user followed. Unfortunately, this will produce a lot of data. We need some experience with the system to see, if the amount stays within a reasonable range.

The previous behaviour for the current node can be easily obtained by filtering the history with the current node. An interesting aspect e.g. is the relative frequency of a command c for a fixed node n and a fixed location l in the history $\mathbf{H}_{u,g}$:

$$f_{n,l}(c) = \frac{|\{h_{n,l} \in \mathbf{H}_{u,g} | \text{command} = c\}|}{|\mathbf{H}_{u,g}|} \qquad (4.25)$$

In addition to context data that is obtained by observing the user's navigational behaviour the user's educational level about the current task has to be taken into account. Moreover the task can provide additional context data that has to be evaluated. This is treated in section 4.8.3.

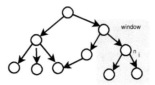

Figure 4.19: Window for the current node

4.8.3   Environment or Activity

In section 2.2 we spoke about the four main categories of context. Gross and Specht named only artifacts of physical locations under the term *environment or activity*. We think that things are different in the audio only world. Here artifacts of electronic locations of the current situation can be added to this category. For the audio browser we have a context located in the electronic location that cannot be described via a URI or a URL, see section 4.8.1. Hence it is not clear why physical location should be the only item describing the environment.

As mentioned in [SKHM04] we have to distinguish between linear and hierarchical topologies. In this section we show that context has to be treated different for those two topologies.

Current Node

When the user traverses through the graph she sees only a small part of it. This is illustrated as a window in figure 4.19.

The window w for node n_i can be expressed by

$$w(n_i) = n_{i-1} \frown n_i \frown (n_k \in C(n_i)) \qquad (4.26)$$

The window regards the current node n_i, the way, the user navigated to it n_{i-1} and the possibilities to proceed to a child node n_k. Special forms of the latter are choice, see section 4.8.3, and sub-graphs, which are explored in the following section.

Sub-graphs

In section 4.6.2 we discovered that sub-graphs may occur in hierarchical or linear topologies. According to section 4.7.1 sub-graphs are located after detail links or choice links. A sub-graph $\mathbf{H'} = (\mathbf{N'}, \mathbf{L'})$ of $\mathbf{H} = (\mathbf{N}, \mathbf{L})$ with $N' \subset N \wedge L' \subset L$ and the root node

$$n_r \in N' : \exists n_p \, in N \setminus N' : n_p \in P(n_r) \qquad (4.27)$$

is defined as

$$H'(N', L') = \{(n_i, l_k) | n_i \in N' \wedge l_k \in L' \wedge path(n_r, n_i) \neq \emptyset\} \qquad (4.28)$$

This means that a sub-graph provides a closed navigation space which is part of the entire graph context.

Detailed Information Links to detailed information occur somewhere within the voice stream, see figure 4.10. If the user wants to get detailed information, she may follow the link. Targets of such links may be a single node or a more complex DAG without any connections to other parts of the graph. The only exception is an audio document that is shared among multiple detailed sub-graphs.

Choice We use SCRIPTED INTERACTION, see section 4.7.1, to select an item from a list. Large lists are divided into smaller parts so that the user can easily skip parts of the list of no interest. The user has to understand intuitively how the list is sorted so that she is able to navigate quickly to the desired item.

SCRIPTED INTERACTION is chosen because it can be handled with our set of 15 basic navigational commands. A better choice would be direct naming of the desired item. It is obvious that SCRIPTED INTERACTION will perform worse than that and will be more boring for the user. We have to explore how big this drawback is and if it would be advisable to load the needed vocabulary from the environment to offer a faster navigation as a second possible input, thus leaving the self contained command set.

In contrast to detailed information sub-graphs choice nodes appear as a single node in the path.

Task

The task or process context provides information about the current task. First of all, providing information about the process is the audio document author's responsibility. We can only offer some solutions for recurring problems. These are

- knowledge about the current task

- pause and resume

- notification after a predefined delay

- parallel execution of tasks

Knowledge About the Task Knowledge about the task can be used to preprocess the graph using alternative representation as it is described in section 4.8.2.

Pause and Resume The user may pause browsing at any time. If a continuation at this point makes sense depends on the scenario. If it is allowed we create a link of the current physical and electronic location and the user context in our prototype of an audio browser. This link may have an expiration date if it is unlikely it will be used afterwards.

There are two uncertainties trying to determine values for two of the involved classes:

1. The position within the current audio document and

2. the location.

The position of the current audio document is determined by the current node, see section 4.8.3, and the path. The current audio document is delivered as a single voice stream. If the user requests a pause while this stream is being played, the only way to get the current position is by evaluating the number of bytes that were sent. This, however may only be reasonable, if the user interrupts for a short time. For a longer time we have to go back to the beginning of the document or a marker within.

In a system using relative positioning it is possible that the user's profile cannot be associated with a certain location. In this situation there are two possibilities to solve this problem:

1. use the last known position and

2. ask the user to associate a location.

There is no general concept to solve this. The current handling must be obtained from the task context.

Notification After a Delay   Some process may have pauses where the user has to wait for a certain time before she can continue with the next step. We call this waiting time a delay. A delay is similar to the previous situation. In contrast to the previously described pause, where the user was the initiator, here, the system initializes the pause. We have to inform the user about this pause and must get back to her after the delay.

The same information as before is needed to proceed browsing, but it is easier in the sense that there is no uncertainty about the position within the document and about the location. For both of them the the author is responsible.

In addition to the location based entry an alarm based entry to the audio browser is required.

Parallel Execution of Tasks   Parallel execution of tasks is an extension to the notification after a delay. To manage this situation the system must store the information for multiple graphs in parallel. In addition inter-dependencies of the involved graphs are possible.

This is explored in detail in section 6.4.

4.9   Use of Contextual Information

In the previous section we presented the type of the context data which we plan to use for our audio browser. In order to see how they can be used, we need a classification according to the definition of Dey, refer to section 2.2.

For the main categories, the applying class is marked with a • in table 4.5.

Aiding the user not to get lost in the audio world is one of our most important goals. Nearly all of the context data presented in section 4.8 focuses on this goal. The only exception is the physical location. Physical location is primarily used to identify anchor points for a graph. Besides it can be used to aid the user in identifying objects.

Table 4.5: Context classification according to Dey

	presentation	execution	tagging
physical location	•	•	•
electronic location	•		•
identity	•		
history	•		•
task	•	•	

In this section, we will explore only the location context, since this is the key context which we are using. A careful investigation of the categories identity and history are not part of this thesis, but the key concepts that are presented here can be transferred to include them. Task is a category that is better handled by a workflow engine, see section 2.4. Workflow engines are not integrated into the audio browser at this point. We will have a closer look at it in section 6.4.

4.9.1 Identifying Graphs

The objects of interest are starting points for our information browsing. This section describes how the physical location can be mapped to the root node of our document graphs.

In section 4.8.1 we differentiate between absolute and relative positioning. With absolute positioning we can simply attach the identification of the tag to the root node of our hyperbase.

Things are more complicated with absolute positioning. Independent of the used technology, scene analysis or triangulation, the location is represented in world coordinates. In order to determine proximity, a world model is needed. This can be done e.g. using Java3D [Jav06a]. The advantage of Java3D is not the possibility to draw but to model objects. It will not be necessary to model everything, but at minimum all objects of interest and the borders of the room. The borders are necessary to determine if the user is really able to look at the object. The objects of interest are starting points for our information browsing. It must be possible to attach a root node of a hyperbase to a modeled object. But this is not enough. When the user navigates through the documents she may listen to a document that is related to an object of the real world. The Java3D universe uses a directed graph for modeling whose items can be mapped to the nodes of our graph. Due to the differentiation between absolute and relative positioning this, modelling the world with Java3D satisfies only the absolute positioning system. For relative positioning we need a simple mapping of the tag id to a modeled object.

4.9.2 Informing the user

When the user looks at an object that has an associated root document we want to inform the user with an auditory icon. Since physical location is the only context with an executional category it has to be treated different to other context data.

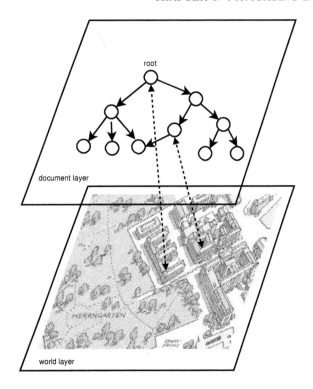

Figure 4.20: Mapping of world model and documents

Hence the decision to play the auditory icon can be influenced by some factors like

1. the user is busy navigating through another graph

2. the user is currently not navigating but there are lots of objects around that are associated with a root document

3. the user is currently not navigating and does not want to be interrupted

We can summarize these factors under the term *interruptibility*. Interruptibility is important since it can have a negative effect on the memory capabilities of the user. Hence it increases the *lost in space* problem. Especially the last one is hard to determine and has been focus of several researches, like [HA03]. In this research Horvitz calculates the expected cost of interruption ECI as

$$ECI_j = p(A_j|E)u(D_i, A_j) \qquad (4.29)$$

where $p(A_j|E)$ is the probability of the attentional state A_j conditioned on evidence stream E and $u(D_i, A_j)$ is the cost of a user in attentional state A_j disrupted by a task or communication event D_i.

For a complete evaluation we need more sensor data for an analysis of the user's state. For example, detecting the presence of a conversation by an audio signal process analysis would be helpful.

This is beyond the scope of this thesis. We assume that the user is busy with the audio browser and can be interrupted within this system at any time. This means we will not take respect to item 3 of the list above. Nevertheless we use this to determine if we can interrupt a user when she is browsing another graph. In our case we restrict the number of communication events to

D_L the user leaves the last visited location with an associated document,

D_E the user reenters the last visited location with an associated document,

D_O an object outside the current graph is reachable and

D_T another user wants to talk to the user.

For all of them the costs $u(D_i, A_j)$ have to be determined by user studies. The resulting interruptibility factor ECI_j is a key factor in the decision, if we allow the system to interrupt the user. The required context data can be obtained from the history.

While the user is performing the task, she may receive instructions that demand her full attention. Authors of audio documents have to take this into account and leave a pause after such an instruction to minimize the cognitive load.

4.9.3 Identification of Objects

The mapping mentioned above does not only refer to root nodes. Other nodes may be related to objects of the real world, too. These objects must not serve as root nodes, because they are embedded into a context which the user does not know. In the case that a node within a graph has a relation to an artifact of the real world is also a root node that can be used as a starting point for browsing the user can use this as her entry point into the application. If she utters the command *start* to jump to the root node, which she expects to be the starting point of the current context, will cause the application to jump to the root node of the overlaying context. This can confuse the user since she does not know anything from the overlaying context.

The advantage of linking sub-nodes to object is the possibility to aid the user in locating objects that are named in the documents. This may vary from a short description where to find the described object to playing an auditory icon to inform the user that he looks at the object of interest. Especially the goal oriented scenarios would benefit from it. This goes beyond the scope of listening to documents but would be incredible helpful. It will require a *location link* besides the document link and a *location node* besides the document node.

From the user's history and her background knowledge we can conclude if the system should help the user to identify the object or if she is familiar with this scenario.

The history uses a general purpose rule based on a simple threshold for the decision. We simply count all occurrences of the root node n_1 of the graph g in the history

$$\sum_{l_i \in \mathbf{L}} |\{h_{n_1, l_i} \in \mathbf{H}_{u,g}\}| > \theta_{h_g} \qquad\qquad (4.30)$$

Another factor that has an influence on equation (4.30) is time. If the user did not visit the graph for a long time she may have forgotten about parts or all of it. We can take respect to this by limiting the history $\mathbf{H}_{u,g}$ to a certain time interval. The threshold θ_{h_g} has to be determined through user studies.

4.10 Conclusion

This chapter introduced the concepts for browsing audio documents in ubiquitous environments. Starting with existing solutions for audio rendering of HTML we transferred this concept to the ubiquitous environment, where users on the move access documents using voice commands to control the browser.

We identified several scenarios where these concepts are applicable and discussed them, based on the limitation inherent to the medium, and on the underlying network topology. Several user studies have been conducted to determine topologies that can be supported by this infrastructure.

We discovered, that the amount of deliverable information is strongly limited by the human cognitive capabilities, especially short term memory. This is the main reason why the concept of browsing documents on a desktop PC cannot be easily transferred to audio. The operational range of an application is limited to browse a small set of documents. More information requires the help of other modalities, like displays. This finding is also in conjunction with observations of real world applications. Users prefer to use applications with a visual feedback but it is acceptable to use audio based control in small applications or to perform some small interaction with the user in a bigger process.

With respect to our target architecture we developed a prototype of an audio browser to browse audio documents in an ubiquitous environment. We used a distributed speech recognizer and developed a simple architecture to handle detail links.

This audio browser uses a general purpose basic command set which allows the creation of all the topologies of our use case scenarios. This basic command set is close to the ETSI standard satisfying the need for easy speech recognition since the commands are acoustically different and natural.

Chapter 5

Patterns for Voice User Interface Design

5.1 Motivation

Nowadays, the design of efficient speech interfaces is considered to be more an art than an engineering science. This idea is also supported by Junqua in [Jun00] who concludes his book *Robust Speech Recognition in Embedded Systems and PC Applications* with the demand:

> Today building the dialog component of a conversational system is more an art than engineering or science. We need to develop techniques for dialog design that are grounded on strong theoretical frameworks.

Several guidelines exist, but are more or less hints about what should be avoided. This chapter introduces a first set of patterns integrating many guidelines and solution approaches developed during the past 15 years. The goal is to document and share this knowledge with new designers as well as to provide a language to talk about *Voice User Interface* (VUI) designs

"Patterns and pattern languages offer an approach to design with much potential" [DF06]. There are many reasons to use patterns which are motivated in the following sections.

The organization of this chapter is shown in figure 5.1. After this motivation, a short historical background of patterns is given in section 5.2, followed by a discussion of the different intentions of patterns and guidelines in section 5.3. The voice user interface design pattern language is presented in section 5.5. The chapter ends with a conclusion about the benefits of the pattern language in section 5.6.

5.2 A Short Historical Background of Patterns

In the 1970s the architect Christopher Alexander introduced the concept of *patterns* and *pattern languages* to have a vocabulary to discuss reoccurring problems in the area of town building [AIS77, Ale79]. The use of patterns allows sharing knowledge of experience and design. "Each pattern is a three-part rule, which expresses a relation between a certain context, a problem and a solution. The pattern is, in

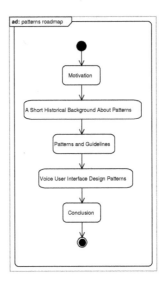

Figure 5.1: Road map to handle Patterns for Voice User Interface Design

short, at the same time a thing which happens in the world and the rule which tells us how to create that thing, and when we must create it. It is both a process and a thing; both a description of a thing which is alive, and a description of the process which will generate that thing" [Ale79]. "Each pattern describes a problem which occurs over and over again in our environment, and then describes the core of the solution to that problem, in such a way that you can use this solution a million times over, without ever doing it the same way twice". [AIS77]

Alexander describes his idea as *design pattern*:

Definition 25 *A **design pattern** describes a design problem and a general solution for this problem within it's context.*

In 1987 Kent Beck and Ward Cunningham used the idea of patterns for GUI design with the smalltalk programming language [BC87]. This was the first time that the concept of a *pattern* has been used in software development. It became popular with Gamma et al. famous book *Design Patterns: Elements of Reusable Object-Oriented Software* [GHJV92].

Reoccurring problems in object oriented software design can be solved by a procedure described as a pattern. This procedure is written down by someone in an abstract but usable way to make it applicable to different usage scenarios. The main idea is to share the knowledge and experience with people who have less expertise in a certain domain. This requires the author of a pattern to describe the problem and the context for their solution. Software engineers were the first to use patterns to have good solutions for known problems. Nowadays patterns are frequently used in software-architecture, -design and -development. During the past years, patterns and pattern languages have attracted increasing attention in HCI (**H**uman **C**omputer **I**nteraction) for these reasons. Some of them are more general interaction design patterns [Tid05, vWvdV03, Laa03]. Some cover even aspects of multimedia [Bor01], or hypertext and hypermedia [RSG97], but all rely on visual interfaces. There is hardly any work on audio only interfaces.

5.3 Patterns and Guidelines

Common ways to share knowledge about design principles are *guidelines*.

Definition 26 *A **guideline** is a statement or other indication of a policy or a procedure by which to determine a course of action.[ea00]*

Design guidelines in that sense are more principles for design. In HCI, they can also help to develop efficient user interfaces by capturing design knowledge into small rules. Patterns, in contrast, are capturing *proven* design knowledge and are using a well defined format. But this well defined format is not enough. In addition it is important that it is a proven solution. Moreover it is required that designers agree upon it.

Van Welie [vWvdVE00] summarizes the problems of guidelines that were reported in [DABF98, MJ98].

- Guidelines are often too simplistic or too abstract

- Guidelines can be difficult to select

- Guidelines can be difficult to interpret

- Guidelines can be conflicting

- Guidelines often have authority issues concerning their validity

Patterns "provide the context and problem explicit and the solution is provided along with a rationale. Consequently, compared to guidelines, patterns contain more complex design knowledge and often several guidelines are integrated in one pattern" [vWvdVE00].

Pattern usually relate to each other and form a network of patterns. If a community agrees upon this network, it is possible to speak of a *pattern language*.

Definition 27 *A **pattern language** is a network of patterns with grammatical and semantic relationship among the patterns. Each pattern describes its relationship to other patterns and to the language as a whole.*

5.4   Pattern Format

Alexander demands that each pattern has to be well formulated:

> "Every pattern we define must be formulated in the form of a rule which establishes a relationship between a context, a system of forces arising in that context, and a configuration, allowing these forces to resolve themselves in that context" [Ale79].

To ensure this requirement, a general format is needed. This format should have pointers to the needed components. There are two main formats [DKW99]. One of them is the *Alexandrian Form*, which has been used by Alexander. This form is also known as *canonical form*. The other is the *GoF Form*, used by Gamma et al. [GHJV92]. Both formats differ in the headings of the sections, but the information that a pattern should give to the designer is almost the same in both templates [Teš05].

In this thesis an own format, based on the GoF Form is used. The following is a description of each section, some of which are taken from [Teš05].

Name Meaningful name of the pattern. A good and understandable name helps by making analogies to general experiences to describe the idea of the pattern.

Intent A short description of the intention of this pattern in a single sentence.

Context Preconditions under which the *problem* and its *solution* occur and for which the solution is applicable. A pattern describes a solution in a given context, and it might not make sense in other contexts.

Problem Description of the problem, which this pattern tries to solve.

Force Patterns represent a concrete scenario providing the motivation to use of pattern in a certain context to solve a certain problem. Forces make clear intricacies of a problem, since all problems are clear cut. This section encapsulates all the forces upon which it might have an impact.

Solution Guidelines to solve the described *problem* in the given *context*.

Structure A graphical representation of the solution, showing the relations of all involved objects.

Consequences Postconditions after the pattern has been applied. Consequences may be both, positive and negative, and other problems that may arise from the resulting context.

Known uses Known occurrences of the pattern and it's application within existing systems. This helps to validate the pattern, e.g. verify that this pattern is indeed a proven solution to the problem. They can also serve as instructional examples.

Related Patterns Description of static and dynamic relationship between this pattern and other patterns.

Sample code Code fragment illustrating an implementation.

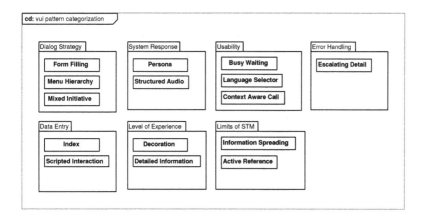

Figure 5.2: Categorization of Voice User Interface Design Patterns

5.5 Voice User Interface Design Patterns

In this section a pattern language is presented that is helpful in the domain of voice user interface design. The language has been presented at EuroPLoP 2005 [SLW05] and EuroPLoP 2006 [SL06] and discussed with the community. In addition, some known uses are presented for several patterns to show that these are proven solutions.

The patterns can be categorized according to their main purpose. An overview is given in figure 5.2, and connections between them are shown in figure 5.3. This pattern language is just a starting point and is not complete in all categories. There is a need to mine more patterns, for example to handle errors.

Our focus is on ubiquitous computing environments, where users can walk around and retrieve information about items of the real world. Artifacts of the real world are starting points for navigating to the desired information. The user makes an *utterance*, a special command or a complete sentence in natural language, to start browsing. This is evaluated by the *recognition engine* and handed over to the *audio browser* to generate a response in audio. The response consists of natural language, generated by a *text-to-speech engine* (TTS engine) and some *auditory icons*, pre-recorded sounds used as a means for structuring the presented information.. To present a complete picture, we mention all known existing dialog strategies, but leave mixed initiative unhandled in our further investigation.

Although this scenario is different from the scenarios where typically audio based user interfaces can be found, such as the telephone, many of the problems faced are common to all kinds of VUIs. Hence, the task of navigating to a desired service in a telephony application, has a similar structure like browsing for a certain *audio document*. Most of the patterns are useful in a audio-only user interface, although some of them, for example the patterns for data entry, can also be used in multimodal applications.

An example implementation of each pattern is given. We choose a car repair

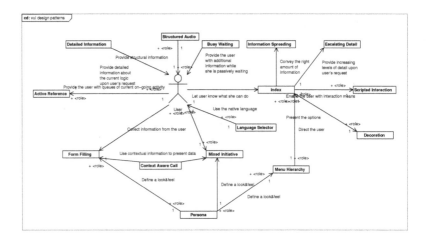

Figure 5.3: Relation of Voice User Interface Design Patterns

shop as our example scenario, where a worker processes a list of work items. We use VoiceXML for the example code and a specification of the tags can be found in [Voi04].

5.5.1   VoiceXML

VoiceXML is a language in the XML format that has been developed by the Voice-XML forum. The forum was founded by IBM, Motorola, and AT&T to access networked services via a telephone. Version 2.0 of the VoiceXML specification has been release in February 2003. In 2004, it was standardized by the W3C [Voi04].

The goal of VoiceXML was to have a means for easy development of voice based applications. The main domain is telephony based applications. However, the concept can also be used to serve mobile devices.

VoiceXML documents consist of several dialogs (<form> or <menu>). These dialog elements describe the interaction with the user. Besides there are tags to support input fields, control elements, variables, event handler, and blocks containing procedural logic.

5.5.2   Additional Background Information

An application designed for audio only input and output faces several challenges which were discussed in section 2.6.1. These are forces which are met in all patterns of the language.

Some of the pattern descriptions feature a section about known uses. In general, this is a real telephony application which can be called. Some of the phone numbers may incur calling charges. It is also possible that they are not accessible from outside of Germany.

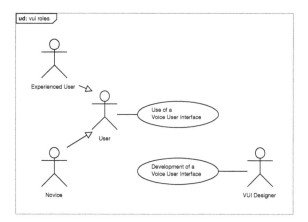

Figure 5.4: Simplified view on roles involved in VUI design

Figure 5.4 shows a simplified overview of the roles involved in VUI design. *Novices* are users that have not used the application before, and are neither familiar with the concepts of the application nor the grammar they can use. *Experienced users* have a systematic understanding of the application and its functionality. They are accustomed to interrupting the system to quickly navigate to the information they want. In the world of telephony this is known as *barge-in*. The *VUI designer* develops the application and the concepts on how to present it to the user.

For some of the patterns we suggest to use a *wizard-of-oz* experiment [FG91]. This is a well known strategy taken from the field of human-computer interaction. Test persons interact with an application which they believe to behave autonomous. Actually it is operated by an unseen human being, the *wizard*. Instead of real voice recognition, the user's input is manually entered into the system and processed as a text stream rather than an audio stream. These experiments should reveal information about use and effectiveness of the application.

The name of the experiment comes from *The Wonderful Wizard of Oz* story, in which an ordinary man hides behind a curtain and pretends to be a powerful wizard.

5.5.3 Dialog Strategy

Like GUI-based application interaction, voice applications interaction consists of *user input* and *system output*. User input can be an audio recording of a user, touch tone, or more commonly voice recognition of a user's voice entry [Dug02]. Similarly, system output can be text-to-speech or pre-recorded sound.

This section addresses various interaction styles, the *dialog strategies*. Command & Control is not listed, since it is handled exhaustively in chapter 4. All these patterns feature a common set of forces:

- Dialogs have to to be efficient and short

- Dialogs have to be clear and structured

- Novices have to be guided. They need to know what kind of information to provide

- Experienced users know what to say and need a fast way to enter the data

Form Filling

Intent   Gather information from the user based on a structured flow of questions and answers.

Context   The user has to provide data that can't be gathered through a selection process. Forms are a well known concept of the real world to provide information in a sequential order, one at a time.

Problem   How to collect structured information from the user?

Forces

- Forms are forcing users to provide one data at a time

- Natural language communication allows to provide more than one data in a single utterance

- Speech is invisible: Users might forget what they entered in the beginning

- Speech recognition performance: Users need feedback about the entered data

Solution   Identify the fields and the order in which they should be filled. Identify a short description or label for each field to be filled in and prepare a variable to store the entered information. Use comprehensive instructions for the label [Shn86] using a consistent, brief, and clear terminology the user is familiar with. Prepare a grammar to retrieve the valid values of the fields. Ensure the label contains clues about the format of the user's utterance. To ensure the correctness of the data, an own error handler for each field may be used.

Present the label to the user, followed with an optional input prompt and silence to let the user enter the data, as if she were filling out a form.

Present a summary of all collected data and let the user confirm or correct them.

Structure   This is illustrated in the following figure. The user is requested for an utterance in node *Field 1*. If she does not make an utterance within a predefined period of time, or made an erroneous input, she will be re-prompted. If all goes well, the dialog proceeds to the next field until she reaches the node *Summary*, where she is asked to confirm a summary of her inputs. If she rejects the summary, the dialog proceeds with the first field for another try.

In an alternative approach, the user can be prompted to confirm each field separately.

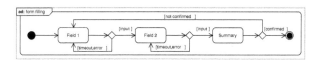

Consequences

+ Dialogs are clear and structured

+ Good for beginners/novices

+ System messages are not confusing

o System controls dialog flow

- Dialogs appear rigid and inflexible

- Dialogs become lengthy

- Does not solve the problem to provide more data at a time

Known Uses The Poldi Gewinnspiel of the 1. FC Köln used FORM FILLING to request the desired information about the caller, like membership of the 1. FC Köln and to enter the answers to the quiz. The application went offline in 2005. Until then it was callable at +49 (180) 5 29 00 29.

The dating line L.U.C.Y. from Com Vision uses FORM FILLING to request the data of the caller, i.e. *sex, age* and *ZIP code*. Having entered all data, the system summarizes all data in one step. The application can be called at +49 (12) 345 662 662.

The Citiphone Banking application uses FORM FILLING to enter the data, i.e. *account number* or *bank code* for a bank transfer. After the caller has entered a value for a field, she is asked for confirmation. The application can be called at +49 (180) 33 22 111.

Related patterns FORM PATTERN [Tid05] solves a similar problem for graphical user interfaces.

ESCALATING DETAIL as a means of error recovery.

MIXED INITIATIVE is an alternate approach and enables the user to provide more than one datum at a time.

Sample code In a car inspection scenario, the worker enters the data after a car has been repaired. He enters his worker *id*, the *order number* and other data that belongs to the order such as *part numbers* in a form before the back-end system continues with the billing process.

Note: The VoiceXML `<form>` element must not be confused with the form concept that is described in this pattern. `<field>` elements are just one side of the elements which a `<form>` may contain.

```
<form id=" prepare_bill">
    <field name=" id" type=" digits">
        <prompt>Please say your id.</prompt>
    </field>

    <field name=" order" type=" digits">
        <prompt>Please say the order number</prompt>
    </field>
    ...
    <block>
        <submit next=" http://www.example.com/servlet/bill"
                namelist=" id , order , part_number"/>
    </block>
</form>
```

Also Known As DIRECTED DIALOG, SYSTEM INITIATIVE

Menu Hierarchy

Intent Guide the user to the information of interest

Context The user has to provide data that can be gathered through a selection process. The options to be presented to the user are interrelated in a hierarchy, or can be made to appear that way.

Problem How to guide the user to a certain piece of information?

Forces

- Hierarchical structures are easy to understand

- Not all options can be grouped in a hierarchical structure

- Long menus are more efficient [SFG01]

- Speech is one-dimensional: Long menus force the user to wait until the wanted option is presented

- Speech is one-dimensional: The system's response time to present a menu is very high

- Speech is invisible: Users cannot see the structure of the data

- Speech is transient: The user has to remember the path

Solution   Form categories of similar option items to create a tree structure [Nor91]. If this is not clearly solvable, the initial design can be improved upon the user's feedback. Use a natural sequence of the items to determine the presentation sequence [Shn86]. In case there is no natural sequence, choose an order that is obvious to the user, such as most frequently used items first or alphabetic sequence of terms. Present these options in a menu to the user. Avoid listening to long prompts by using barge-in. Aid the user by naming the appropriate commands in the prompt [Yan96]. Enable the user to deviate from prompted words by specifying alternative words in the the grammar or use the touch tone key-pad. Conduct *wizard-of-oz* experiments to evaluate the menu with respect to the wording of the prompts and the grammar. Once, the user makes a selection, the system offers another sub-menu until the application settles on the one item or action the user wants. Remember the user's path to allow going up in the hierarchy.

The limitations of the short-term-memory have been studied by several authors and are still discussed in the HCI field. Some authors like Miller [Mil56] suggest that a person can only remember 7+/-2 information chunks. In an ongoing project we conducted a user study where we found that more than 6 options are rejected by most users. Since the path must also be kept in the memory, we assume that this limit is also applicable for the depth of a menu tree. Therefore, the length and the depth of such a menu tree should be as flat as possible, and should also not exceed the *magical number 7*.

Structure   This is illustrated in the following figure. The user is requested for a choice in node *Option 1*. Depending on her answer the dialog proceeds with the appropriate next option until it reaches a leaf.

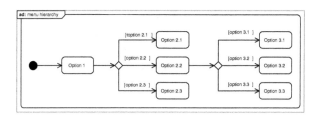

Consequences

+ Dialogs are clear and structured

+ Good for beginners/novices

+ The user is guided by the system and gets more details on demand

+ The user is able to control the leaves she wants to enter or leave

o System controls dialog flow

- Dialogs are too structured

- The *lost-in-space* problem increases when the number of options or the depth of the hierarchy are too high

- Poorly chosen categories force the user to navigate back and forth the menu to find the category that matches their reason for calling [SFG01]

Known Uses   The traffic information InfoTraffic from Viasuisse uses a hierarchical structure to enter the route, in which the caller is interested. Since Switzerland is multilingual, the application first asks for the desired language. It continues in the chosen language to enter the desired means of transportation, like highways, train, etc. Having chosen i.e. highway the application turns to FORM FILLING to enter the id of the highway. The application can be called at +41 (900) 400 500.

Related patterns   Typical applications use FORM FILLING and MENU HIER-ARCHY at different points, depending on the information and the user's mental model [CGB04].

INDEX or SCRIPTED INTERACTION may be used to present the available options. ACTIVE REFERENCE can be used to help the user stay oriented in the hierarchy.

HIERARCHICAL SET [Tid05] solves a similar problem in visual oriented applications.

Sample code   At the car inspection the worker browses for information about a part that needs to be exchanged. The parts are sorted in a hierarchical structure. Having navigated to the exhaust system, she is been asked for the sub-part in which she is interested.

```
<menu>
    <prompt>
        Say the part of the exhaust system <enumerate/>
    </prompt>
    <choice next="http://www.example.com/pipe.vxml">
        Exhaust pipe
    </choice>
    <choice next="http://www.example.com/converter.vxml">
        Catalytic converter
    </choice>
    <choice next="http://www.example.com/rear_muffler.vxml">
        Rear muffler
    </choice>
    ...
</menu>
```

Mixed Initiative

Intent   Collect information from the user with respect to her level of experience.

Context   Users with a different level of experience have to enter some pieces of information that may have interdependencies. The dialog should imitate a natural human-to-human conversation.

Problem How to collect information from the user seamlessly?

Forces

- Users want to enter data without too many restrictions

- It is possible to say the same thing in *endless* different ways.

- Combination of user data grows by a factorial order

- Grammars can cover only part of the ways to capture user input

- Speech is invisible: Users may not know what to say

Solution Start the conversation with an open ended prompt, e.g. *How may I help you?*. Create a field, also known as *slot* for each piece of information to obtain from the user. Allow the user to provide more information than the current question expects, e.g.

System: Where do you want to go?
User: I want to go to Darmstadt by train at 17:00.

Also allow filling or corrections of field that are out of focus, e.g.

System: At what time do you want to go to Darmstadt?
User: No. I want to go to Mannheim.

Use references in the dialog context, e.g.

System: Bayern München lost 2:3
User: What is their current rank

Use barge-in to enable the user to interrupt system prompts. If the application's task can be divided into multiple sub-tasks, do not stick to the principle of *Say what you want at any time you want to* described above. This reduces the occurrence of the system's misbehaviour in the presence of recognition failures.

Use suitable follow-up prompts, once the field gets filled. Present the collected information in a final prompt and ask the user for confirmation. Use ESCALATING DETAIL to aid the user in case of a timeout (the user did not say anything) or in case of a reject (the utterance could not be mapped to the grammar). Use FORM FILLING as the last escalation level. Conduct *wizard-of-oz* experiments to evaluate the grammar.

Structure An example of a structure is shown in the following figure. The user is requested to provide information for *field1* and *field2* after the initial *InputPrompt*. If she provides information for *field1* she will be prompted for *field2* in *PromptField 2*, whereas if she provides information for *field2* she will be prompted for *field1* in *PromptField 1*. Having provided the missing piece of information she will be asked to confirm the entered information in *ConfirmAll*. As an alternative she can provide information for both fields at once and will be asked to confirm all in the next dialog step.

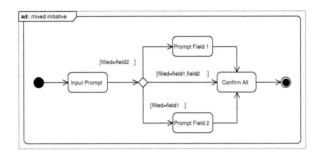

Consequences

  + Dialogs are more natural

  + Users can provide more than one information item at once

  + Dialogs can become more efficient and shorter

  + Users can take control of the dialog flow

  - Recognition rate decreases since the user is free to make any utterance

  - User is fooled to think she is in a real free form entry, which will cause her to use words that might not belong to the grammar

  - *Turn taking* (When should or can the user speak?) and *intention recognition* (What are the goals of the user?) come up as new problems [Hea99]

Known Uses   The cinema Cinecitta in Nuremberg offers a voice portal as cinema information. After calling the system gives a short overview of its capabilities. The user is free to interrupt the system at any time. If the user does not make an utterance or calls for help, the system falls back into a FORM FILLING like dialog strategy, by asking first for the hour and then presents a list of movies that are shown at the given time. The user is free to resume the initiative again at any time. The application can be called at +49 (911) 20 66 67.

Related patterns   ESCALATING DETAIL is used to aid the user to get back on track.

  If the user fails to enter the data, the dialog strategy may fall back into FORM FILLING.

  PERSONA might be used to make the dialog appear more natural.

Sample code   In a car inspection scenario, the worker enters the data after a car has been repaired. She enters his worker *id*, the *order number* and other data that belongs to the order, such as *part numbers* into the system before the back-end system continues with the billing process. The worker can enter all data in one single utterance or in a sequential order.

```
<form id="repair_done">
    <grammar src="repair.grxml"
             type="application/srgs+xml"/>

    <initial name="get_info">
        <prompt>Say the data for the bill</prompt>
        <catch event="nomatch">
            <prompt>
                Let us try getting each field separately.
            </prompt>
            <reprompt/>
            <assign name="get_info" expr="true"/>
        </catch>
    </initial>

    <field name="id">
        <grammar src="reapair.grxml#id"/>
        <prompt>Please say your id.</prompt>
    </field>

    <field name="order">
        <grammar src="repair.grxml#order"/>
        <prompt>Please say the order number</prompt>
    </field>
    ...

    <block>
        <submit next="http://www.example.com/servlet/bill"
                namelist="id,order,part_number"/>
    </block>
</form>
```

Command & Control

Intent Provide a means for the user to control an application using voice.

Context In Command & Control environments the application can handle a voice command menu that contains voice commands.

Problem How to enable the user controlling an application by voice?

Forces

- The user has to learn a special vocabulary

- Does not scale.

- Commands may sound similar and are hard to distinguish by the recognizer

- Commands should be easy to learn and natural

Solution   Determine the commands that the user should be able to initiate by voice commands. Associate a command for each action to perform. Invoke the action, if the user said the word. Expect the next command.

Structure   This is illustrated in the following figure.

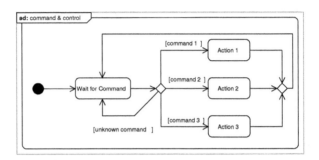

After the start, the application waits for a command. If the user enters a command by voice, the appropriate action, e.g. *Action 1* is invoked. After invocation, the application waits for the next command.

Consequences

+ Easy to understand

o System controls dialog flow

- Hard to recover, if an unwanted action was triggered.

Known Uses   The new Windows Vista allows to control the desktop using voice commands, e.g., the command *open notepad* launches the notepad application.

Katalavox [Kat06] offers a voice control for phocomelic drivers. Drivers can control all functionalities, like turning signals or controlling the whiper by voice commands.

Sample code   The following code expects the commands *start* and *stop*. Depending on the command, the application executes the corresponding method in a Java archive *application.jar*. Afterwards it returns expecting the next command.

```
<form id="entercommand">
        <field name="command">
    <grammar src="http://grammarlib/commands.grxml"
        type="application/srgs+xml"/>
    <filled>
        <if cond="command=='start '">
            <goto next="#startapp"/>
        <if cond="command=='stop '">
```

```
          <goto next="#stopapp"/>
       <else/>
          <reprompt/>
       </if>
    </filled>
  </field>
</form>

<form id="startapp">
  <object name="start"
     classid="method://start"
     data="http://application.jar"/>
  <goto next="#entercommand"/>
</form>

<form id="stopapp">
  <object name="start"
     classid="method://start"
     data="http://application.jar"/>
  <goto next="#entercommand"/>
</form>
```

Also know as USER INITIATIVE

5.5.4 Error Handling

In contrast to visual user interfaces speech recognition as an input medium is still error prone. Errors can be reduced by improving the technology but not totally eliminated. Consequently an application that uses speech recognition has to make to think about error handling.

Junqua says in [Jun00]:

> The cost of an error is application dependent, and so is the error correction technology used. Errors have serious consequences because they can destroy the user's mental model.

This is especially true for our purposes. Consequences of an error are that the user navigates somewhere where she didn't want to go. This increases the lost in space problem and the feeling of not being in control.

Escalating Detail

Intent Provide an error recovery strategy when the speech recognizer does not return a recognition hypothesis.

Context The performance of speech recognition is still a problem. The most common results in case of errors are *reject*, which means that the utterance could not be mapped successfully to the grammar, and *no-speech timeout*, because no speech was detected at all.

Problem   How to aid the user to recover from an error?

Forces

- In case of a timeout, it is likely that users did not listen carefully and do not know what utterances they may perform. They need more guidance to provide the required data.

- In case of an error, experienced users are forced to listen to long explanations, as a consequence of the one-dimensional medium, even if they just need another try. They want to have a faster system response.

- Users do not know what to say and need more detailed explanations. This hinders them from using the application..

- Different types of errors, *reject* and *no-speech timeout*, need different strategies to handle those errors appropriate.

- Low recognition performance and background noise result in a misinterpreted type of error.

- An error can only be detected, if the recognition result is not allowed in the current context.

Solution   Write handlers for different types of errors. Use a counter for the occurrences and levels of the affected type in a row. Write prompts to increase the amount of help provided at each level.

The higher levels may also offer alternative approaches, e.g. a form-based data entry for a date versus free-form input, to enter the required data. Within these repetitions the initial prompt can be reused to provide information about the input possibilities.

Structure   The structure is shown in the following figure. The introduction of choices is in node *Intro* and the actual presentation of the options in *Choice*. The error document is chosen depending on the error count and the type of the error.

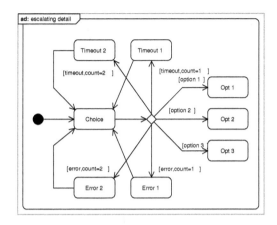

Consequences

+ The error recovery strategy matches the type of the error and adapts to the dialog state. The application gives only so much help as it is needed for the current dialog state.

+ The user is guided and does not need to listen to lengthy and general explanations.

- Difficult to find the right amount of help at each level.

- Not suitable for open-ended prompts, e.g., *How may I help you?*

Related patterns DECORATION can be used to reuse the initial prompt.

Sample code At our car inspection, the worker can get more information about the items of the inspection process while the items, introduced by the auditory icon *item.raw* are read and during the break before the next item starts, by the simple utterance *Yes*.

```
<field name="answer">
    <nomatch count="1">
        Please say next to proceed.
    </nomatch>

    <nomatch count="2">
        I could not understand you.
        Please say next to proceed, or help to get a list
        of valid commands.
    </nomatch>

    <noinput count="1">
```

```
    Please say something.
</noinput>

<noinput count="2">
    <reprompt/>
</noinput>

<prompt>
    When you are ready, please enter the car
    and sit in the drivers seat.
    Say next when you are there.
</prompt>
    ...
<filled>
    <if cond="answer=='next'">
        <goto next="#nextDialog" />
    </if>
</filled>
</field>
```

5.5.5 Design of the System Response

Developing voice based applications with VoiceXML is straightforward. The design of quality speech interfaces on the other hand, is a non-trivial task. This section introduces some patterns that can help to design the system's response to the user input.

Persona

Intent   Define a *look & feel* for voice based applications.

Context   Users of voice based applications build their own mental image of a personality or character that they infer from the application's voice and language. Such mental image relates certain properties to the virtual dialog partner, where systems responses should fall within a foreseeable range of possibilities.

Problem   How to realize a *look & feel* for voice based applications?

Forces

- Interests of the target groups are different

- Interaction with voice based application should provide an underlying coherent and stable personality

- The system's responses must be consistent. New characters distract the user.

- Dialogs should appear more natural

- Users know that they are talking to a machine

- The character must match the user's mental image of the application

Solution Identify the audience and enumerate the benefits to members of the intended audience. Specify what impressions and feelings the application should convey to the audience. Describe the fictional persona by writing a short biography of her to get hints, how to phrase messages and prompts. Define the wording of each message and prompt so it conveys the persona's message and personality. Compare several synthesized voices and select the voice with the tone, accent and energy that matches the persona. Determine the speed, tone and prosody of each prompt. Use markup languages like SSML [Spe04], to encode the voice characteristics or a voice actor emulating the persona, when recording the messages and prompts. Assure congruence of synthesized and prerecorded audio if both techniques are combined. In addition, choose the appropriate non-verbal sounds, background music or pauses to improve the clarity of prompts and messages. Make sure, that the usage is consistent throughout the whole dialog.

Consequences

+ VUI anticipates the caller's needs

+ Callers of the target group are satisfied

+ Common *look & feel* for the application

  - Callers outside the target group feel sidestepped

  - Users are distracted if the the persona is chosen wrong

  - Not applicable if the target group varies widely

Known Uses BERTI, the soccer information service from Sympalog uses the fictive person BERTI to interact in a MIXED INITIATIVE dialog with the caller. The application can be called at +49 (9131) 61 00 17.

The Poldi Gewinnspiel of the 1. FC Köln used a very famous person to create their PERSONA: Lukas Podolski. The application went offline in 2005, but was callable at +49 (180) 5 29 00 29.

Related patterns PERSONA is often used as an extension to the chosen dialog strategy, FORM FILLING, MENU HIERARCHY, or MIXED INITIATIVE, to make the dialog appear more natural.

Sample code In our car inspection scenario, the customer can call to get information about the progress of the repair. He has to identify herself with her customer id to retrieve the current repairs that are associated with this customer.

The sample code provides an example, how SSML tags can be used to use prosodic information within an application to control the TTS output. This example can give only an idea about this pattern. The decision for a persona is more or less a philosophical question, that has to be consistent throughout the whole dialog.

```
<field name="customer">
  <prompt>
    Hi, my name is Bill. I can give you some information
    about the status of your car repair.<break/>

    Please say your
    <emphasis level="strong">customer id</emphasis> that
    is printed on your copy of the
    <emphasis level="strong">order</emphasis>.
  </prompt>
  <grammar mode="voice" root="customer_id">
    ...
  </grammar>
</field>
```

Structured audio

Intent   Provide structural information in audio.

Context   Graphical documents offer many possibilities to structure the contents by means of headlines, different fonts and many other. This structure helps the user to stay oriented and allows for easy and fast access to the desired information.

Problem   How to provide information about document structure in audio?

Forces

- Structural information helps the user to access to information easy and fast

- Visual content is a fundamental part of any document

- Structural meta information gets lost while reading the document

- Voice applications have no direct means to represent structural information

Solution   Use sounds in form of *auditory icons, earcons* or *background sounds* to represent the structure. As an alternative, different speakers may also be used [Jam98].

Structure   The following figure shows an example, how an auditory icon *item.raw* is used to introduce the distinct items, *Item 1* and *Item 2* read by the TTS engine.

Consequences

+ Use of structural information in audio

+ Easier for the user to concentrate on the content

- A sound may have a different meaning to users

- Exhaustive use may distract user's attention

Known Uses The AHA framework [Jam98] uses STRUCTURED AUDIO to render structural information of web pages in audio.

Sample code At our car inspection scenario, the worker listens to a list of repair works that have to be done. Each item is marked with an item sound to indicate the list structure.

```
<field name="detailChoice">
    ...
    <prompt>
        This car needs the following repairs:
        <mark name="oilChange" />
        <audio src="item.raw"/> oil change <break />
        <mark name="changeTyres" />
        <audio src="item.raw"/> change tyres <break />
        <mark name="checkNoise" />
        <audio src="item.raw"/> check noise from exhaust
            <break />
    </prompt>
    ...
</field>
```

5.5.6   Data Entry

Since speech is invisible, users may not know what to answer or do not know which words they can use. Even if explained by a prompt, they may have forgotten about it, due to to the transient nature of speech, and may utter a command which is not in the grammar. This in combination with recognition errors of not successfully recognized valid commands can make the application unusable.

The dialog strategy patterns, see section 5.5.3, are also means of entering data. They describe, in contrast to the patterns presented in this section, the overall appearance of the application.

Index

Intent   Present a menu of options to the user.

Context   To use an application, users must be able to recognize the available functionality in order to operate the software. In VUI applications, it is particularly difficult to let users become aware of the available options and how to perform a selection. User selections can be performed in different modalities (voice or keystroke), and given a chosen modality, how the selection is actually performed (voice commands or keystroke sequences) must also be defined. Finally, the imperfect performance of speech recognizers forces the introduction of further complexity in the application in order to recover from errors while sustaining user's confidence and interest.

Problem   How should a VUI reveal the available functionality to the user?

Forces

- Novices require more detailed information about each option in order to use the most convenient one.

- Experts do not want to be bothered with the same long explanation they already know by heart, nor do they want to hear all the options every time they access the system.

- Voice activation is simpler

- Button selectable options are faster

Solution   There are two aspects involved in the solution that need to be addressed: letting the user learn the system's vocabulary, and providing different means to perform the selection of an option. To introduce the system's vocabulary there are three common techniques that can be combined:

1. Explaining the options at every point in the discourse (*a directive prompt*), guiding the user towards issuing a valid command.

2. Give directive prompts only if the user fails to issue a command within a few seconds (*a timed prompt*).

3. Provide context sensitive *help on demand*. Users may become confused which state the conversation has reached and what the system would accept as a valid command. Thus, users have the chance to re-establish the context, recall the available options, and ultimately find a way out.

Structure   This is illustrated in the following figure. The user is requested for an utterance in node *Choice*. If she does not make an utterance within a certain time, more information is given in *Info 1*. If she again does not know what to say, she gets more info in *Info 2*. At any time, she can get more help in *Help* by the corresponding command or by selecting the desired option to continue with *Option 1* or *Option 2*

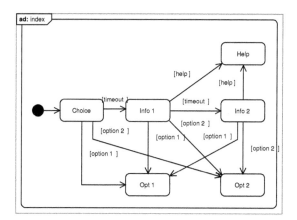

On the other hand, there are a number of approaches to enable more opportunities for the user to perform the selection of an option using voice and buttons. Again, we can divide the approaches in two:

- *Transient*: Options can be unambiguously selected while they are being conveyed to the user, until the next option is named. Usually activation is enabled by stating *Yes* or pressing the equivalent button on the phone.

- *Persistent*: Options are indexed and assigned an ID that is always the same for the same list of options and the current task. Options become active immediately after the user accesses the current list, thus enabling experienced users to quickly navigate to a known option. Furthermore, keeping the coding of options persistent enables users to memorize sequences for common, repetitive tasks.

Finally, since audio interfaces are mostly linear, it is important to provide users with the possibility of skipping (*barge-in*) options. Such skipping could be again triggered by voice (*next* or *previous* voice commands) or by pressing a number for other options.

Consequences

+ Users are provided with a wealth of choices to make a selection, making it easier to use new systems using conventions and assistance to effectively completing a required task.

- Enabling the selection of options using buttons typically limits the number of choices to about 12, where 10 (0..9) can be used for item selection and the remaining 2 (typically "#" and "*") for control purposes.

Sample code At our car inspection, the worker can get more help on how to behave after a timeout. This is an extension to the example given at SCRIPTED INTERACTION to provide more guidance.

```
<field name="detailChoice">
    ...
    <prompt>
        If you are not familiar with the procedures of this
        station , you can get more help on:
        <mark name="oilChange" />
        <audio src="item.raw" /> Oil change <break />
        <mark name="changeTyres" />
        <audio src="item.raw" /> Change tyres
        <mark name="checkNoise" />
        <audio src="item.raw" /> Check noise from exhaust
    </prompt>

    <timeout count="1">
        Say next, when you want to proceed.
    </timeout>

    <timeout count="2">
        You can also say repeat, to listen again.
    </timeout>
    ...
    <filled>
        ...
        <goto expr="'#detail '_+_detailChoice$.markname" />
        ...
    </filled>
</field>
```

Scripted Interaction

Intent Guide the selection of an option with a limited vocabulary.

Context It is common use to map each list item to a certain keyword. Dynamically generated lists thus enforce a change in the active grammar.

Problem Selection from a list is a problem for users of speech based applications, especially novices. Menu driven applications, which are used in most telephony applications, share the same problem, since menu selection can be reduced to a list selection. Novices need more guidance to choose the desired option or service in menu driven applications. They do not know the content of the list, and the appropriate keyword. If the list content varies, this is also true for all users, so the problem turns to handling dynamic lists with a limited vocabulary.

Forces

- Selection of items by name enables fast selection.

- List items may not be acoustically different.

- Items of the list are unknown to the user.

- Utterance of the user must match the grammar.

- Not all speech recognizers allow a dynamic change of the grammar.

Solution   Write the items as a script which leads the user through the selection process, as proposed in [Jam98]. Read this script to the user. Expect a single command to activate the selection.

Add the possibility to navigate forwards and backwards within the list, to the first or last section or repeat the current section by corresponding voice commands to allow for a faster access to the desired list item.

Structure   This following figure illustrates the structure of this list. After the choice introduction in node *Choice* has been read, the system continues with naming the first option in node *Desc 1*. The user can select this option *Opt 1* through a confirmation. If she says nothing, the next option in node *Desc 2* is read after a short timeout.

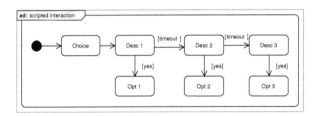

Note that *Choice*, *Desc 1*, and *Desc 2* will appear as a single node in the graph. They form their own navigation space.

Consequence

+ Guidance of the user through the selection process.

+ Processing of any list with a fixed and small vocabulary.

- Navigation to an item may require many interactions from the user, especially for larger lists.

Known Uses   The Deutsche Bahn AG offer in their travelling service the possibility to select an option, such as an earlier or a later train, after the schedule has been read. The user can select the command by *yes* after the option has been named. The application can be called at +49 (800) 150 70 90.

Borussia Dortmund offers a ticket reservation system via telephone. While the matches are read to the user, she can select the named match by the voice command *stop*. The application can be called at +49 (1805) 30 9000.

Sample code   At our car inspection, the worker can get more information about the items of the inspection process. The items are read out and introduced by an auditory icon *item.raw*. During the break before the next item starts, the worker can select the item by the utterance *Yes*.

```
<field name="detailChoice">
    ...
    <prompt>
        If you are not familiar with the procedures of this
        station , you can get more help on:
        <mark name="oilChange" />
        <audio src="item.raw"/> Oil change <break />
        <mark name="changeTyres" />
        <audio src="item.raw"/> Change tyres
        <mark name="checkNoise" />
        <audio src="item.raw"/> Check noise from exhaust
    </prompt>
    ...
    <filled>
        <goto expr="'#detail '+ detailChoice$.markname" />
    </filled>
</field>
```

5.5.7   Different Levels of Experience

An application that has cope with different types of users, e.g. experienced users (expert) and novice users (novice), has to provide information with different levels of detail for each user type

Since speech is only one-dimensional, the expert would have to listen to all the information, which she already knows, whereas novices may not get enough information to use the application.

Decoration

Intent   Present the same choices to users with different background information.

Context   Selection of an option is a common task in menu based telephony applications. While the commands are unknown to novice users, the expert knows what to say and does not need any explanation.

Problem   How to present the same choices to users with different background?

Forces

- The same options must be presented differently to users with different background knowledge or experience.

- The users to be supported and their domain knowledge may be unknown and can change over time.

- Not every prompt is suitable as a candidate to be decorated.

Solution   Use a profile to classify the expertise of the user with the system. This can be achieved by an identification mechanism as it is used i.e. in a banking application or by observing the speed of the user's interaction with the system and making guesses about the user's experience. The solution is built reusing the design concept of the GOF's Decorator Pattern [GHJV92]. The intent of a decorator is to provide a flexible alternative to extend functionality. In this way, VUI can provide a simple and extensible adaptation mechanism by transparently adding or *decorating* existing options with further information. Transparency refers to the actual definition of the option remaining unchanged. The decoration procedure is very simple and can only happen either before or after the given option is conveyed to the user, by inserting or removing explanatory information according to the user's profile.

Structure   The following figure illustrates the structure. *Info 2* is the node to be decorated. Decoration can be done by either *Pre 2* before or after this node by *Post 2*. using both, pre- and post-decoration for one node is also possible.

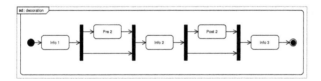

Consequences

+ Users are provided with different description of the options available.

- It might be difficult or impossible to obtain the user's profile.

- Decoration cannot be used until the user's profile is obtained.

- Guessing maybe wrong, if the user knows only parts of the application very well.

Related patterns   The GOF DECORATOR pattern. ESCALATING DETAIL can
be used to recover from wrong guesses. DETAILED INFORMATION can be used if the
profile cannot be determined.

Sample code   The following example is again taken from a car inspection. The
list of items is dynamically generated from a database.

This list is decorated when it is read to the worker with a short introduction to
the list:

```
<var name="decoration"
    value="This_car_needs_the_following_repairs"/>
...
<prompt>
    <value expr="decoration" />
    <audio src="item.raw"/>Oil change
    <audio src="item.raw"/>Change tyres
    <audio src="item.raw"/>Check noise from exhaust
</prompt>
```

Detailed Information

Intent   Deliver information with a different level of detail on demand.

Context   An application that has to deliver information with different levels of
detail and that has to address novices and experts has to deliver all the needed
information with respect to the user's background information. Solutions for this
problem are solved in written documents by a footnote or in the hypermedia world
by a link. They enable the user to retrieve more detailed information about a certain
passage on demand. Thus, users are able to control the amount of information being
delivered on their own. In addition, this does not hinder the normal reading process.

Problem   How to control the amount of information users get?

Forces

- Users with different background knowledge require different levels of details.

- Expert users do not want to be bothered with the same long explanation they
  already know by heart.

- The users to be supported and their domain knowledge may be unknown and
  can change over time.

Solution   The mechanism of a footnote can be copied to audio information delivery.
Use an auditory icon or a different voice to mark the passage where users can follow
a link to more detailed information. Provide a single command to activate the
link and define an anchor point where the user can continue after listening to the
detailed information, e.g., the start of the passage or an earlier point to return to

the previous context. Provide a command to continue at this anchor point. If the detailed information is long or requires thinking by the user, it might make sense to provide more commands to control pause, resume, and repeat of the detailed information.

The change of context can be introduced by another auditory icon. A repetition of the whole document is not needed.

Structure   This is illustrated in the following figure. After *Info 1* has been delivered to the user, the system passes the anchor point *Anchor* and continue with *Info 2*. The user may utter a command to get more detailed information in *Detail 2* and continue with another command at the anchor point. If she decides not to request more details, she continues with *Info 3*.

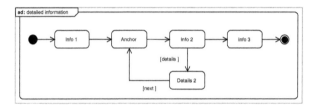

Consequences

+ Users get enough information to work with an application, independent of their background knowledge.

+ No profile needed.

+ Novice users can follow a link to get more information to enhance their background information and can easily get back into the main context.

+ The added auditory icon has less impact on the amount of information to be delivered to the user than any explanation given at this point.

- Too many occurrences in a row for short paragraphs will overload the memory capacities of novice users.

- This pattern cannot be applied if the information cannot be grouped or sorted in a way that is not obvious to the user.

- An additional, reserved, word is needed.

Related patterns   If the user's profile is known, DECORATION can be used to provide additional information.

Sample code   The following example extends the list of items of the car inspection to get a more detailed description of the item.

```
<field name="detailChoice">
    ...
    <prompt>
        This car needs the following repairs:
        <mark name="oilChange" />
        <audio src="item.raw"/> oil change <break />
        <mark name="changeTyres" />
        <audio src="item.raw"/> change tyres <break />
        <mark name="checkNoise" />
        <audio src="item.raw"/> check noise from exhaust
            <break />
    </prompt>
    ...

    <filled>
        <goto expr="'#detail '+ detailChoice $.markname" />
    </filled>
</field>
```

The worker can ask for more detailed information by uttering *details* from the start of the marker while the item is being delivered by the Text-to-speech (TTS) engine and throughout the pause after the item. The detailed information for the the item *change tyres* may look like this:

```
<prompt>

<audio src="section.raw"/> Change tyres

<audio src="paragraph.raw"/>
This car needs tyres of size 185/55 R15 S82.

</prompt>
```

The worker can resume with the command *next* after the detailed information has been read to return to the initial context, or get the document repeated with the command *repeat*.

5.5.8   Limits of the Short Term Memory

An application that has to deliver a large amount of information faces the problem that users are not able to keep all the information, or extract the information in which they are actually interested. The main reason for this is the limitation of the short term memory (STM).

Information Spreading

Intent   Divide the amount of information for the user into manageable pieces.

Context   Treating all the information to be delivered as a single logical entity conflicts with the limits of STM. Furthermore users cannot navigate to the information in which they are actually interested and have to listen to all the information that is given.

Problem   How to handle large amounts of information?

Forces

- A large amount of information has to be delivered.

- The short term memory capabilities of users are strongly limited.

- It might be impossible to find logical entities within the piece of information to split.

Solution   Group the information to be delivered into several sub nodes. Groups can consist of information items that meet certain criteria or are limited by their number. In the latter case they have to be sorted in an order that is obvious to the user.

A command or a timeout after each information subnode can be used to proceed with the next subnode. Add commands to allow to navigate back and forth and to handle the case that users realize that the information of interest cannot be in the current subnode, but may appear in a previous subnode or a subnode to come next.

Structure   This is illustrated in the following figure. The information is spread over the node *Info 1*, *Info 2*, and *Info 3*. The user can proceed by a utterance.

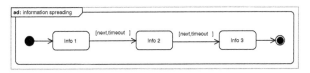

Note that this structure forms its own navigation space.

Consequences

+ The information that is delivered to the user is split up into pieces that the STM can handle.

+ Users gain control about the information being delivered at once. They may also navigate within this information. This allows for easier concentration on information of interest.

+ From application side, the spread information can still be treated as a single logical entity.

- Each information node must form a logical entity and additional effort is necessary to split the information appropriately.

Known Uses   The FAZ Electronic Media GmbH reads columns, e.g. sports, to the user. The headlines and the corresponding contents are read one by one. The user has the possibility to navigate in these headlines using voice commands. The application can be called at +49 (1805) 32 91 000.

Sample code   If the worker at our car inspection has to check the radio, the information about the use of the radio is spread over several documents. She can navigate through them by simple browsing commands *next* and *go back*. Note that only the first document contains the title.

```
<form name="start">
    <field name="start">
        ...
        <prompt>
            <audio src="section.raw"/> Radio

            <audio src="paragraph.raw" />
            The radio is located under the clock and the
            volume knob is green. To turn on the radio, turn
            the volume knob clockwise.
        </prompt>
        ...
        <filled>
            <if cond="start == 'next'">
                <goto next="#tuning" />
            <else />
                <reprompt />
            </if>
        </filled>
    </field>
</form>

<form name="tuning">
    <field name="tune">
        ...
        <prompt>
            <audio src="paragraph.raw"/>
            Turning the volume knob further clockwise
            increases the volume. To tune the radio, use
            the two buttons marked with arrows which are
            located on top of the volume button.
        </prompt>
        ...
        <filled>
            <if cond="start == 'next'">
                <goto next="#frequency" />
            <else />
                <reprompt />
            </if>
        </filled>
```

```
    </field>
</form>
```

Active Reference

Intent Help the user stay oriented.

Context Designing a voice interface requires careful planning of the functionality exposed to the user. The design of the navigational space is particularly complex, as it tends to be modeled spatially, which makes voice navigation difficult to map [MD90]. As the number of options and amount of information available increases, it relies more and more on the user's attention and memory. It becomes complex to identify successive actions as a part of the same task, remembering the options available and making the right decisions to reach one's goal. Furthermore, limitations of speech recognition performance may cause an indefinite number of extra navigational steps of error recovery and action confirmation. Due to the invisible nature of speech, after confirming, repeating options, selecting, listening instructions, correcting selections, the user may face the *lost in space* problem.

Problem How to help the user not to become lost in the audio space?

Forces

- Lack of permanent marks or cues as in visual interfaces, due to the transient nature of audio.

- STM is limited and cannot be constantly exercised to operate the application.

Solution The problem of orientation is similar to the hypertext domain and it is centered within 4 cardinal questions: *Where am I?*, *How did I get here?*, *Where can I go from here?* and *Why am I here?* (*What am I doing?*). This means the solution must address all these aspects. However, the linearity of the aural environment forces us to address each aspect separately. Furthermore, some of the solution proposals are split into transient and permanent aspects.

- **Where am I?**: Name the point in the navigational space the user has reached.

- **How did I get here?**: Name the navigational path the user has taken so far.

- **Where can I go from Here?**: Usually implemented as an INDEX (see Section 5.5.6).

- **Why am I here?** (What am I doing?): Give a sense of unity to the steps a user is performing. Create auditory indicators serving as a binding for related steps to the current task. In that way, users can distinguish whether current point belongs to the ongoing activity of if the latest action implied a change of activity.

Consequences

+ Users are provided with different cues that help them improve their awareness of their current status

- Excessive cues pushed to the user increases overhead, and may trigger user resistance

Related patterns   ESCALATING DETAIL can provide help depending on the current navigational point and experience of the user. SCRIPTED INTERACTION is used to navigate to the current path item.

Sample code   As an example we modify the example given for SCRIPTED INTER-ACTION to play back a prerecorded *radio* sound, before or while the information is being delivered.

```
<form name="start">
    <field name="start">
        ...
        <prompt>
            <audio src="radio.raw" />
            <audio src="section.raw"/> Radio

            <audio src="paragraph.raw" />
            The radio is located under the clock and the
            volume knob is green. To turn on the radio, turn
            the volume knob clockwise.
        </prompt>
        ...
        <filled>
            ...
        </filled>
    </field>
</form>
```

Note   Unfortunately VoiceXML is not capable to play audio in background. As a workaround, the whole audio can be prerecorded and mixed manually. Since we wanted to show the mixing, we decided to add the text as a prompt.

5.5.9   Usability

We present some of the most common usability issues in publicly available voice applications. In particular, these problems and cardinal aspects that we consider should be addressed in voice applications that are expected to become a central part of the communication and information strategy of any organization.

Language Selector

Intent   Support of language selection for users.

Context   Voice applications usability is affected by a number of objective factors such as response time, noise and attention, but also by other more subjective, such as vocabulary, expressions, intonation and pronunciation. All these factors introduce different degrees of complexity when accessing content through a voice interface. However, the language remains as the biggest barrier.

Problem   How to provide users with an effective language selection mechanism?

Forces

- Global companies and currently increasing migration within multilingual economic regions such as the EU or Mercosur are demanding services to be offered in multiple languages

- Users want to access a service in their native language

- Service has to be translated into the target language

- The default language of the company that offers the service is unknown to users

- Recognition of multiple languages concurrently is not supported by all speech recognizers

Solution   Order the languages to be supported according to their importance in the host country or the area of the country. Use the list of official languages of the country in case of doubt. Greet the caller in all languages that are supported or in the language to be considered dominant. Ask the user for the language to use in each language in the determined order. If the speech recognizer does not support concurrent recognition of multiple languages, use SCRIPTED INTERACTION to ask simple *Yes/No* questions in each language

Structure   This is illustrated in the following figure. After the *Greeting*, the application prompts the option of interaction with the language *L1* in that language and the option for *L2* in language *L2*. After the user has chosen the language, the application continues with the selected language in *L1 Application* or *L2 Application*.

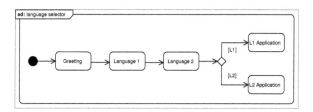

Consequences

+ Allow users to easily recognize an option

+ Enable users with little foreign language skills to access the system

- Listening to options in many different languages can be confusing

- The problem of translating the application remains unsolved

Known Uses   An example can be found in major airlines services such as the
United Airlines customer service: +49 (69) 50 07 03 87.

The traffic information InfoTraffic from Viasuisse asks the user in all official
languages of Switzerland in the language to obtain the language the user want use.
The application can be called at +41 (900) 400 500.

Related patterns   SCRIPTED INTERACTION can be used to ask for the language.
CONTEXT-AWARE CALL can be used to automatically suggest the language from
the caller's ID.

Sample code   If the customer calls our international car repair shop, if her car is
ready, the application asks for the language, sh wants to use.

```
<form id="language">
    <field id="language">
        <prompt>
            Welcome to the car inspection.
            <p xml:lang="en">Do you want to use English?</p>
            <p xml:lang="de">
                Moechten Sie Deutsch verwenden?
            </p>
            <p xml:lang="es">Desea acceder es Espanol?</p>
        </prompt>
        <grammar src="language.grxml"
                 type="application/srgs+xml"/>
        <filled>
            <if cond="language='english '">
                <goto next="en/car.vxml"/>
            <elseif cond="language='deutsch '">
                <goto next="de/car.vxml"/>
            <elseif cond="language='espanol '">
                <goto next="es/car.vxml"/>
            </if>
            <reprompt/>
        </filled>
    </transfer>
</form>
```

Busy Waiting

Intent   Provide a meaningful interaction to users waiting to be attended.

Context   Personal attention is a scarce resource. More and more, companies are rapidly moving to provide their customers to centralized call-centers with an increasing number of self-service functionality in order to cope with the ever-growing demand and to reduce costs. However, human intervention to resolve conflicts cannot be totally replaced. In these scenarios, bottlenecks are more likely to appear as human attention (operator) does not scale well but only through the addition of more operators. As such, customers looking for human attention often find themselves waiting to be attended.

Problem   How to transform the passive user waiting in a phone line into a more active, engaging experience (and keep them waiting!)?

Forces

- Waiting is avoided by customers

- Avoid users leaving the service (possibly in favor of a competitor)

- Minimize the time users spend waiting to be attended

- Physical limitations of the telephone system or used services to attend more people at the same time

- The company wants to offer the service, but adding more operators is costly

- Users expect a 24x7 service

- Not all call centers are available 24x7

Solution   The solution needs to address the uncertainty of the waiting status (Am I going to be attended? Will it take long? How many people are already waiting? Why keep waiting?). There are number of information that can be conveyed to the user to bring clarity and sense of the time spent *queued*:

Clearly state if the service is available 24h or not. Mention the time-zone, if the application covers an area over multiple time-zones. At regular intervals of time provide some information.

This information can be one or a combination of the following modules. This can vary, depending on the target group.

- Let the user know that the system is aware of the waiting, apologize and reinforce the message that the user will be attended as soon as possible.

- Provide information about how many people are in the queue (as a subjective delay measure) or better, provide an estimate of the waiting time

- Offer alternative ways to perform a request. For instance, offering the user self service options or directing users to the customer website.

- Provide short advertisements about new services, products and last minute offers.

- Play a smooth and calming music in the background. This can be combined with brief corporate or branding messages and intervals where only the music is heard.

Structure   This is illustrated in the following figure. In *Connect* a caller should be connected to a technician. During the transfer she hears music. If the connection was successful, she gets transferred to the technician. If a timeout occurs, she can be provided with some other information, i.e. numbers of persons waiting, before she hears the music again.

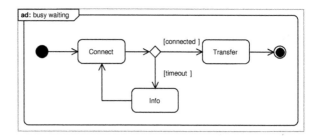

Consequences

+ Users become more satisfied because they know more.

+ Changes the waiting period into informative moments

- It doesn't solve the need for more operators

- Users might feel caught by the application if they get information in which they are not interested

- Telephones usually have a lower sound quality than a radio. Therefore, playing advertisements originally prepared and recorded for radio broadcasting may not be easy to follow and understand

Known Uses   The customer service at T-Online informs the user about alternative request possibilities, if all technicians are busy. While the user is in the waiting queue, she gets notified that she will be connected to a technician as soon as possible from time to time. The application can be called at +49 (180) 5 30 50 00.

Related patterns   A Place To Wait [AIS77] with the constraints of the audio domain and a virtual environment

Sample code If the customer calls the car repair shop, if her car is ready, she may end up in a queue. Each 60 seconds, she will be informed about the number of persons to be served first.

```
<form id="xfer">
    <transfer name="mycall" dest="tel:+1-555-123-4567"
              transferaudio="music.wav" connecttimeout="60s"
              bridge="true">
        <prompt>
            Say cancel to disconnect this call at any time.
        </prompt>
        <grammar src="cancel.grxml"
                 type="application/srgs+xml"/>
        <filled>
            <object name="size"
                classid="method:///queue.size"
                data="http://www.example.com/queue.jar">
            </object>
            <prompt>
                There are only <value expr="size"/>
                persons to serve before you.
            </prompt>
            <reprompt/>
        </filled>
    </transfer>
</form>
```

Note, that this example would not really work, since the caller would be disconnected and enqueued again, if the connection timeout expires. The reason is the limitation of the `<transfer>` element in VoiceXML. A workaround for VoiceXML is to dynamically create the audio file *music.wav* and synthesize the announcements to this file. Proprietary implementations with a CTI connection to the telephony system do not have this limitation.

Context-Aware Call

Intent Provide more meaningful interaction to the users.

Context Requesting services and goods over the phone is a common part of our lives. These voice applications are continuously applied everyday into the most diverse purposes. From making appointments and accessing bank services to ordering a pizza or a taxi, spoken requests are an every day activity.

A certain amount of context information is often required for any request in order to be meaningful. In voice interfaces, such information must be provided by the user.

Problem How to minimize the overhead of gathering information to perform a request?

Forces

- The process of conveying directions and specifications of what is being asked can be time consuming when the amount of information is large

- A request cannot be fulfilled unless all the required information is available

- When a service must be repeatedly requested, providing the same information is time consuming

- Users do not feel annoyed, if they do not use the service frequently

- Users need feedback about the information which the system already has, and temporal orientation

- A low speech recognizer performance makes that data entry more error prone

- Context information is not available for third parties yet

Solution   Context information can help voice interaction systems be more responsive and better adapt their response to the users. A common source of context information in voice applications is brought for instance in each phone call by the caller ID service. Use this information to determine actions and default values for data that the user has to provide to use the service.

Structure   This is illustrated in the following figure. If contextual information *ctx* is available, it is obtained in *GetContext*. If *ctx* is not available, the user has to enter it manually in *Enter* before the information can be processed in *Process*.

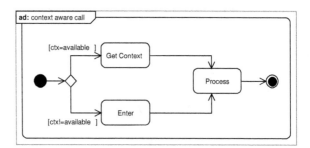

Consequences

- + Personalized service. The information about who's calling and potential needs and preferences is already available

- + Less mistakes on the overall process of attending a request. Elimination of repetitive data entry favors accuracy

+ More efficient interaction between the user and the operator. Substantially more calls can be attended in the same amount of time

+ Other planning and logistic systems can be integrated and use the contextual information to schedule service according to other criteria such as logistics or customer relation

- Cannot be applied for services requiring authentication, since a caller ID might not be enough to identify the caller for critical applications

Known Uses A very popular application is the Memobox implemented by communication providers, which uses the user ID in order to automatically enable the access to the private recorded messages. In this case, the telephone (either fixed or mobile) becomes an identification (not authentication) token.

Another example is the case of a taxi request system available in Argentina (+54 221 427 4500), which by default uses the caller ID information to determine the address where a Taxi should pick up its passenger, unless otherwise instructed. When the call is made from mobile phone, this fact is reflected to the operator who in that case asks the customer if the pick up location is the same as last time or should be found somewhere else. The use of context information helps the taxi company improve its efficiency keeping the average customer call very short (8-12 secs), just enough to acknowledge the existing address is correct and confirm the request.

The Israeli Electric company prints a *Contract Number* field on the electricity bills as a single *handle* that is typed when calling their VUI system. This handle replaces a whole group of numeric entry fields that were required to bill with a credit card.

Related patterns In FORM FILLING, context-aware call can help with automated filling of fields with known information about the caller.

Sample code In a car inspection scenario, the worker has to get a list of which repairs have to be done for the next car. This information can be entered manually by reading the license plate to the system or by a location system, that automatically detects that the worker is standing near to a certain car.

```
<form id="get_order">
    <object name="location"
            classid="method://Locator/locate"
            data="http://www.example.com/location.jar">
        <param name="worker" expr="id"/>
    </object>

    <block>
        <if cond="location">
            <submit next="http://www.example.com/read.jsp"
                    namelist="location"/>
        </if>
    </block>
```

```
<field name="enter_location">
    <grammar src="order.grxml"
             type="application/srgs+xml"/>
    <prompt>Please read the license plate</prompt>
    ...
    <filled>
        <submit next="http://www.example.com/read.jsp"
                namelist="enter_location"/>
    </filled>
</field>
...

</form>
```

5.6 Conclusion

We have introduced a set of patterns that repeatedly appear in voice based applications. These patterns comprise several known design guidelines for VUI design. The complexity of designing VUI applications has its roots in the inherent transience and invisibility of the medium, the user's memory capabilities and the varying performance of currently available speech recognition technology. These three factors introduce a particular set of problems and requirements to the application that must be addressed, and that we have documented in this paper.

The design patterns we presented in this work aim to help the designer of a VUI understand the nature of the problems and thus successfully analyse and solve these issues to provide a successful voice interface.

SCRIPTED INTERACTION, ESCALATING DETAIL, and INDEX offer guidance for data entry, while ESCALATING DETAIL focuses on recovering from a recognition error.

DECORATION and DETAILED INFORMATION address the problem of supporting users with different background information and experience.

INFORMATION SPREADING and ACTIVE REFERENCE tackle the problem of the Short Term Memory limitations. ACTIVE REFERENCE helps the user stay oriented by providing different cues that help improve the awareness of the current status, and INFORMATION SPREADING provides the means to avoid overloading the cognitive capabilities of the user.

An overview of how these patterns can be combined and how they behave in action is illustrated in figure 5.5. This is a very dynamic process which we show in four usage scenarios (a to d). Each scenario is shown with the time line in the middle. Above the time line the active grammars are shown. For scenario a, this is the permanent grammar *1—2—3—4* and the transient grammars *yes—no* which are only active while an option is delivered to the user. The system's output and the user's answers, in grey, are shown below the time line.

The menu with four options is presented to the user using the INDEX pattern. SCRIPTED INTERACTION defines how the user can perform a selection. Some commands are active all the time, while others are time constrained.

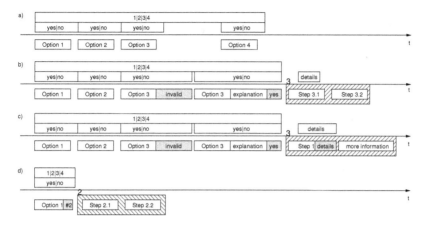

Figure 5.5: Audio Navigation Patterns in action

Usage scenario b shows how ESCALATING DETAIL can be used, if the option was not recognized because the user may not have understood the option. A detailed description of the item is presented using DECORATION. The *explanation* decorates the description with further information.

The next usage scenario c shows how DETAILED INFORMATION delivers the information with another granularity according to the user's need if she asks for *details*.

The last usage scenario d shows how a user can activate an option efficiently, i.e. by pressing the *#2* button without waiting to hear the index. ACTIVE REFERENCE is used in the form of a background sound to bring unity to a set of actions that occur over time. This is indicated by the hatched background. The large amount of information is delivered using INFORMATION SPREADING.

This subset of patterns from the language demonstrate that it is possible to have a language to talk about VUI designs. It enables designers to get a quick overview of the benefits and drawbacks of each design decision they make. We have started building a new pattern language which we hope will continue to grow with the help of the VUI community.

Chapter 6

Integrating VUIs, Context and Workflow

6.1 Motivation

In chapter 4 we described the fundamentals of an audio browser that can be used in mobile environments. This is only a part of the picture of a system supporting workers on the move that we sketched in section 1.1.

In this chapter, we will focus on the integration of all techniques, introduced so far, and explore the *Business Process* component, see Figure 1.2, with respect to voice user interfaces and context. These techniques comprise the results in the context of the multi-purpose audio browser for smart environments introduced in chapter 4 and the workflow engine to handle the Business Process, see chapter 2. In this chapter we shall replace the audio browser with a workflow engine, retaining the browsing concept. Both components are not as different as they appear at first sight. Table 6.1 shows the direct analogy between an audio browser and a workflow. We choose the workflow specification in XPDL, see section 2.4.1.

Both can be regarded as a state machine where the user can influence the path traversed. If a certain location has been reached, the audio browser starts and the user begins to browse by saying, e.g. *details*. In XPDL, a process can be started either in *manual mode*, requiring explicit user interaction to invoke the start, or in *automatic mode*, where the start of process is fully controlled by the workflow engine. The mode used is specified in the *Execution Control Attributes*. Hence, the user interaction to start the browser is comparable to manual mode. Each node of the audio graph is an audio document. In the world of workflows, we do not have the terminology of documents, but rather activities. It is possible to map an audio document to an activity. However, an activity is designed to handle more than one simple document, which we will explore later in this chapter. The traversal from one node to another is called a *transition* in both worlds. Each transition may have a guard condition. For the audio browser this may be the user's *utterance*, e.g., *next*. In fact, it is possible to omit the utterance, to automatically traverse to the next node. Workflows must know the more general term of a *condition* to check if this transition should be taken.

From the discussion above, we can conclude that it is possible to implement an audio browser using a workflow engine. In addition we gain a lot more, mainly built-

Table 6.1: Analogy of the Audio Browser and Workflow

Audio Browser	XPDL
document link	execution control attributes
audio document	activity
transition	transition
utterance	transition

in task support, a better integration into business processes and data flow. From our prototype of an audio browser we observed also some recurring problems where we try to support the workers performing their tasks, see sections 4.8.3 and 4.8.3.

Knowledge about the current task In order to create the graph and help the user to navigate it, knowledge about the task, especially its relationship to the environment that, we can retrieve as context is needed.

Conditions Utterances are the first type of condition that needs to be supported. When the worker interacts with the environment, we need a more complex support of conditions for the transitions.

Pause and resume Some tasks require a certain waiting time, e.g. the laboratory worker waiting for a certain amount of time before she can continue with her task. Another option is that the user triggered the pause, e.g., the telephone rings and she wants to continue after finishing her call.

Notification after a predefined delay If the interruption is triggered by the system we may need a notification to inform the user that she may continue.

Timeout Some time critical tasks may only proceed within a certain time span. If the user does not complete the task within that time span, an error path might be required to follow.

Parallel execution of tasks Interruption also leaves time for other tasks.

Workflow systems are designed to handle these problems. The following sections focus on the integration of workflow systems into the target architecture. Figure 6.1 shows the roadmap of this this chapter.

Section 6.2 deals with the use of context information in workflow engines, thus focuses on the first two items: *Knowledge about the task* and *Conditions*. The basic requirements have been defined in section 2.5.

Section 6.3 introduces the new concept of voice based interaction with a workflow engine based on the definitions that were introduced in section 2.7.

This serves as a basis to consider the remaining items of the above list: *Pause and Resume*, *Notification after a predefined delay*, *Timeout* and *Parallel execution of tasks*.

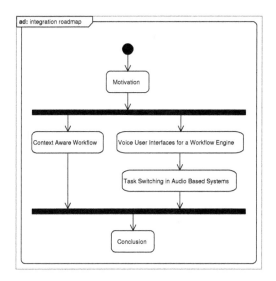

Figure 6.1: Roadmap to handle the Integration of Voice User Interfaces, Context and Workflow

6.2 Context-Aware Workflow

In section 2.5 the requirements for a context-aware workflow system were discussed. Some of the requirements came up again in section 4.8.3, when we talked about the use of environment and activity. As pointed out in the previous section, workflow engines are ideal candidates to cope with these issues. In this section we present how context information can made accessible to workflow engines. First, we discuss the core challenges to achieve such integration.

Use context information in transitions As pointed out in section 2.5.3 a basic requirement of a context-aware workflow is to use context information in transitions of the workflow process.

The following example workflow has an activity *Activity 1* waiting for an RFID event of an object. There are only three cases to distinguish:

1. If the object is o_1 proceed with *Activity 2.1*

2. If the object is o_2 proceed with *Activity 2.2*

3. If the object is unknown, continue waiting.

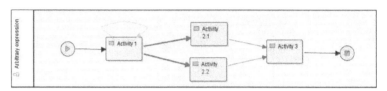

In this case, the evaluation of the transition condition is a simple comparison of two integers. Complex comparisons, e.g., determining equality of parts of a complex object, cannot be handled easily. We need to be able to compare

- equality of primitive values like integers
- equality of complex objects
- partial equality of complex objects

The latter one is important, if we are only interested in certain properties of the object, e.g., the event is coming from a certain type of RFID tags, regardless of the ID. In this case, the type information has to be used in the transition, but we might also be interested in keeping he object for further processing.

Timing Issues *Activity 1* in the above example is waiting for an event to come from the environment. There are no problems, if the events are received at any time t_2, after the corresponding activity has been activated t_1 and before it ends t_3, as shown in the following figure.

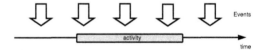

Events that have been received at any time $t_0 < t_1$ are not considered. If the activity has to wait for such an event, it may wait infinitely, since the event has already been sent, but the workflow was not able to process it. If we want to get rid of timing constraints, we need a mechanism to know in advance, in which events we are interested and also need mechanisms to store them for a later retrieval. A similar issue is know from the Java Message Service [Jav06b], where we can have *durable* and *non-durable* subscription for messaging events. The durable/non-durable concept is not enough for our purposes. There may be cases, where we are not interested in all events, but only events that were received after t_k. An example is to detect, if a worker pressed a button to start a process. She must do it in the current process and we are not interested, if she pressed it last week.

Separation of unhandled data from already handled data Imagine an activity processing context data from a sensor that is constantly publishing events. An example is shown in the following figure.

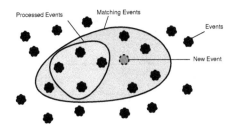

Figure 6.2: Separation of unhandled data from already handled data

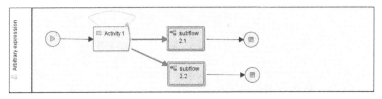

The process waits in *Activity 1* until it receives an event. If an event arrives, either *subflow 2.1* or *subflow 2.2* is started asynchronously, depending on the kind of event. After starting the subflow, *Activity 1* continues waiting. Events that do not match are ignored.

Again the incoming events and the receiving activity are not synchronized. In addition to the previous point, that we do not want to miss an event, we have to make sure that only events that are not processed are delivered to the activity and that the data is kept for future processing, as illustrated in the Figure 6.2.

The events e_i that are relevant for *Activity 1* are in the set E marked in blue. The events e_k that are already processed are contained in the set $E_p \subset E$, marked in green. It must be sure, that only events $e_l \in \{E \setminus E_p\}$ are processed.

6.2.1 Limitations of the Context Server

The requirements for context-aware applications are solved by Mundo, see section 2.3. Mundo allows to publish context events over a predefined channel and also to receive them. The missing part is an integration of Mundo to Workflow Engines. Nøthvedth et al. showed in [NN04] that this can be done using the Interface 2, see section 2.4. They used the Context Toolkit from Dey [Dey00], which is comparable to our context server, to preprocess context data coming from the environment. Nødveth's approach does not offer solutions for problems that come with the use of contextual information in transitions and the use of contextual data in the workflow, but leaves it to the preprocessing in the context toolkit.

As shown in section 2.3 the context server is able to derive high level context from lower level context, like pure sensor data. This enables us to solve the above named challenges, but lacks a reusable concept.

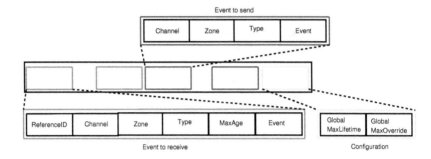

Figure 6.3: Data container structure

In order to use context information in transitions, a concept is needed to make the possible comparisons as easy as possible, but also keep the data for later use to transform complex objects into manageable pieces. This works in principle but lacks a reusable concept tom compare

6.2.2   The Data Container

Currently there is no standard to exchange data with the environment. In the following we will develop an first approach towards a standard by a demo architecture. Mundo offers great support for context-aware application development. Thus we need to integrate Mundo with the workflow management system at a first step.

The definition of XPDL poses some restrictions on the exchange of data with applications. The number and types of parameters is defined to be fix for each application, although the ToolAgents are designed to handle a variable number of parameters. This means, that it would be necessary to define different applications with a different set of parameters for each combination of events that the ToolAgent wants to publish or receive. We wanted to use only one ToolAgent, so we had to use a data-type that enabled us to encode all data in a single parameter. XML allows for such a encoding or multiple data in a single string.

A possible structure, which we call the *data container* is illustrated in Figure 6.3. The data container consists of three main building blocks

1. events to receive,

2. events to send and

3. configuration.

A Data Container can contain multiple receive and multiple send blocks and one configuration block. The contents of the blocks are described below.

Receive Block

Events to receive must contain at least the following items

ReferenceID As mentioned above, we need a unique identifier for the event, to retrieve the data of the event and an easy comparison in transitions.

channel The channel name, where the event is published. This is Mundo specific and has to be replaced by a corresponding concept of other implementations.

zone The Mundo zone, which again is Mundo specific.

type Identifier to mark this as a receiving block.

MaxAge Maximal age of events, that are accepted.

Event The receiving component must know in which type of event the current activity is interested. Thus we need a description of the events to wait for.

Send Block

Sending events is easier than receiving them. In order to send an event, we just have to fill the variables for the sending block, which must contain at least the following data.

channel The channel name, where the event is published. This is Mundo specific, like the corresponding block to receive events.

zone The Mundo zone, which again is Mundo specific.

type Identifier to mark this as a sending block.

Event Event to be sent.

This makes it possible to interact with the environment, i.e. control switches or trigger the output of a text-to-speech engine.

Configuration Block

The last block offers the possibility to provide some configuration parameters. One configuration block per Data Container is enough to address all requirements. Send blocks and receive blocks requiring different configuration parameters can be sent via multiple data containers.

6.2.3 Reference Implementation

Demo Scenario

We developed a prototype as a proof of concept. As an example we regard a simple workflow at a coffee machine, shown in Figure 6.4. The basic idea is that a user approaches to the coffee machine, puts her cup under the dispenser, identifies and gets a cup of coffee. If the machine needs a filter change the user is guided by a TTS output through the change process. Identification of the user happens via an RFID tag which the user carries with her. We use a transponder used at the Technical University of Darmstadt, Figure 6.5, which is normally used to as a door key.

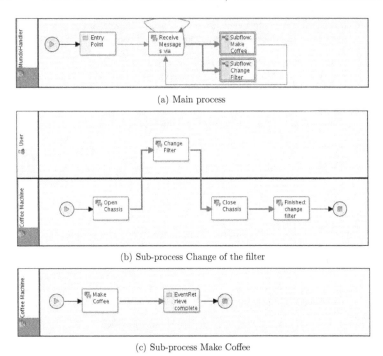

(a) Main process

(b) Sub-process Change of the filter

(c) Sub-process Make Coffee

Figure 6.4: Example workflow for a filter change of a coffee machine (bold arrows indicate conditional transitions)

Figure 6.5: RFID transponder used at the Technical University of Darmstadt with a receiver

This simple workflow addresses all the functional requirements that were named in section 2.5.3. We can enact a preplanned process by receiving an RFID of the user's transponder. The ID is used, e.g., as a condition to traverse to the corresponding next subflow. In addition, we are able to trigger services in the environment from the workflow by sending utterances to the synthesizer. We did not look at exceptional situations and enact unplanned processes.

The workflow starts with the main process, see Figure 6.4(a) consisting of the following activities.

Entry Point This is a dummy activity that serves as an entry point to the workflow. Unfortunately XPDL does not allow having only one main activity that is part of a loop.

Receive Messages via Mundo This activity waits for an event to arrive over Mundo. Dependent on the event, the workflow proceeds with one of the following subflows. If the event is unknown, the event is ignored and we wait for the next event.

Subflow: Make Coffee This subflow is used to control the coffee machine in making coffee.

Subflow: Change Filter This subflow aids the user in changing the

The subflow *make coffee*, see Figure 6.4(c) comprises the following activities:

Make Coffee This activity starts the machine to make a cup of coffee.

EventRetrieve complete After the start, this activity simply waits until the output is finished.

The subflow *Change Filter*, see Figure 6.4(b), comprises the following activities:

Open Chassis This activity sends a signal to the synthesizer with instructions to open the chassis. Afterwards the activity waits until the user opened it, which is received by a signal from a sensor.

Change Filter This activity is performed by the user. If the user has performed the task, she terminates the activity by a voice command.

Close Chassis This activity sends a signal to the synthesizer with instructions to close the chassis and waits until the user closed it. Again, this is detected with the help of a sensor.

Finished: change filter This again is a dummy activity that serves to mark the end of the subflow.

As mentioned above, we developed a general model that can be used, to receive events, access the data, and that also allows for easy use in transitions. The basic architecture is described in the next section. The following sections describe how our model is used for receiving and sending events.

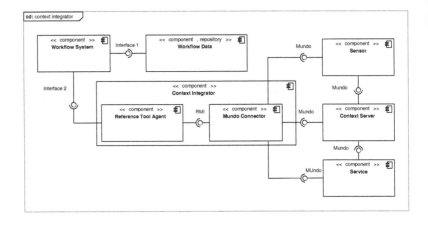

Figure 6.6: Context Integrator architecture

Prototype Architecture

Our target architecture of a context-aware workflow that was introduced in Figure 2.1 named the *Context Integrator* component being responsible to make data coming from sensors and services in the network accessible by the *Business Process* component. In our prototype, we focused on the implementation of the Context Integrator Figure 6.6. The definition of Interface 1 and Interface 2 is given in section 2.4. We use Interface 2 as a hook to communicate with the environment handled by the *Context Integrator*. The *Context Integrator* consist of two components: the *Reference Tool Agent* and the *Mundo Connector*. The *Mundo Connector* is responsible for the communication over Mundo and as storage for event data. It is designed as a Singleton [GHJV92] which is shared among all workflows. We regard the setup of the communication and storage of event data as to heavy-weighted to be done by each activity that needs communication capabilities. The *Reference Tool Agent* thus serves as a means to get access to the *Mundo Connector*. It is implemented as a Tool Agent

The following sections describe the concept of the usage to receive and send events using this prototype. The concept is based on XPath which is described in the following section.

XPath

The **XML Path** language (XPath) was developed by the W3C [XML99] to address parts of an XML document. XPath is a basic technology that is used in several other standards, like XSLT, XPointer and XQuery. The newer version 2.0 has been released in January 2007. We use the previous release 1.0, which was released in 1999.

XPath regards an XML document as a tree structure, the so called **Document Object Model**. Parts of this tree can be addressed by XPath expressions. Nodes of the tree are XML elements, attributes, comments, namespaces and processing instructions.

Starting from an arbitrary node, the rest of the document can be described via XPath *axis*. The five main axes in total describe the complete tree. We use the definitions of section 4.5 to describe these axes. In addition, we need a relation to describe the order within the tree. The relation is based on an order set of of links $\{(n_i, c_1), (n_i, c_2), \ldots, (n_i, c_m)\} \in \mathbf{L}$ from n_i to all children c_k with $C(c_k, n_i)$. Then, a node n_k is after a node n_l if the following equation holds.

$$\text{after}(n_k, n_l) = \exists n_p : P(n_p, n_k) \wedge P(n_p, n_l) \wedge k > l \tag{6.1}$$

A node n_k is before a node n_l if

$$\text{before}(n_k, n_l) = \exists n_p : P(n_p, n_k) \wedge P(n_p, n_l) \wedge k < l \tag{6.2}$$

self The arbitrary node n_i.

ancestor All nodes n_k on the path from the root n_r to n_i such that $\{n_k | A(n_k, n_i)\}$

descendant All partial trees having a root node n_k being an immediate child to n_i such that $\{n_l | \exists n_k \in \mathbf{N} : C(n_k, n_i) \wedge A(n_k, n_l)\}$

following All nodes n_k that are sequentially after n_i and are neither contained in ancestor nor descendant. $\{n_k | \exists n_l, n_m \in \mathbf{N} : A(n_l, n_i) \wedge \text{after}(n_l, n_m) \wedge A(n_m, n_k)\}$

preceding All nodes n_k that are sequentially before n_i and are neither contained in ancestor nor descendant. $\{n_k | \exists n_l, n_m \in \mathbf{N} : A(n_l, n_i) \wedge \text{before}(n_l, n_m) \wedge A(n_m, n_k)\}$

These axes can be used to navigate the DOM tree. We use the Xalan library [The06] from the Apache project to evaluate XPath expressions.

Receiving events

Use of Context Data in Transitions We use the Data Container that was introduced in section 6.2.2. The event description is based on XPath [XML99]. The activity *Receive Messages via Mundo* waits for an RFID event of an object, sent by the RFID reader, once it discovers the object. We use the XML serialization and deserialization capability of Mundo to create an XML representation of an object and instantiate objects from such an XML representation.

The listing below shows an example of a serialized RFID event.

```xml
<?xml version="1.0" encoding="ISO-8859-1"?>
<message
  xmlns:xsi="http://www.w3.org/1999/XMLSchema-instance">
  <main xsi:type="map" activeClass="org.mundo.rt.TypedMap">
    <object xsi:type="map"
             activeClass="org.mundo.rt.TypedMap">
      <object xsi:type="map"
               activeClass="ga.mundo.service.rfid.RFIDEvent">
```

```
   <serialnumber xsi:type="array" activeClass="[I">
     <object xsi:type="xsd:int">181</object>
     <object xsi:type="xsd:int">238</object>
   </serialnumber>
   <command null="1"/>
   <data null="1"/>
   <status null="1"/>
   <tstmp xsi:type="xsd:long">0</tstmp>
   <id null="1"/>
   </object>
  </object>
 </main>
</message>
```

The information of interest, which identifies the owner of the tag, is encoded as the *serialnumber*. We can retrieve it using the following XPath expression:

```
//main/object/object/serialnumber
```

The result is as follows:

```
<serialnumber xsi:type="array" activeClass="[I">
 <object xsi:type="xsd:int">181</object>
 <object xsi:type="xsd:int">238</object>
</serialnumber>
```

The following listing causes the *MundoConnector* to compare this result to a predefined value. This is the case, for example if we are waiting for a certain event from a certain sensor.

```
<?xml version="1.0" encoding="UTF-8" standalone="yes"?>
<dataContainer>
  <DCEvents>
    <entry>
      <key>1731916119</key>
      <value>
        <channel>RFID</channel>
        <dataContainerQueryResults>
          <entry>
            <key>//main/object/object/serialnumber</key>
            <value>&lt;serialnumber xsi:type="array"
                    activeClass="[I"&gt; &lt;object
                    xsi:type="xsd:int"&gt;181&lt;/object&gt;
                    &lt;object
                    xsi:type="xsd:int"&gt;238&lt;/object&gt;
                    &lt;/serialnumber&gt;</value>
          </entry>
        </dataContainerQueryResults>
        <maxLifetime>-1</maxLifetime>
        <referenceID>1731916119</referenceID>
        <type>0</type>
        <zone>lan</zone>
      </value>
```

```
    </entry>
  </DCEvents>
  <globalMaxLifetime>−1</globalMaxLifetime>
  <globalMaxOverride>false</globalMaxOverride>
  <returnVar>result</returnVar>
</dataContainer>
```

Once the event is received, the *ReferenceID* 1731916119 is returned to the workflow. This single value can be easily tested for equality to determine the next transition. WfMOpen allows using simple Java-like expressions to be used as a conditional expression for the transition. These expressions are based on standard data types, i.e. string, float, integer. Complex comparisons, e.g. determine equality of parts of a complex object, cannot be handled easily. We use the XPath expression for this purpose. This way, we can reduce the comparison of complex object to a simple string comparison. Note that we use the ReferenceID only for decision purposes. The only information that we get at this point is, that at least one event matches our query.

Accessing Context Data   If we are interested in the real data, we have to do some additional work. It is possible, that our query matches not only one single event, but a group of events, as illustrated in Figure 6.2.

The *MundoConnector* remembers the events that have already been returned by the calling activity. These events are contained in $E_p \subset E$. The MundoConnector selects one event e_l, marked in red, from the set $E \setminus E_p$. Since the selection via the ReferenceID is not unique, we need an additional parameter that uniquely identifies such an event. We generate a unique *EventID* for each event that is also returned by this ToolAgent as an additional parameter. Then, this event can be selected using this EventID by the *RetrieveEventToolAgent*, which returns the XML representation of the event.

In some cases, we are interested in the event data without the need for comparison with a defined object, for example if we waiting for any event from a certain sensor. In this case we build the Data Container as follows to receive the RFID event

```
<?xml version="1.0" encoding="UTF−8" standalone="yes"?>
<dataContainer>
    <DCEvents>
        <entry>
            <key>1327206957</key>
            <value>
                <channel>RFID</channel>
                <dataContainerQueryResults>
                    <entry>
                        <key>//object/@activeClass</key>
                        <value>
                            ga.mundo.service.rfid.RFIDEvent
                        </value>
                    </entry>
                </dataContainerQueryResults>
                <maxAge>−1</maxAge>
```

```
          <referenceID>1327206957</referenceID>
          <type>0</type>
          <zone>lan</zone>
       </value>
     </entry>
  </DCEvents>
  <globalMaxLifetime>-1</globalMaxLifetime>
  <globalMaxOverride>false</globalMaxOverride>
</dataContainer>
```

This causes the MundoConnector to return the ReferenceID if an object of the type ga.mundo.service.rfid.RFIDEvent has been received. Again, the EventID can be used to retrieve the received data.

Sending events

Sending events is easier than receiving them. In order to send an event, we just have to fill the variables for the sending block. The event to send is delivered to the tool agent in an XML serialized format.

The following Data Container sends the above event over channel *RFID* and zone *LAN*

```
<?xml version="1.0" encoding="UTF-8" standalone="yes"?>
<dataContainer>
  <DCEvents>
    <entry>
      <key>1873937867</key>
      <value>
        <channel>RFID</channel>
        <dataContainerQueryResults/>
        <maxAge>-1</maxAge>
        <referenceID>1873937867</referenceID>
        <sendCon>&lt;main xsi:type="map"
            active-Class="org.mundo.rt.TypedMap"&gt;
&lt;object xsi:type="map"
            activeClass="org.mundo.rt.TypedMap"&gt;
&lt;object xsi:type="map"
            activeClass="ga.mundo.service.rfid.RFIDEvent"&gt;
&lt;serialnumber xsi:type="array" activeClass="[I"&gt;
&lt;object xsi:type="xsd:int"&gt;240&lt;/object&gt;
&lt;object xsi:type="xsd:int"&gt;160&lt;/object&gt;
&lt;/serialnumber&gt;
&lt;command null="1"/&gt;
&lt;data null="1"/&gt;
&lt;status null="1"/&gt;
&lt;tstmp xsi:type="xsd:long"&gt;0&lt;/tstmp&gt;
&lt;id null="1"/&gt;
&lt;/object&gt;
&lt;/object&gt;
&lt;/main&gt;</sendCon>
        <type>1</type>
```

```
        <zone>lan</zone>
      </value>
    </entry>
  </DCEvents>
  <globalMaxLifetime>-1</globalMaxLifetime>
  <globalMaxOverride>false</globalMaxOverride>
</dataContainer>
```

This makes it possible to interact with the environment, for example controlling switches or triggering the output of a text-to-speech engine.

Configuration

The last block offers the possibility to provide some configuration parameters. Currently we support the following parameters

GlobalMaxLifetime This is the time that events are stored in the EventCache.

GlobalMaxOverride If the value is `true`, the value of GlobalMaxLifetime is been used without respect of the current value. If the value is `false`, the value is set, if the current value is smaller than the one in GlobalMaxLifetime.

We implemented an EventCache that serves exactly that purpose. If there is no activity listening for an event that is currently being received, it is stored in the EventCache. The time that an event is stored in the cache can be configured. A thread checks at configurable time intervals, if there are any events that can be deleted from the cache.

Further Functionality

It is possible, that multiple activities of different processes use the same channel. In this case, it is possible that one activity a_1 ends, while the second a_2 is just starting. The end of a_1 will cause the removal of the subscription to the channel. If a_2 starts, before a_1 ends, there is no need to start a new subscription, since such a subscription already exists. a_1 will then close the subscription and as a result, a_2 will never receive events, until another activity starts a new subscription to that channel.

In order to avoid this misbehaviour, it is possible to explicitly registering and deregistering the subscription to a channel. Subscriptions are handled by the *RegisterToolAgent* and the *DeregisterToolAgent* whose main parameters are the Mundo zone name and the Mundo channel. The principle of registering channels is based on *reference counting*, a technique that is also known from smart pointers in C++ programming. The Mundo Connector simply counts the registering calls and increments an internal counter for a channel. Each deregistering call decreases this counter. If there are no more references left, the subscription is removed.

6.3 Voice User Interface for a Workflow Engine

This section focuses on the generation of voice user interfaces for a workflow engine in smart environments. Our basic understanding of voice user interfaces and code

Figure 6.7: Shopping Task

generators was introduced in the sections 2.6 and 2.7. Generation of user interfaces is handled by the *Voice Controller* component of the target architecture which was introduced in section 2.1. In section 6.3.1 we show that current approaches use modality dependant task descriptions for their task model which result in task models that can not be easily transferred to other modalities. We explain our implementation of a dialog model with the help of a demo scenario (section 6.3.3) . Section 6.3.7 demonstrates how our approach can be applied to different modalities. Finally we conclude this section with a short summary and an outlook to further enhancements.

6.3.1   Limits of Task Decomposition

It is obvious, that the reuse of the dialog model is not suitable to satisfy the needs of different modalities, which is probably also a reason, why this model is the one least explored [Ols92]. Olsen's statement is still true as Luyten points out in [Luy04].

This becomes clearer in the following example. Consider a shopping task, where the customer first has to select the items to buy and then proceeds to entering the billing address. Figure 6.7 shows how the task *Shopping* is decomposed into the sub-tasks *Select an item* and *Purchase the items*. This is exactly the way as it is proposed by Luyten et al. [Luy04]. According to Luyten, a task t can be recursively decomposed into a set of sub-tasks:

$$t \xrightarrow{d} \{t_1, \ldots, t_n\}_{n \geq 2} \tag{6.3}$$

We concentrate on the purchasing task, which is further decomposed into the sub-tasks *Enter address information* and *Enter credit card information*.

The designer of a graphical interface would stop modelling at this stage, since these are tasks, which can be handled by a single view in the user interface. Note that it is also possible to expand these tasks, but it is not necessary. An example implementation of the address entry from Amazon is shown in Figure 6.8.

The same level of expansion would not work in audio, since each input field of the address entry is a complex operation in audio and has to be treated separately.

Apart from the problem, that free-form voice entry of names is still an unsolved problem, several other challenges inherent to the medium have to be considered, which were introduced in section 2.6.1. As a consequence, the task *Enter address*

Figure 6.8: Amazon: *Enter address information* form

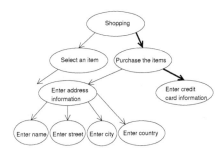

Figure 6.9: Expansion of *Enter address information* for voice

information must be expanded for voice as shown in Figure 6.9. Stopping decomposition is no longer an option.

This means, that a task decomposition d may have modality dependencies M, where M is a set of targeted modalities $m_1, \ldots, m_k$. Moreover, the task t itself supports only a set of modalities M, expressed by t_M.

Therefore we extend equation (6.3) to:

$$t_M \overset{d_{M'}}{\to} \{t_{1,M'}, \ldots, t_{n,M'}\}_{n \geq 2} \qquad (6.4)$$

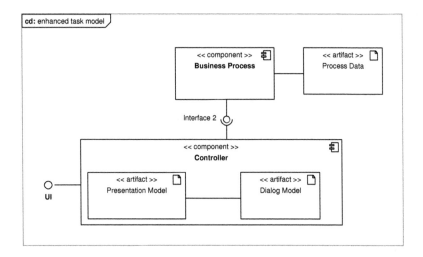

Figure 6.10: Division of the task model into a modality independent and a modality dependent part

where M' is a set of supported modalities of the decomposition with

$$M' \subseteq M \qquad (6.5)$$

The decomposition $d_{M'}$ decomposes the current task into subtasks supporting all modalities of M'. As long as $M' = M$ we do not loose a modality. Decomposition starts in $\hat{t}_{\hat{M}}$ with $\hat{M}$ being a set of all known modalities, which means modality independence.

In the rest of this chapter, we introduce an approach that splits the tasks of the tasks into a modality independent and a modality dependent, as illustrated in Figure 6.10. The modality independent part of the task model can be handled by the workflow engine. Modality dependent tasks are part of the dialog model and require an additional handler in the *Controller* component. This approach is used to create higher quality UIs and meets all requirements in reusable business logic. Task decomposition stops at a point where we loose a modality, which means $M' \subset \hat{M}$. All these tasks $t_{M'}$ must not be part of $\mathcal{M}_T$ but part of $\mathcal{M}_D$. More mathematically

$$\{t_{M'}|M' \subset \hat{M}\} \notin \mathcal{M}_T \qquad (6.6)$$

In other words: Tasks with a modality dependency are treated as a modality dependent view on the corresponding modality independent task.

The following section presents a reference implementation of our approach.

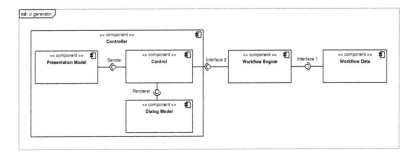

Figure 6.11: Architecture of a workflow based UI generator

6.3.2 Reference Implementation

User interfaces for workflow engines have been considered to be graphically-oriented desktop PC applications only. The MOWAHS [MOW04] project extended this approach to mobile users using heterogeneous devices. Moreover it tried to integrate contextual information from the environment into workflows. In section 6.2 we enhance their approach by a data oriented solution. However, research in this project concentrated on graphical devices. Our approach tries to fill the gap between the world of workflow engines and the world of voice-based UIs.

Our basic architecture is shown in Figure 2.1. The task model is stored as *Workflow Data* and is accessed by the *Workflow Engine* as an execution environment. The *Controller* reads the current activity from the workflow engine and asks the *Dialog Model* through the *Renderer* interface for the next dialog specification. Currently the output of the *Renderer* is limited to markup languages. But this is only a minor issue, since markups for Swing-based Java user interfaces and others exist [Abs06] and are well explored. The dialog specification is passed through the *Sender* interface to the *Presentation Model* to be transformed into a concrete UI.

To illustrate how this architecture can be applied to ease the development of ubiquitous computing systems, we will discuss how it could be used in an exemplary scenario, which is introduced in the following section.

6.3.3 Demo Scenario

The scenario is a ticket machine which overcomes the bottleneck of its single graphical user interface by allowing different modes of access depending on the resources available to the user.

Imagine the following situation: A user is rushing to the station to catch a specific train. As she arrives at the platform, the train is already pulling into the station. Unfortunately she still needs to buy a ticket and the queue in front of the ticket machine kills any thought of taking that train.

The bottleneck in this situation is the ticket machine. More specifically it is the fact that there is only a single, sequentially working user interface to the ticket machine which has to be shared by all users. A known solution for this problem is

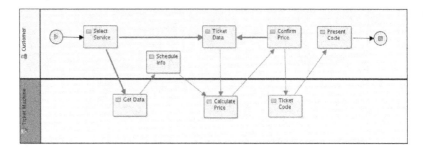

Figure 6.12: Ticket Machine workflow example

the possibility to buy a ticket using mobile phone SMS, but this is strongly limited to the medium SMS. Imagine a ticket machine that is able to extend its user interface to external devices like PDAs, mobile phones or bluetooth headsets. A user that who to use the ticket machine can connect to it wireless with her device. The machine determines the capabilities of the mobile device and renders an appropriate user interface.

The first activity asks the customer which service she wants to use. Depending on her selection, the *Get Schedule Information* or *Edit Ticket Details* tasks are executed. For simplicity the remainder of the *Get Schedule Information* workflow has been omitted. *Edit Ticket Details* presents default ticket details to the customer and gives her the opportunity to change them. When she finishes this activity, the values are transferred to the *Calculate Ticket Price* activity which calculates the final fare for the ticket. Next, the calculated amount is presented to the customer who can decide to make further adjustments or confirm the purchase. If she confirms, the ticket machine computes a ticket code as a replacement for a *real* ticket. This code is again presented to the customer. Once this is done, the workflow finishes.

Our implementation is based on XForms and XSLT. Both will be explained in the following sections, before we focus on their use in our implementation of a dialog model.

6.3.4   XForms

XForms aim at collecting form based data and is standardized by the W3C [W3C06]. XForms is platform independent and can be used on various devices like desktop computers or mobile phones.

The target of the development of XForms was to offer support of forms in HTML and XHTML, the XML based successor of HTML, and to combine these forms with XML technology. Consequently XForms is part of the upcoming XHTML 2.0 standard. However, XForms can also be used independent to XHTML.

XForms uses the MVC pattern, see section 2.7. The model is described in XML format using the `<xfm-model>` tag. An example of a model will be shown later in section 6.3.6.

XForms does not contain many clues for the presentation, leaving it to the language that is used to embed XForms. The controller uses widgets to combine the elements of the model. These widget feature properties for the presentation, like smaller, importance, and the schema of the datatype. The latter one can be exploited, e.g, by web applications to validate the entered data in order to avoid validation on the server or using JavaScript on the client. This is especially important for smaller devices, since it saves resources like memory or network bandwidth.

The widgets are defined in elements like `<xfm:trigger>` or `<xfm:submit>` to activate certain actions like `<xfm:setvalue>` or `<xfm:insert>`. Some of these widgets do not have a meaningful implementation in voice-based UIs. One of them is `<xfm:setfocus>`. In our prototype, the voice renderer, who is responsible for the evaluation of the XForms description, simply ignores these tags. Again it is noteworthy that the weakest medium limits the expressions of a UI markup language. Current implementations ignore this or are just able to produce UIs with limited capabilities [HKM+03].

We use XForms as a language in XML format to control the presentation in VoiceXML. The benefit of the XML format is that we can use XSLT transformations to transform the XForms into VoiceXML, which is also in XML format.

6.3.5 XSLT

The **XSL T**ransformation (XSLT) is part of the **E**xtensible **S**tylesheet **L**anguage (XSL). XSLT is a programming language that can be used to transform XML documents. It uses the DOM tree, refer to section 6.2.3, to define transformation rules in XML format. XSLT processors read the stylesheets and transform one or more documents into the target format according to these transformation rules.

The transformation rules are called *templates* in the XSLT jargon. Each template features a pattern based on XPath, see section 6.2.3, to describe the part of the DOM tree for which it applies. If the pattern applies, the content that is described by the template is taken as the part of the tree in the output DOM tree.

XSLT is standardized by the W3C. The current version 2.0 was released in January 2007. We used version 1.1 and the Saxon [Kay] implementation, since this implementation satisfies all our needs and is fast enough.

6.3.6 Dialog Model

We will explain the architecture using the ticket process example shown in Figure 6.12.

In the example, we concentrate on voice-based user interfaces. We use VoiceXML to handle speech input and output. Other modalities can be supported by other markup languages, see section 6.3.7. Figure 6.13 shows the core components of the VoiceXML renderer.

The *VoiceXMLRenderer* implements the *Renderer* interface of the *Control* component. The renderer transforms XForms [W3C06] forms, stored in the correspondent artifact into the targeted markup language, e.g. VoiceXML.

Each activity of the workflow engine can have multiple forms. This enables a modality dependent decomposition into sub-tasks as shown in Figure 6.9. In fact the *Control* component is a state machine, that handles all interactions belonging

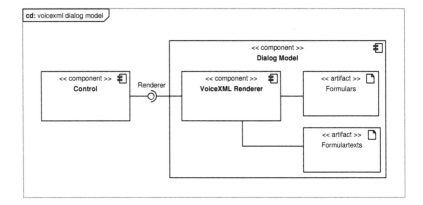

Figure 6.13: VoiceXML Renderer based on XForms

to a single activity. The process designer can concentrate on her task to establish a workflow and has little stimulation to over design the workflow, since she need not care about the UI.

Modelling of Data

XForms is based on an `<xfm:model>` element. The following listing shows the model for the schedule:

```
<xfm:model>
    <xfm:instance id="schedule">
    <data>
        <TrainNumber>RE2475</TrainNumber>
        <Departure>Darmstadt</Departure>
        <Destination>Mannheim</Destination>
        <DepartureTime>10:24</DepartureTime>
        <DestinationTime>10:59</DestinationTime>
                <DepartureTrack>6</DepartureTrack>
                <DestinationTrack>2</DestinationTrack>
    </data>
    ...
    </xfm:instance>
    <xfm:instance id="selection"/>
    ...
</xfm:model>
```

We use the workflow engine to retrieve the data. In our case the data is obtained from a database in the *Get Data* activity and stored as a copy in the *selection* parameter..

Definition of Forms

Next we have to define that the destination and arrival time should be read to the user, before she is prompted to select the current train from the schedule. This is shown in the next listing.

```
<xfm:output id="train"
   ref="instance('schedule')/data/TrainNumber"/>
<xfm:output id="destination"
   ref="instance('schedule')/data/Destination"/>
<xfm:output id="destinationTime"
   ref="instance('schedule')/data/DestinationTime"/>
<xfm:input id="select"
   ref="instance('cart')/data/selection">
```

Besides simple input and output for the default data types known from XPDL, we also implemented support for selections from lists and complex data types like structures.

The **ref** attributes indicate, that the text resides outside this document. This can be used, e.g., for internationalization. It is defined in its own document. This makes it possible to write texts independently of the XForms data model and the workflow activity. The following listing shows the text for the shopping task.

```
<Item isa="text">Train</Item>
<Item isa="output" id="trainNumber"/>
<Item isa="text">arrives in</Item>
<Item isa="output" id="destination"/>
<Item isa="text">at</Item>
<Item isa="output_id="destiationTime"/>
<Item_isa="text">Do_you_want_to_select_this_train?</Item>
```

In addition, a form can have internal variables which are used to control the selection of the next form or to transfer data from one form to another.

A possible output would sound like this:

System: Train RE2475 arrives in Mannheim at 10:59. Do you want to select this train?

The Form State Machine

Next we have to define how to process the data. An action to perform such a processing step is defined by the `<xfm:action>` tag. The following listing shows how this action is defined in our example to select a train from the schedule.

```
<xfm:action>
    <xfm:insert at="1" ref="instance('schedule')/selection"
        position="before"/>
    <xfm:setvalue ref="instance('schedule')/.../TrainNumber"
        value="instance('schedule')/data/..[...]/TrainNumber"/"/>
____<xfm:setvalue_ref="instance('schedule')/.../Departure"
_____value="instance('schedule')/data/..[...]/Departure"/"/>
    ...
</xfm:action>
```

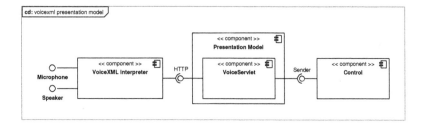

Figure 6.14: VoiceXML Frontend

We look upon the forms as a description of input and output elements, linked with the actions. Each activity defined in the workflow engine can have multiple assigned forms. The logic to *display* a certain form is then comparable to a state machine. This is where we enhance XForms with the <Transition> tag. After submission of a form, the state machine decides, whether there is another form to display or if the activity is complete. In the latter case, control is returned to the workflow engine. A transition can be defined like in the following example:

```
<Transitions>
    <next to="schedule">
        <test var="todo" op="eq" value="n"/>
    </next>
    <next to="schedule_again"/>
</Transitions>
```

Checking for the next next transition is done by the eq attribute of the <next> tag. Currently we are able to check data for equality in combination with logical operators <and> and <or>, which can surround the <next> tags. An empty <next> tag is the default value, where control is returned to the workflow engine.

Some media may require certain renderer parameters, like fonts and colors for XHTML or voice for VoiceXML. These parameters depend on the renderer. They can be defined in a <RendererParam> node and are delivered to the renderer without further evaluation.

The benefit from using a state machine is that the UI tasks are separated from the business process. We gain a separation of concerns. The business process is defined in the workflow engine without any information of the display medium. UIs are defined in an independent repository with all the specific parameters that are required for rendering.

The *VoiceXML Renderer* is implemented using an XSLT transformation.

Presentation Model

The presentation model can be defined via a plug-in architecture through the *Sender* interface. As an example implementation, we show a VoiceXML presentation model based on XForms (Figure 6.14).

The user communicates with the VoiceXML interpreter over the phone. The

VoiceXML documents are retrieved from the *VoiceServlet*, stored on a Tomcat servlet container. The *VoiceServlet* communicates with the *Controller* using Mundo, see section 2.3.

6.3.7 Prototype

This section shows our reference implementation at work. Although different interaction techniques (e.g. VoiceXML, XHTML) are supported, they all share the same basic workflow to determine the overall structure of the application and how information is exchanged between different activities. This scenario demonstrates key strengths of the architecture provided. By decoupling the business logic from the implementation of the user interface, the implementation of different modalities is greatly simplified while still providing enough flexibility for the UI designer to build the interface most appropriate for a specific interaction technique. Also by having the same workflow beneath all variants, the user does not have to relearn the logic behind the application when switching devices.

Voice-Only Interface

The voice-only interface can be used when no visual interface is available. Low-end mobile phones or wireless headsets would be examples of devices using this mode of access. This is also true when visual user interfaces are not an option as for visually impaired people.

Sample Dialog:

System: Which Service can I provide? Say 1 for buying tickets and 2 for schedule information.
User: 1

System: Do you want an adult ticket for zone 1? Say 1 to change the ticket type, 2 for another zone and yes to confirm.
User: 1
System: Name the number of the destination zone.
User: 1
System: Say 1 for adult, 2 for student and 3 for child.
User: 2
System: Do you want a student ticket for zone 1? Say 1 to change the ticket type, 2 for another zone and yes to confirm.
User: yes

System: The student ticket for zone 1 costs € 1.20, buy that ticket?
User: yes

System: Your ticket code is ABZ723S. Shall I repeat the code?
User: yes
System: Your ticket code is ABZ723S. Shall I repeat the code?
User: no
System: Good bye and thank you for using our service.

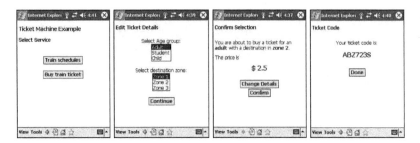

Figure 6.15: Ticket Machine Example XHTML Interface

Notice that the architecture is flexible enough to accommodate UI patterns specific to the voice-based nature of the interface. That is repeating important information is one of these aspects that is not necessary with visual interfaces, but which is required in audio-based interfaces due to its transient and invisible nature.

The task model could also be used for a hand crafted mixed initiative dialog.

System: What can I do for you?
User: I need a ticket for zone 1
System: Do you want to buy an adult, a student or a child ticket for zone 1?
User: student

System: Do you want to buy a student ticket for zone 1 for € 1.20?
User: Yes

System: Your ticket code is ABZ723S. Shall I repeat the code?
User: No.
System: Good bye and thank you for using our service.

This dialog is only hand crafted, but demonstrates the flexibility of our approach. It is even possible to generate user interfaces like that with another type of renderer. Currently, the knowledge about the patterns which we mined, see chapter 5, is crafted in the XSLT transformation. A next step would be to develop renderers that automatically create renderers, using the patterns, from the dialog model to produce high quality voice user interfaces. This is beyond the scope of this thesis, since it is necessary to get deeper into code generators.

XHTML Interface

When a PDA or smartphone is available, the architecture uses a different renderer with its own repository of UI forms to deliver the service to the customer. Figure 6.15 shows sample screenshots from an XHTML renderer.

The forms for this renderer are been optimized for PDA and smartphone interfaces to improve the user experience. At the same time, the overall business process and associated links into the back-end system are reused. Therefore the user interface designer can concentrate on the user experience and is not concerned with back-end integration.

6.3.8 Recap of Results

In ambient intelligence environments, multiple devices are used to interact with the environment. Each device has its own characteristics, depending on the modalities used. Declarative markup languages are considered to be a solution for single authoring user interfaces targeting different devices and modalities. In this section we introduced a novel architecture to combine model-based UI generation from declarative markup languages with a modality independent task model.

We showed that current approaches to use task models are not modality independent. The separation of modality independent tasks and the integration of data flow, see section 2.7, enabled us to use a workflow engine as the runtime environment for the task model. Since workflow engines are already adopted by companies, we hope that this is a first step to make generated user interfaces ready for industrial settings. Our approach is a generalization of the MVC pattern to model-based architectures as proposed in [Luy04].

We identified modality-dependent components of the task model and moved those to the dialog model. As a positive consequence, the business logic, which is stored in the remaining task model, is fully reusable for different modalities. This makes it also possible to integrate other systems or trigger events.

We implemented our architecture and showed that it is possible to generate higher quality user interfaces which take respect to the current modality. The current implementation focuses on voice interfaces. Other markup languages like XHTML are currently being implemented, see section 6.3.7.

For our target architecture we enhanced the *Control* component to generate VoiceXML documents for a workflow engine. The *Business Process* component is fully replaced by the *Workflow Engine*.

6.4 Task Switching in Audio Based Systems

This section focuses on tasks which are described as a process in a workflow definition language. The execution of a task is often interrupted by external events or by the user who wants to suspend the task, or switch to another task. If the user later wants to resume the task she has to be aware of her current position in the workflow. Due to the transient nature of speech, see section 2.6, she does not have the possibility to review what she has done before. The user has to know how she can ask for information about the current state of the process, which leads to a decreased usability, especially for novice users. This section presents a novel approach to assist the user in getting back into the context of an interrupted task. The basic assumption, based on psychological theories, is that goals are the most important information to be remembered for a task's resumption. All relevant information about the state of a task focusing on information about the current goals and about the current position (what the user has already done) in the workflow is stored in an proprietary XML-structure. This structure is retrieved from the task's workflow-description. In order to determine the amount of necessary information for a given situation, the development of an estimate for the adverse effect of an interruption is required. Finally, the usability of this recovery concept was tested in a user study.

6.4.1   Definitions

We use the concept of task decomposition that was introduced in section 2.7 to determine the tasks that are stored as a process in a workflow engine. In that sense, tasks share a common goal. Examples of tasks are a *system-task* like writing an email, an *external task* like talking on the phone, or just even the task of doing nothing (*idle task*).

Corragio [Cor90] defines an interruption as

Definition 28 *An **interruption** is a discrete event that breaks continuity of cognitive focus on primary task*

Covey states in [Cov89] that interruption typically "requires immediate attention" and "insists on action" and therefore causes a temporary shift of the user's focus. An interruption can be caused by an external source (for example another person), by the task-handler (e.g. by informing the user about an incoming email) or by the user herself. The external sources can be classified in other applications beyond the control of the task-handler and other sources from the environment independent of the computing system (for example someone knocking at the door).

Definition 29 *A **task switch** is the process of stopping or pausing the execution of a task for the benefit of a second task.*

A special case of a task switch is the *termination* of a task. If one task ends, a new task has to be started or an interrupted one resumed. A task switch decomposes in its components *start, interrupt, resume* and *end*. The second task can also be an external task which leads to the statement, that interruption is also a kind of a task switch.

6.4.2   Problems with task switching

If the user wants to resume a task, she has to recapitulate its context. At this point several challenges are faced:

- How much information is needed to help the user to resume the task?

- Which information is necessary for the resumption?

- How should the user interact with the task-handler considering the transient and invisible nature of speech?

We are interested in finding a general approach to answer these questions, in order to be relatively independent of the application area. The key requirements for this approach are shown in Figure 6.16.

One possibility for determining the appropriate amount of information is to ask the user how much information she needs (e.g. *much, normal* or *little*). Another option is that the system estimates the amount of information. An approximation of the factors has to take the disruptive effect of the interruption into account. Hence, a concept for adapting the amount of repeated information is needed.

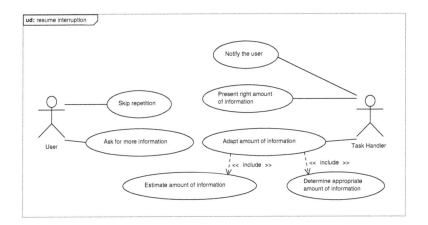

Figure 6.16: Requirements to resume interrupted tasks

Having determined the amount of information, it has to be decided which information shall be presented to the user. Which information is relevant to build up the context of the primary task?

A fundamental aspect of the task context is the goal that the user wanted to achieve. In order to obtain an understanding of the cognitive background on how users process tasks, we follow the studies of Anderson [AL98] and Newell [New90], assuming goals to be in a stack-like cognitive structure, ensuring that the items belonging to the control flow reside in memory. The newest goal on such a stack directs the behavior [AL98, New90] In this cognitive architecture goals are sources of activation without requiring active maintenance or rehearsal and they are linked associatively to other goals, which are related via task constraints. This model is based on the cognitive architecture ACT-R (*Adaptive Control of Thought, Rational* [AL98]), which consists of a set of inter-related mechanisms to simulate and explain human cognition. Its basic processing assumption states that, when the central cognition queries the memory, it returns the most active item in memory, which then directs the behavior. Activation therefore means relevance to the current situation.

It is probably more comfortable for the user to simply listen to the information, especially when she is not used to the system. It is much more difficult to design interaction in an audio-only environment than in a visual one, because of the audio inherent challenges, refer to section 2.6. The user has to be aware of the possibilities she has at a certain point in the interaction. Therefore she has to know all available commands. However, at least two voice commands have to be supported, because it is never for sure that the appropriate amount of data is repeated. The user has to be able to skip the repetition or to ask for more information.

On the other hand, longer texts, summaries utilizations of detail-links require the possibility to interact with the system in order to turn the summaries off or on.

The design of an interactive recovery process needs a decision about the commands that should be used for it. They have to be intuitive to reduce the learning time, and be well distinguishable, to decrease the error-rate of the speech-recognition system, refer to section 2.6. Moreover, the user has to be able to quickly find her way through the task without having much experience.

Hence, a concept for adapting the amount of repeated information is needed. Other facts that we have to consider are reminders and situational awareness. The execution of the interrupting task can take a while or the user might want to perform some more tasks before getting back to the primary task and thus the user might forget the existence of the interrupting task. Therefore a more complex handling of reminders is needed which also regards suspended tasks.

Franke, Daniels and McFarlane [FDM02] divided an interruption into three phases (Pre-, Mid- and Post-interruption).

pre-interruption The pre-interruption phase takes place before the actual interruption. It should enable the user to rehearse some information, to help and to differentiate between primary and interrupting tasks.

mid-interruption The mid-interruption phase should support user control of context switching and help the user maintain situational awareness of the interrupted task.

post-interruption The post-interruption phase consists of the resumption of the primary task. Thereby the interface should aid the user in recalling the context of the interrupted task. The user has the possibility to use special commands to query the interface about aspects of the previous task. This can be general queries like *Where was I?* and also specific questions, e.g., which supplies have been ordered. Additionally the user can request a full progress review of the interrupted task.

For the mid-interruption phase Franke noted that negotiation was the best approach for all kinds of user performance, except when even small temporal differences were of importance. Based on this experiment Franke et al. chose an intelligent, automated selection of interruption strategy on a case-by-case basis. In order to decide which strategy to use they compared the relative importance of the current and the interrupting task. If the interrupting task is mission critical compared to the current task, the user is interrupted immediately. If the current task is critically important compared to the interrupting task, the alert is held until the user is finished with the current task and thus until the next cognitive break. In all other cases, the interruption is negotiated. In addition they vary the default action taken after a negotiation. If the interrupting task is slightly more important than the primary task, the default action is to accept the interruption (interrupt), otherwise the default action is to delay the interruption until the next cognitive break.

6.4.3   Related Work

There is already a lot of research focusing when and how a user should be interrupted to reduce the adverse effects, but there is hardly any research how to help the user resuming a task, especially in the audio domain. The closest is an interface developed by Franke et al. [FDM02], which considers most of the problems, which are also important in our work.

Franke, Daniels and McFarlane developed a "spoken dialog interface system for a radio-based human-software agent military logistics task" [FDM02].

For the pre-interruption phase they decided to use a different voice as cue for incoming alerts, e.g. the primary dialog uses a female voice, and the system switches to a male voice as soon as an interruption should be introduced.

In comparison to our approach, Franke et al. focus on very simple and short tasks, with a specific application area with very formal standardized military communication, while we are interested in a more general approach. For using Franke's approach, the user has to be trained which questions she can use for getting the information she wants. Additionally Franke et al. do not vary the amount of repeated information, e.g., depending on the elapsed time, because they only handle with short tasks and short interruptions, whereat only little information accumulates. In contrast, this approach deals with an amount of data which would be too annoying to listen to, when the interruption was not really disruptive. Another fact that Franke et al. did not consider are reminders. They do not support any situational awareness of the interrupted task, despite that the primary task is automatically resumed after the completion of the interrupt. Such a procedure is not sufficient for a general approach. A more complex handling of reminders is needed which also regards suspended tasks, which are not taken into consideration in Franke's approach.

Franke et al. transfer the result of McFarlane's experiment from the visual domain to the audio domain. It is doubtful that the results are the same in this domain, because the processing of auditive interruptions differ from the processing of visual interruptions as shown e.g. by Latorella [Lat98].

Furthermore using the prototype realization shows too few differences between the different negotiation strategies (varying in the default option). The user needs to spend too much attention to the interruption to be aware of this little difference (*...Accept now?* vs. *...Defer now?*), which hampers the performance on the primary task. Additionally the implemented negotiation takes too long, which also disrupts the memory for the primary task.

6.4.4 Concept

We use the principle of task decomposition, that was introduced in section 2.7 and which we already used in VoiceXML frontend for a workflow engine, see section 6.3. The use of task decomposition start with the assumption that a workflow has one main goal (in the example: *Repairing a car*) which can be split in several subgoals (in the example: *Error diagnosis* and *Repair part* ...). These can in turn consist of some subgoals (for example *disassemble*, *clean* and *reassemble*). Each subgoal can thereby be associated with a subtask of the workflow.

We also assume that it is sufficient for short interruptions to restore the context of the subtask, which was interrupted, because the goals are better encoded, can therefore be better remembered and are not affected that much by retention loss. If the interruption takes longer the user also needs help to restore the goals, thus

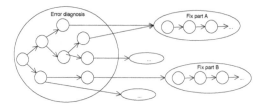

Figure 6.17: Example workflow for a car repair

more information has to be presented.

Determining the amount of required information

In order to determine how much information the user needs in order to resume a task, the adverse effect of the interruption has to be estimated. Several factors can be identified. They can be divided in four categories that have an impact on the disruptive effect of an interruption. These factors are rated on an unique scale and its weighted sum estimates the adverse effect of the interruption.

The factors can be grouped into the following categories:

- Characteristics of the interrupting task

- Characteristics of the interruption and its announcement

- Characteristics of the interrupting task

- User Characteristics:

Characteristics of the primary task are

Timing / Cognitive load The higher the cognitive load at the moment of the interruption, the more harmful is the effect of the interruption and the more information needs the user for resuming the primary task.

Characteristics of the interruption and its announcement are

Predictability Unpredictable and uncontrollable events cause stress and thus increase the adverse effect of an interruption.

Defocusing This refers to the shift in focus caused by the announcement of an impending interruption. Aurally presented interruptions are more quickly attended to than visually presented interruptions. Additionally, an announcement via speech is more distracting than using auditory-cues or ambient sounds.

Frequency A high frequency of interruptions results in an increased recovery time and an increase in the number of potential errors. The frequency should therefore be kept as low as possible.

Interruption lag A delay between the alert to a pending interruption and the interruption proper can be utilized by the user for enhancing the memory representation for the primary task. This results in a shortened time needed for resuming the primary task.

Initiator If the user herself interrupts the primary task it is most likely, that she chose the point in time, where the disruptive effect is minimal. However, if an external source initiates the interruption, the task-handler does not have any possibility to lessen the adverse effect.

Characteristics of the interrupting task are

Duration The longer the primary task is interrupted the more the user forgets about it, due to the temporal decay of the memory traces.

Interference Is there any interference of the interrupting task with the primary task?

Capacity interference This is due to the limitations of the working memory. The more complex the interrupting task is, the more disruptive is the interruption

Structural interference If the same modality is used for the interrupting task as for the primary task, the adverse effect of the interruption is increased

Task similarity The greater the amount of shared information between the two tasks, the more distorted gets the memory representation for the primary task

User Characteristics are

Involvement in the ongoing system or external task If the user is heavily involved in the current task, an interruption is more harmful as if the user does not pay much attention to it. In this case an interruption can be even of avail, because it can help the user narrow his attention to the ongoing task and thus increase his performance on this task.

Expertise / Training People have the ability to dynamically adapt their behaviour to accommodate interruptions. The more trained a task is, the lesser is the disruptive effect of interruptions.

Gender Women are more easily distracted than male when performing complex tasks.

Social characteristics, which affect the processing of the interruption. These are

- The form of the interruption,
- the person who or the object that generated the interruption and
- social expectations that exist regarding the responsiveness to the interruption.

The expected costs of an interruption (ECI, refer to section 4.9.2) are calculated from these factors. All characteristics of the primary task, the kind of interruption and the user's characteristics impact the adverse effect of interrupting a user. Section 6.4.5 introduces a simplified calculation of ECI.

Knowledge Representation

A task consists of several steps to achieve the goal of the task. The activation of a task includes activation of the goal. If the goal of a task is activated, it superposes the individual propositions of the task and therefore facilitates the task resumption. Furthermore goals are crucial for solving problems. An experiment conducted by Trafton et al. [TABM03] also indicated that being aware of the current goals is more important than remembering the current position. 62% of participants used prospective goal encoding and only 38% used retrospective rehearsal. All this shows how important it is to be aware of the current goals and subgoals. Additionally, the user needs to know at which point of the current task she was interrupted (position information). However, the goals are sometimes not explicitly stated (it is not possible to know always what the user is really up to), in this case the user can be helped with the repetition of the shared history (position information), which induces the priming of the user's goals. The goals and position information are stored hierarchically and build a stack which grows from top to bottom. Thereby, the goal-items describe the aims of the task in different granularities and the position-items are describing what the user has already done. Figure 6.18(b) illustrates such a goal-hierarchy in form of a tree which contains all possible goals during a shopping task. The actual workflow activities are represented by its leaves. The state of the goal-stack for a given workflow activity consists of all goals which are located between the root of the tree (the task's goal) and the node corresponding to the activity. The position items are specified by all already achieved goals that are directly linked to a goal on this path. The goal and position items of the goal-stack are pointed out for the activity *entering credit card number*. The order of elements in the stack is determined by the breadth-first search of the corresponding goal-tree (see figure 6.18(a)).

How much information (goals and position information) is really repeated is determined by the value of `amountInformation`. If the user needs only little information the system only provides her with the current minimal goal and the last position information, because it can be assumed that higher goals are still sufficiently activated (goals persist longer in memory [AG00] or that at least the presentation of some cues (like the current minimal goal) suffices for reactivating them. If the user needs little more information the system starts at a higher subgoal and repeats all underlying goals, and all position information. Finally, if the user requires the maximum amount of information the system repeats the task's goal (the aim of the whole task), all subgoals which lead to the current position and the position information. Every item can also feature some detail information, which are read with the corresponding item and must never be repeated alone.

Every goal and subgoal marks a starting point, at which the system can start reading the information. However, only the last position item can act as a starting point, because the last performed action is sufficient to prime the higher goals for short interruptions.

Interaction

In order to keep simple, information presentation and repetition must be possible without the user's interaction. If the user is not satisfied with the presented amount

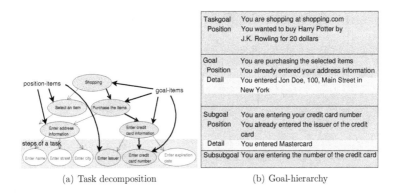

Taskgoal	You are shopping at shopping.com
Position	You wanted to buy Harry Potter by
	J.K. Rowling for 20 dollars

Goal	You are purchasing the selected items
Position	You already entered your address information
Detail	You entered Jon Doe, 100, Main Street in
	New York

Subgoal	You are entering your credit card number
Position	You already entered the issuer of the credit
	card
Detail	You entered Mastercard
Subsubgoal	You are entering the number of the credit card

(a) Task decomposition   (b) Goal-hierarchy

Figure 6.18: Example of a goal-hierarchy using the example of a shopping process with highlighted goal and position items for the point of entering the credit card number

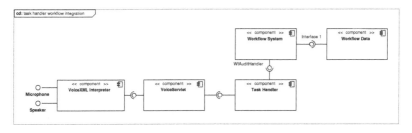

Figure 6.19: Integration of the TaskHandler with the workflow engine

of information, she may ask for more information, or skip the repetition, if she does not need that detail of information.

Additionally, she can use the same interaction, to request data about her current position or any other available information during the execution of the task. This way, we are able to provide a consistent way of interaction with the system.

If we summarize larger texts, the user must also have the possibility to turn the summaries off and on.

6.4.5 Reference Implementation

This section describes how the information is represented which is collected during the performance of a task. The core architecture of our reference implementation is shown in Figure 6.19 . The *TaskHandler* uses the *WfAuditHandler* interface

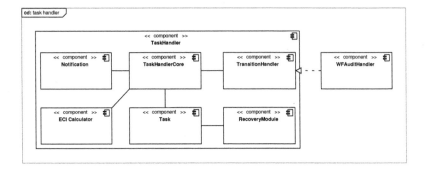

Figure 6.20: Modules of the TaskHandler

of the workflow engine. A *WfAuditHandler* gets invoked, whenever the workflow engine throws an event. This is used to update the knowledge representation as soon as a transition is performed. Additionally, the *TaskHandler* is responsible for the VoiceXML output, which is requested by the *VoiceServlet*, and coordinates the communication between most modules. A more detailed view on modules involved is shown in Figure 6.20.

TaskHandlerCore is the core component of the *TaskHandler*, implementing most of the functionality. The *TransitionHandler* implements the *WfAuditEvent* interface and notifies the *TaskHandlerCore* about ongoing transitions in the workflow engine. This information is used to update the *Task* module. The *Task* module encapsulates all method invocations, which deal with the corresponding workflow process. Hence, it is a lightweight implementation of the concept, introduced in section 6.3. The *RecoveryStorage* encapsulates the access to a specific *RecoveryXML* document, which is needed by the modules *Task* and *TransitionHandler*.

The *Notification* module represents a notification to be send to the user, which can be linked to a workflow activity. It uses the information given by the *ECI Calculator*. The *ECI calculator* calculates the expected costs of interrupting the user performing a specified task with a specified interruption at a specified time.

At first the structure of such a knowledge representation file is described, which is called **R**ecovery**XML** (RXML). Next, it is explained how the knowledge information is retrieved from the task's XPDL-representation and which entries have to be added there.

ECI Calculator

The expected cost of interruption is calculated to determine, the best point of interrupting a user. The different factors were introduced in section 6.4.4.

Timing / Cognitive load The cognitive load was examined in section 4.7. With equation 4.9 the cognitive load λ can be expressed by

$$\lambda = \delta_c |C(n_i)| + \delta_h n_{i-1} + \delta_i |I(n_i)| \tag{6.7}$$

Frequency In a simplified view, if the minimal gap t_ϵ between the current time t and the timestamp of the last interruption t_λ is minimal the disruptive effect of the interruption can be rated as maximal. Afterwards, this effect decreased linearly until it reaches t_ϵ and is appraised as 0. Then, the frequency ν is expressed by the following equation.

$$\nu = \begin{cases} 0 & \text{if } t - t_\lambda > t_\epsilon \\ \max_s - \frac{\max_s}{t_\epsilon}(t - t_\lambda) & \text{else} \end{cases} \tag{6.8}$$

Interruption lag For an estimation, each kind of interruption has to be related to a scale S. The interruption lag θ_l should be set to 0 if the interruption was predictable and $\max_s$ if not.

Predictability For an estimation, each kind of interruption has to be related to a scale S. The predictability θ_k should be set to 0 if the interruption was predictable and $\max_s$ if not.

Interruption type We assume that an interruption caused by the user is less disruptive than an interruption caused by the system. The determination of the factors defocus θ_d, interruption lag θ_l, and predictability θ_k is only possible, if the system initiated the interruption. In that case, the weighted sum of these coefficients builds the interruption type θ. However, if the user initiates the interruption, we assume that she chooses the most suitable timestamp for the interruption, which allows us to set this factor to 0 in this case. If an external source causes the interruption, we assume that this is the worst case and set $\theta = \max_s$.

$$\theta = \begin{cases} 0 & \text{if initiator} = \text{user} \\ w_d\theta_d + w_l\theta_l + w_k\theta_k & \text{if initiator} = \text{system} \\ \max_s & \text{if initiator} = \text{external} \end{cases} \tag{6.9}$$

Involvement in the ongoing system or external task The involvement in the current task ι_i depends on the number n of current workflow steps, and the time that passed since the last interaction with the system. The latter can be measured as the number of no speech timeouts $|t|$. If $|t|$ exceeds a predefined maximum $|\hat{t}|$ we regard the user as no longer involved in the current task. Then, the involvement ι is expressed

$$\iota_{n,i} = \begin{cases} \frac{1}{2}\iota_{n-1,i} & \text{if } |t| > |\hat{t}| \\ \frac{1}{2}\iota_{n-1,i} + \frac{1}{2}(\max_s - \frac{\max_s}{|\hat{t}|}|t|) & \text{else} \end{cases} \tag{6.10}$$

The involvement in external tasks ι_e as they are used by Horvitz [HA03] and Kern [Ker05] require the use of sensors. Since we do not have the possibility, to make use of such sensors, we simply ignore this parameter by setting ι_e to 0.

A detailed calculation of the ECI factor is beyond the scope of this thesis. We use a simplified calculation that takes respect to these factors as a weighted sum:

$$ECI(t) = w_1\lambda(t) + w_2\nu(t) + w_3\theta + w_4\iota_i + w_5\iota_e + w_6\chi \qquad (6.11)$$

The cognitive load λ and the frequency ν are time dependent, since they can be estimated at a later point in time, whereas the other factors describe how the user is mentally involved in the current task.

RecoveryXML

The purpose of RecoveryXML is to obtain all the relevant information that is described in section 6.4.4. We use a simple file featuring an XML structure for this purpose. One file is saved for every instance of a task as soon as the task terminates or is aborted the system deletes the file. The information stored in the RecoveryXML is taken from the workflow description. Every goal and subgoal needs to be specified. Additionally the details and position information eventually have to be updated by every transition in the workflow.

This XML-structure cannot only be used to help the user get back into the context of the interrupted task. It can also aid the user orienting during the task execution. For that purpose she simply has to have the possibility to ask for this information. Further, this structure can be used to store some additional information which might be useful during the task's execution, for example the content of the shopping cart. Thus, there is an easy and uniform way of providing the user with additional information.

An RXML-file is stored persistent in the user's folder for every task instance. The file names contain the task's ID (its name) for identification. The file consists of two parts:

Header-section: contains additional information about the task, for example the key of the corresponding process within the workflow system and the task's current state. This data is used to restore the user's session (even after a reboot).

Data-section: contains all information the user can ask for during the execution of the task and which is used to help the user to resume a task.

The data-section embeds the actual information containers. They can be identified and referred to by the "'name"'-attribute. The most important container is the position-container which is mandatory. This container consists of *goal* and *position* information. Thereby, the position items represent what the user has done before (for example, *you have already chosen a destination*) or minimal goals (for example, if the user searches an item in a category tree like the one used at amazon.com, the chosen categories are stored in position items). These goal and position information are presented if a user wants to resume a task. The remaining containers serve just for providing additional information to the user during the performance of the task. Thereby, the user can ask for the content of every container using special commands. Each container holds a multitude of information items and can optionally provide some details for the items. These details are never read alone, only in combination with the corresponding item. The information is read to the user from top to bottom starting at a given point, specified by the calculated amount of required information. For the position-container every *goal*-entry and for all other containers every *item*-entry can act as starting point. However, only the first position-item can act as a starting point, because it can be assumed that the last performed action is sufficient to prime the goals for short interruptions.

An ID can be assigned to each information item, which is used for facilitating the modification of the file during the task execution and to identify the different goal-levels.

The goals are stored in a hierarchical order. The main goal is specified by the item with the ID *taskgoal*. The following goal has the ID *goal*, the next *subgoal*, and then *subsubgoal* and so on. Every time a new goal arises the old goal with the same ID is transformed to a position-item and as all dependent goal-, detail- and position-items are replaced.

The following listing shows an example of a recovery file using the shopping task example at the point of asking for the credit card information.

```
<Recovery>
    <Header>
        <ProcessKey>456</ProcessKey>
        <State>running</State>
    </Header>
    <Data>
        <Container name="position">
            <goal id="taskgoal">
                You are shopping at abc.com
            </goal>
            <position>
                You already selected three books and a CD
                for 30 dollars
            </detail>
            <goal id="goal">
                You are purchasing the selected articles
            </goal>
            <goal id="subgoal">
                You are entering your credit card
                information
            </goal>
            <position id="current">
                You already entered the issuer of the credit
                card
            </position>
            <detail>You entered MasterCard</detail>
        <goal id="subsubgoal">
            You were entering the credit card number
        </position>
        </Container>
        <Container name="shopping_cart">
            <item id="firstItem">
                You bought two books.
            </item>
            <detail>
                These books are Harry Potter and The Client
```

```
      </detail>
    </Container>
  </Data>
</Recovery>
```

The file is maintained by the *TaskHandler* that listens to the transitions in the workflow engine. The following section describes how the *TaskHandler* collects the needed data and how it is stored in the workflow descriptions.

Transforming Workflow to RecoveryXML

The information which shall be stored in the RecoveryXML document has to be added as extended attributes in the corresponding XPDL-File. The goals and position information should be formulated to answer a user's question like *What am I doing* for goal-items and *What have I done?* for position-items. The main goal (taskgoal) is specified in the extended attributes of the description of the corresponding workflow process. For example

```
<ExtendedAttribute Name="taskgoal"
    Value="You_are_shopping_at_abc.com" />
```

All other goal- and position-items are specified in the extended attributes of the activities, at which these goals become valid. As mentioned before a goal loses its validity as soon as a goal with the same or higher ID arises. Addi-tonally it is transformed to a position-item and all underlying goal-, detail- and position-items are replaced. The position and all additional items are added and edited during the transition between two activities. It makes sense, for example, to change the used tense of some items, like changing *You are entering your shipping address* to *You have already entered your shipping address*. For that purpose, the extended attributes of the transition contain a `recovery_mode` and a `recovery_value` parameter. The `recovery_mode` specifies how the recovery-file shall be edited. Possible values are:

text this is used if the transition marks the end of a goal. recovery_value specifies the text of the emerging position-item (the transformed goal).

code the developer can enter some specific functions in recovery_value for modifying the recovery-file

external a developer-written function (identified by recovery_value) is called for more complex modifications

If the mode *text* or *code* is used, `recovery_value` can contain placeholders (have a leading dollar sign), which are filled by the system with the corresponding user input (e.g. `$amount` is replaced by the value which the user entered in the appropriate field named amount). The code which can be used to modify the recovery-file consists of functions for creating, deleting and modifying detail-, item- and position-items and containers. For the identification of an item the developer can use ids she has entered at its creation. If no ID is given the last item is used per default. The following code snippet illustrates an example for the usage of extended attributes.

```
<ExtendedAttribute Name="recovery_mode" Value="code"/>
<ExtendedAttribute Name="recovery_value"
    Value="appendItem("Shopping cart",
                          "You bought \$amount items");"/>
```

6.4.6 User study

We conducted a user study to test the usability of our recovery concept. In this section the goals, the proceedings and the results of the study are presented.

The participants had to perform a shopping task and were interrupted twice. The system supported them in resuming the task with different amounts of information and tested if this had any influence on the users' performance or experience.

Objectives

The principal objective was to test the usability of the recovery concept. Therefore, the performance of users was measured when resuming an interrupted task and when they were thereby supported by the repetition of different amounts of information. The intention was to find out whether the amount of information has an influence on the user's performance and on the user experience. The participants were divided into three groups. Each group received a different quantum of repeated information. Further, it should be determined how much information should be repeated to be helpful and without being annoying.

Test setup

The shopping workflow chosen for our test consists of two phases: searching and purchasing. In order to search an item the user had to navigate in a category tree where the books and CDs, which can be bought, represented the leaves. To purchase the selected items, the user had to enter her credit card information, a billing and a shipping address. The search process was a hierarchical task, whereas purchasing could be deemed linear. During the whole process the system stored and modified all information which supported the user in resuming the task according to our recovery concept.

The category tree in which the users had to navigate, was built with many ambiguities, each item which should be bought could fit in several categories. The target items were added dynamically to the tree, so that the participants always found the item when they reached the second category in which the item could possibly fit. This ensured that the users had to navigate up and down the category-tree to find the items, and that the users found the target item after a short period of time.

Each user got interrupted once in every subtask (search, purchase). For the task's resumption some context information about the task was read to the user before the workflow continued at the point where it was interrupted. Thereby, the amount of information depends on the recovery strategy the user is assigned to.

There are three different recovery strategies, which differed in the amount of information presented:

ALL repeat all information collected from the shopping task so far

LAST ITEM repeat only the last stored information item (the current subgoal)

NONE The shopping task continues without giving any additional information (control group)

The system should use as few commands as possible, to keep the task as simple as possible and the cognitive load for the user minimal:

back goes one step back in the workflow.

For example, *back* can be used to move the user back up a level in the tree, if she realizes that she has followed a branch that does not lead her to what she is looking for

repeat repeats all options the interface can offer to the user at that point

help tells the user all possible global commands

path gives the user's current position in the search tree or in the purchase process (uses the information of the "position" container), for example "You were just looking for a book about astronomy.". If the information given is not sufficient, the user can also ask for more path information by saying "more path"

more path gives more information about the current position in the category tree or in the purchase process. If the information given is still not sufficient, the user can also ask for more path information by saying "more path" (also uses the information of the "position" container).

cart summarizes all items currently in the user's shopping cart (uses the information of the "shopping cart" container), for example "You bought two books for 25 dollars in total". If the information given is not sufficient, the user can ask for more information by saying "more cart"

more cart gives more information about the current content of the user's shopping cart, for example, the title and prices of the different books. If the information given is still not sufficient, the user can also ask for more information by saying "more cart" (also uses the information of the "shopping cart" container).

(More) Path and *(more) cart* were added to avoid the lost-in-space problem, refer to section 4.7.1, to help the user orient herself in the shopping process. The amount of repeated information for these commands was also dependent on the group-assignment. The system read as much information to the user as she would get, if she would be interrupted at that point. An exception were the participants in the NONE-group they get as much information as the members of the LAST ITEM-group, because they do not get any additional data at all when resuming the task.

Other commands were available based on the current step in the process. For example, at each branching point in the category-tree, the system gave a list of options to the participants to select from. During the purchase of the items she could use free speech input to enter the address and credit card data.

Interruption task The users had to perform a memory task during the interruption of the shopping task. The operator read twelve words to the user and repeated them three times. The user had to memorize them and write them down at the end. The words used for this task were all taken from the shopping process, e.g. "credit card" or "fantasy", to reach a high degree of interference with the shopping task and therefore making the interruption as disruptive as possible [AT02]. We define the interference level as the expected (mean) activation of the most active distractor (nontarget item). After Altmann et al. the time course of activation features two phases *strengthening* and *decay*. Strengthening rapidly builds up activation by increasing the number of times the goal has been sampled in a short period of time. This activation cannot be sustained because the cognitive system needs to turn to task-related operations and therefore the activation gradually decays. A functional reason for this is the insurance of a periodic re-evaluation of the system's cognitive direction.

Group allocation Each user was assigned to one of three groups, one for every examined recovery strategy (ALL, LAST ITEM and NONE, see above). The users in each group were counterbalanced so that one half had to perform the memorization exercise A during the search-part and the memorization exercise B during the purchase-part (subgroup a) and the other half of the group vice versa (subgroup b).

The participants were randomly assigned to the six different subgroups by using a random number table taken from the CRC tables [Bec91].

Finally, the number of users assigned to each group was reduced to five, the size of group 1b even to four, because there were only 29 participants instead of the desired 36.

Study Procedure Every user had to perform a shopping task of buying two books with given titles. The participants could choose which item they wanted to buy first.

The users were not allowed to take any notes during the whole process, in order to make it more realistic, because it was not possible to act on the assumption that every phone user is able to take notes. But the participants could rely on some voice commands which informed them about the current content of the shopping cart or the current position (i.e. *(more) path* and *(more) cart*.

At first each user got the general instruction sheets, containing all global commands and their meaning. The participants could refer to this sheet while performing the task. With this the cognitive load is reduced and it facilitates and encourages the usage of the new unfamiliar commands *(more) path* and *(more) cart*. In the pre-study it could be observed that most participants focused only on the shopping application itself and what was missing in the shopping process (e.g. further confirmations). In order to shift the participants' attention to the repeated information, they were made aware that the shopping task was only a really simplified example and we wanted to examine the influence of the amount of represented information on the user experience.

Each participant received a task sheet for the first task, which contained the names of the two books the user had to buy and the credit card information. She should use her own address as shipping address and the one of her father as billing address, because they were asked used two different addresses and that they could easily remember them without writing them down. In order to speed up the process of entering those addresses and to reduce the input errors, the user had asked to write down both addresses and hand them over to the operator. The items, which should be bought, were selected so that they could fit into several categories. The interruption took place after the user had selected the first item. For finding the second item she had to navigate in another subtree where the new target item was located. Our design assured that the target book was found in the second category the user visited in which the item could fit. Thus, the user reached one category in which the book would possibly fit in, but did not find the item there. Therefore, she was forced to inspect another category and to navigate up and down the tree in order to reach it. During this way back the user got interrupted after two steps and had to perform a memory task. After the interruption, a short jingle (*Let's continue with the shopping process!*) was played to prepare the user to switch back to the shopping task. This jingle should also compensate the time needed to switch attention between tasks.

Next, some information was read to the user, also contingent upon his group-assignment, which should help her in getting back into the context of the shopping task. Examples of this repeated information for every group are:

[LAST ITEM]: "You‿are‿currently‿at‿the‿point‿of‿buying‿a book‿for‿children."

[ALL]: "Your‿shopping‿cart‿contains‿1‿book‿for‿45‿dollars. You‿selected‿"Religious settlers on the west coast"‿for 45‿dollars.‿You‿wanted‿to‿buy‿a‿book.‿You‿wanted‿to‿buy‿a book‿about‿fiction.‿You‿are‿currently‿at‿the‿point‿of buying‿a‿book‿for‿children."

The dialog continues with *So, do you want to buy a book about fantasy, a novel or a comic?*. After this recovery, the shopping task proceeded at the same point where the interruption had occurred. Having selected the second item the shopping process continued with the purchase of the items. Here all users got interrupted at the same point of the purchase: by entering the street name of the shipping address. The interruption and resumption of the shopping task went on as in the search-phase. Examples for the repeated texts are:

[LAST ITEM]: "You‿are‿entering‿the‿shipping‿address.‿"

[ALL]: "Your‿shopping‿cart‿contains‿2‿books‿for‿85‿dollars. You‿selected‿"Harry Potter and the Prisoner of Azkaban"‿by J.K.‿Rowling‿for‿40‿dollars. You‿selected‿"Religious settlers on the west coast"‿for 45‿dollars.‿You‿are‿purchasing‿those‿items.‿You‿already entered‿your‿credit‿card‿information. You‿entered‿American‿Express,‿John‿Doe,‿number 5‿5‿5‿5‿6‿6‿6‿7‿7‿8‿8‿8,‿expires‿on‿9‿2008.‿You‿are entering‿the‿shipping‿address.‿You‿entered‿James‿Doe, 3475‿Deer‿Creek‿Road."

The dialog continues with: *Please say the zip code and the city name..*

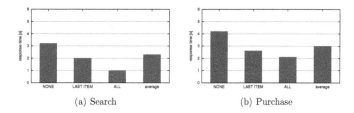

(a) Search (b) Purchase

Figure 6.21: Results of the user study: Response times after an interruption (average: average response time over all groups during the whole search or purchase part)

Finally, the users filled out a questionnaire regarding their subjective feedback on the system.

Results

Response times The response times (resumption lags) of the various groups were compared using a one-way analyze of variance (ANOVA) to test our second hypothesis (H2: "The response time after the interruption is shorter for the participants in the [ALL]- and [LAST ITEM]-group than for members of the [NONE]-group"). The results are illustrated in figure 6.21. The differences for the various groups was significant for the search-part, see figure 6.21(a), ($F_{(2, 25)} = 5.1$, MSE = 12.7, p = 0.014 (<0.05)) and marginal significant for the purchase-part, see figure 6.21(b), ($F_{(2, 24)} = 3.1$, MSE = 12, p = 0.064 (<0.1)). The average response time was lower than the response time for the participants of the [NONE]-group. This is unlikely to be due to the duration of the attention-switch, because a jingle was used before restarting the shopping task for compensating this effect.

Benefit of repeated information For verifying if the first expectation (E1: "The members of the [ALL]- and [LAST ITEM]-group find repeated information helpful") pertains, it was evaluated how helpful the users perceived the repeated information. They were asked to rate the helpfulness of the information with respect to the two different points of interruption (during search and during purchase), whereby 0 means "not helpful at all" and 6 "very helpful". The results can be seen in figure 6.22(a) (M = 4.65, SD = 1.62). Consequently, the results affirmed our first expectation. The rating was not reliably influenced through the point of interruption in the workflow regardless of the group.

Amount of repeated information The participants were asked to judge the amount of repeated information in order to test our first hypothesis (H1: "The members of the [ALL]-group rate the amount of repeated information as more annoying than the members of the [LAST ITEM]-group"), whereby 0 means "not enough information" and 6 "too much information". The result is shown in figure 6.22(b) (group [ALL]: M = 3.20 SD = 1.31; group [LAST ITEM]: M = 3.33,

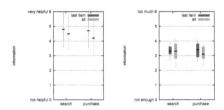

(a) Benefit of information (b) Amount of information

Figure 6.22: Results of the user study: Users' rating of the benefit and amount of repeated information

SD = 0.95). The results did not follow the expectations. Both groups found the amount of repeated information very suitable without any differences between the groups.

This result is rather surprising because the users of the [ALL]-group perceived about 23 seconds of repeated information for the search-part and 38 seconds for the purchase-part, in comparison to 4 and 3 seconds for the members in the [LAST ITEM]-group, respectively. It is doubtful that these ratings would persist, when the participants use the shopping process more frequently. A possible explanation for the positive rating of the [ALL]-group is, that the users felt uncomfortable with the new and rather unfamiliar task, consequently the repetition of already known data was like a confirmation and made them feel more confident.

To get more reliable results, the long-term-effect has to be examined in future user studies. However, the recovery concept is flexible enough to be adapted to future studies.

6.4.7   Recap of Results

A task-handler was developed that supports users to manage audio-based workflow tasks. It allows the users to switch between several tasks, to pause and to resume a task. Further, the system helps the user to keep situational awareness of interrupted and waiting tasks by providing reminders. The task-handler also implements a concept to determine when a user should be interrupted to inform her of emerging events (notifications), for example if a suspended task is ready to be continued. Therefore, a closer look was taken at the factors making an interruption disruptive and proposed an estimate for the expected cost of an interruption (ECI-value) at a given point in time. The task-handler decides on basis of the ECI-value, the priority of the ongoing task and the priority of the notification, how long the notification should be deferred to cause minimal harm, but also without being delayed too long.

However, the core of our task-handler is the management of knowledge about performed tasks, which is used to help the user getting back into the task's context after a pause. Due to the transient nature of speech the user does not have the possibility to review what she has done before. It can be assumed, basing on psychological theories, that goals are the most important information to be remembered for resuming a task. An XML-structure called RecoveryXML was developed to store all relevant information about the state of a task focusing on information about the current goals and about the current position (what the user has already done) in the workflow. The RecoveryXML structure is retrieved from the task's XPDL-description. In order to determine how much information the user needs in which situation, the ECI-value for the point in time of the task's interruption, the duration of the interruption and the degree of interference between the interrupted task and the tasks performed during the interruption were taken into account.

Finally, a user study was conducted to prove the usability of the recovery concept and it was found that the repetition really helped the users getting back into the task's context.

We observed a decreased users' response time after the interruption and that most users rated the repetition as very helpful. Further, it can be noted that the users who received the maximum amount of information were surprisingly not annoyed by its repetition.

Structured Text

This recovery concept is not limited to the usage of goal-oriented scenarios. It can also be helpful for the orientation in structured texts. In order to transfer our concept to the reading of text, meanings of the goal- and position items have be defined. Goals correspond to headings or the currently read sentence. The position items consist of the last paragraph, a text-summary for the currently read section and the already read headings (like for workflows only those items are of interest that are directly linked to the "'goal-path"'). A detail-item can optionally be appended to each heading. It can contain a summary of the corresponding chapter. In order to retrieve the recovery file automatically from the text's structure, automatic summarization of the text is required or another way to speed up the repetition. This expansion to structured text can be useful for many application areas, for example for museum guides. The user might want to interrupt the audio-stream for an exhibit for various reasons, for example she might want to talk to someone or she asks the system for additional information on a specific aspect of the exhibit, like the artist. When the user wants to continue listening to the audio-stream, the system should not start exactly at the point where the user stopped the playback, it should rather start at least at the beginning of the sentence, or at the beginning of the paragraph. Perhaps it is even necessary to read a summary to the user or some context-information. The visitor should be in the position to skip the repetition or ask for more information.

Furthermore, the task-handler can assist the user to search or to jump in audio-documents. Thereby, the user is not aware of the context of the search term or the position she jumped to. Our system can help her in reading some relevant information to her, like headings or summaries, needed to understand the context.

6.5 Conclusion

In this chapter we have shown that the principles of browsing audio documents to support the mobile worker can be easily extended to a workflow enabled architecture.

With this approach, problems that arose in the development of the prototype, such as knowledge about the current task, conditions in transitions or pause and resumption of the tasks could be solved. We enhanced the workflow engine to use information that is obtained from the environment in the form of context events in workflow engines. For this purpose we extended the approach of Nøthvedth [NN04] with a general concept of using context data in the transitions and as workflow data. This approach is based on the publish-subscribe mechanisms of Mundo and allows to use the context events in the workflow. The processing is based on XPath queries which ensures great flexibility not only in handling complex events to control the workflow but also in storing their values in workflow variables. Moreover, we implemented a system that remembers the events. This removes the need for a synchronized receipt of the events. In addition, we are able to send events into the environment and thus control it.

The use of a workflow engine as a basic backbone led us directly to another problem. Workflow engines are able to handle multiple tasks in parallel. Currently there is no concept to switch between several tasks, to pause and to resume a task. We developed a concept of how the system can aid the user to return to the context in order to continue with a paused task. Based on the ECI value our task handler determines the priority of an ongoing task and the priority of the notification, how long the notification should be deferred to cause minimal harm, but also without being delayed too long.

The main task of our task handler is to capture knowledge about performed tasks in order to help the user return to the task's context. Finally, a user study was conducted to prove the usability of the recovery concept and it was found that the repetition did in fact help the users return to the task's context.

To be as flexible as possible we also introduced a new concept for generating user interfaces. We found that current approaches to use task-models are not modality independent, which is possibly the main reason why they are not adopted in industrial settings. Our approach is a generalization of the MVC pattern to model-based architectures. The modality-dependent components of the task model are moved to the dialog model to keep the core of the business logic in the task model, which is handled by the workflow engine. Thus, we obtain a fully reusable task model. Moreover, we are also able to integrate other systems or trigger events.

Figure 7.1: Mobile Worker

Chapter 7

Conclusions and Outlook

The worker on the move needs to access information about her current task, exchange data with the back-end system, enter data, receive instructions on how to proceed and ask for more details or help when needed.

In order to provide sophisticated support for the worker, contextual information about her identity, tasks, and current location is needed. In addition, workers typically have their hands busy with the task. Audio input and output allows for such a hands & eyes free access.

There are several challenges within this scenario of a mobile worker that are difficult to handle.

Due to the invisible and transient nature of speech, the design of voice user interfaces is still an unsolved problem. We have analyzed and structured the limitations of voice-based interfaces. Limitations that are inherent to the audio domain cannot be solved completely using current approaches such as guidelines. Technical problems are less severe when using higher quality speech synthesizers and higher quality speech recognizers. As technical progress is made, these factors will have a decreasing impact on the interface design. In the long term designers will not need to care about these challenges as they do today.

There are two ways in particular to handle these limitations. Existing guidelines are essentially restricted to giving hints about what should be avoided. Patterns are more promising. They offer a well structured documentation to people with less experience in this very specific domain. Patterns also serve as a language to communicate at an interdisciplinary level and they help designers to concentrate on the overall design of a system instead of getting lost in implementation details. In this thesis a first set of patterns was introduced, that are helpful in all design and development phases of a voice based application.

Moreover, we analyzed the structure of the information that the user can browse based on graph theory. The amount of information that can be delivered to the mobile worker is strongly limited by the human cognitive capabilities. Thus the operational range of audio only applications is limited to a small set of documents. More information requires the use of multimodal interfaces, visual interfaces at first place.

Mobile devices do not have the computational power, mainly speed and memory size, of desktop PCs. Since speech recognition is computationally intense, this becomes a challenging problem. Several architectures exist to handle these limitations and enable speech recognition on mobile devices. These approaches can be divided into service dependent speech recognition and device inherent speech recognition. Both categories are not flexible enough to solve the requirements of supporting the user on the move. In this thesis, a standardized base vocabulary was developed, that can be used in conjunction with a small text-to-speech engine as a general purpose device inherent audio interface. Depending on which of the corresponding Mundo services is network-accessible in a given situation, they can be substituted by a high-end recognizer and a high-end text-to-speech engine.

The integration of back-end systems, especially databases, is a common task for voice user interfaces which is mainly achieved using proprietary implementations. A more generic approach is the use of workflow engines. In this thesis a novel MVC-based architecture was developed that is based on XForms and which permits multiple states per activity with a focus on audio. We used VoiceXML to handle the audio input and output. This approach is based on standard technologies which have already been adopted by industry, making it easier for an industrial size use. Our approach has the benefit of a modality independent task model, that is handled by the workflow engine. The use of a workflow engine also introduces the possibility of parallel execution of multiple tasks by a worker. To aid the worker using an audio-only user interface to return to the original context after resumption of a paused task, a novel concept was developed.

The use of contextual information, especially location, can be used to aid the user in solving her task. This requires support of a context-aware workflow. A new data-driven concept was introduced to make events and messages accessible to the workflow engine supporting the worker on the move. Moreover a general concept was introduced to make the environment accessible from the workflow engine.

While the mobile worker is busy with a task she might be interrupted by external events or she may want to suspend the task. The challenges inherent to the audio domain prevent her from reviewing what she has done before continuing after the interruption. We presented a novel architecture, based on psychological theories, to aid the user to return to the context of the task.

The challenges of supporting the mobile worker using an audio interface described above are met within this thesis. However some challenges remain. The generation of voice user interfaces has not yet exploited the pattern concept. A possible extension to the current concept could be to develop a standardized pattern template pool, possibly based on the **Pattern Markup Language** (PML) that would be used to transform XForms forms into high quality VoiceXML user interfaces. Another extension could be to extend the novel architecture of an expandable mobile speech recognition into an industry level standard with guaranteed real-time capabilities. The current prototype proved the concept but cannot guarantee real-time processing. In addition, a concept based on ontologies should be developed to automatically generate grammars for the high-end speech recognizer that would substitute the device inherent recognizer. Depending on the location and services that are available different grammars are needed. A high quality way to generate these automatically does not exist. Finally, the requirement to automatically adapt the workflow based on the services that are available in the network or that are missing remained unsolved.

To summarize, we enhanced existing concepts to provide audio based support support for the worker on the move. We made the first steps towards an engineering oriented approach to develop voice user interfaces.

Bibliography

[Abs06] Abstract User Interface Markup Language Toolkit. http://www. alphaworks.ibm.com/tech/auiml, March 2006.

[AG00] Erik M. Altmann and W. D. Gray. An integrated model of set shifting and maintenance. In *Proceedings of the Third International Conference on Cognitive Modeling*, pages 17–24, Veenendal,NL, 2000. Universal Press.

[AIS77] C. Alexander, S. Ishikawa, and M. Silverstein. *A Pattern Language: Towns, Buildings, Constructions*. Oxford University Press, UK, 1977.

[Ait06] Erwin Aitenbichler. *System Support for Ubiquitous Computing*. PhD thesis, TU Darmstadt, Darmstadt, 2006.

[AL98] J.R. Anderson and C. Lebiere. *The atomic components of thought*. Erlbaum, 1998.

[Ale79] Christopher Alexander. *The Timeless Way of Building*. Oxford University Press, 1979.

[All01] Rob Allen. Workflow: An Introduction. Technical report, The Workflow Management Coalition (WfMC), 2001.

[AM02] Erwin Aitenbichler and Max Mühlhäuser. The Talking Assistant Headset: A Novel Terminal for Ubiquitous Computing. Technical Report TK-02/02, Telecooperation Group, Department of Computer Science, Darmstadt University of Technology, 2002.

[AM03] Erwin Aitenbichler and Max Mühlhäuser. An IR Local Positioning System for Smart Items and Devices. In *Proceedings of the 23rd IEEE International Conference on Distributed Computing Systems Workshops (IWSAWC03)*, pages 334–339. IEEE Computer Society, May 2003.

[AR06] Abderrahmane Amrouche and Jean Michel Rouvaen. Efficient System for Speech Recognition using General Regression Neural Network. *International Journal of Intelligent Technology*, 1(2):183–189, 2006.

[Aro91] Barry Arons. Hyperspeech: Navigating in Speech-Only Hypermedia. In *Hypertext '91 Proceedings*, pages 133–146, 1991.

[Aro93]   Barry Arons. SpeechSkimmer: Interactively Skimming Recorded Speech. In *Proceedings of the ACM Symposium on User Interface Software and Technology*, Video, Graphics, and Speech, pages 187–196, 1993.

[AS68]   R. C. Atkinson and R. M. Shiffrin. Human Memory: A proposed system and it's control processes. In *The Psychology of Learning and Motivation*, volume 2, pages 89–195. Academic Press, New York, 1968.

[AT02]   Erik M. Altmann and J. Gregory Trafton. Memory for goals: An activation-based model. *Cognitive Science*, 26:39–83, 2002.

[Bai01]   Jürgen Baier. Beschreibung von Benutzerschnittstellen mit XML. Master's thesis, Fachhochschule Karlsruhe, Fachbereich Informatik, 2001.

[Bai04]   Alex Bailey. Challenges and opportunities for interaction on mobile devices. Technical report, Canon Research Centre Europe Ltd., 2004.

[BAM04]   Elmar Braun, Erwin Aitenbichler, and Max Mühlhäuser. Accessing Web Applications with Multiple Context Aware Devices. In *Engineering Advanced Web Applications*, pages 353–366, 2004.

[Bar97]   Stephen Barras. *Auditory Information Design*. PhD thesis, Australian National University, July 1997.

[BC87]   Kent Beck and Ward Cunningham. Using pattern languages for object oriented programs. Technical Report CR-87-43, Tektronix Inc., September 1987. Presented at the OOPSLA'87 workshop on Specification and Design for Object-Oriented Programming.

[Bec91]   W. H. Beck. *CRC Standard Mathematical Tables and Formulae*. CRC Press, twenty-ninth edition, 1991.

[BGGM93]   Ladit R. Bahl, Steven V. De Genneraro, P. S. Gopalakrishnan, and Robert L. Mercer. A Fast Approximate Acoustic Match for Large Vocabulary Speech Recognition. In *IEEE Transactions on Speech and Audio Processing*, volume 1, January 1993.

[BH74]   A. Baddely and G. Hitch. The psychology of learning and motivation. In *Working Memory*, pages 47–89. Oxford University Press, New York, 1974.

[BMWr92]   H. Bourlard, N. Morgan, C. Wooters, and S. renals. CDNN: A Context Dependent Neural Network for Contiuous Speech Recognition. In *IEEE International Conference on Acoustics, Speech and Signal Processing*, 1992.

[Bor01]   Jan Borchers. *A Pattern Approach to Interaction Design*. John Wiley & Sons, Inc., 2001.

[Bür02]   Christian Bürgy. *An Interaction Constraints Model for Mobile and Wearable Computer-Aided Engineering Systems in Industrial Applications*. PhD thesis, Carnegie Mellon University, Pittsburgh, Pennsylvania, USA, May 2002.

[Bus06]   Business Process Management Initiative. `http://www.bpmi.org`, March 2006. accessed on 20/24/2006.

[Cas98]   Cascading style sheets, level 2 css2 specification. `http://www.w3.org/TR/1998/REC-CSS2-19980512`, May 1998.   accessed on 08/28/2006.

[CGB04]   Michael H. Cohen, James P. Giangola, and Jennifer Balogh. *Voice User Interface Design*. Addison-Wesley, Boston, January 2004.

[Cho99]   Gerhard Chollet, editor. *Speech Processing, Recognition and Artificial Neural Networks*. Springer, Berlin, 1999.

[CJ02]   J. Chugh and V. Jagannathan. Voice-Enabling Enterprise Applications. In *WETICE '02: Proceedings of the 11th IEEE International Workshops on Enabling Technologies*, pages 188–189, Washington, DC, USA, 2002. IEEE Computer Society.

[CMU$^+$]   Ronald A. Cole, Joseph Mariani, Hans Uszkoreit, Annie Zaenen, and Victor Zue. Universal Speech Interface project homepage. `http://www.cs.cmu.edu/~usi`. Accessed on 04/24/2006.

[CMU$^+$95] Ronald A. Cole, Joseph Mariani, Hans Uszkoreit, Annie Zaenen, and Victor Zue. Survey of the State of the Art in Human Language Technology, 1995.

[CMU$^+$03] Ronald A. Cole, Joseph Mariani, Hans Uszkoreit, Annie Zaenen, and Victor Zue. Speech Graffitti Tutorial. `http://www.cs.cmu.edu/~usi/tutor/SGTutor-MLbrief.ppt`, 2003. Accessed on 04/24/2006.

[Coh04]   Jordan Cohen. Is Embedded Speech Recognition Disruptive Technology. *Information Quarterly*, 3(5):14–16, 2004.

[Cor90]   L. Corragio. Deleterious Effects of Intermittent Interruptions on the Task Performance of Knowledge Workers. In *18th international conference on information systems*, 1990.

[Cov89]   S.R. Covey. *The Seven Habits of Highly Effective People*. Free Press, 1989.

[DABF98]   A. Dix, G. Abowd, R. Beale, and J. Finlay. *Human-Computer Interaction*. Prentice Hall, Europe, 1998.

[dan06]   danet GmbH. WfMOpen. `http://wfmopen.sourceforge.net`, 2006. accessed on 07/27/2006.

[Dey00]   Anind K. Dey. *Providing Architectural Support for Building Context-Aware Applications*. PhD thesis, Georgia Institute of Technology, February 2000.

[DF06]   Andy Dearden and Janet Finlay. Pattern Languages in HCI; A Critical Review. *Human-Computer Interaction*, 21, 2006.

[DH04]   Li Deng and Xuedong Huang. Challenges in adopting speech recognition. *Communication ACM*, 47(1):69–75, 2004.

[DJH⁺02]   Brian Delaney, Nikil Jayant, Mat Hans, Tajana Simunic, and Andrea Acquaviva. A low-poer, fixed-point, front-end feature extraction for a distributed speech recognition system. In *IEEE-ICASSP*, 2002.

[DKW99]   Dwight Deugo, Liz Kendall, and Michael Weiss. Agent Patterns. http://www.scs.carleton.ca/~deugo/Patterns/Agent/ Presentations/AgentPatterns/index.htm, November 1999. accessd on 07/03/2006.

[Duc90]   Philippe C. Duchastel. Discussion: formal and informal learning with hypermedia. In *Designing hypermedia for learning*, pages 135–146. Springer-Verlag, London, UK, 1990.

[Dug02]   Bryan Duggan. Revenue Opportunities in the Voice Enabled Web. Technical report, School of Computing, Dublin Institute of Technology, Kevin St. Dublin 8, Ireland, 2002.

[ea00]   Joseph P. Picket et al., editor. *The American Heritage Dictionary of the English Language*. Houghton Mifflin, Boston, fourth edition, 2000.

[Eag99]   Gene Eagle. Software-Only Vs. Embedded: Which Architecture Is Best For You. *spechTECHNOLOGY magazine*, 1999.

[EL99]   C. Earl and J. Leventhal. A survey of windows screen reader users. *Journal of Visual Impairment and Blindness*, 93(3), 1999.

[Enh]   Enhydra. Open Source Java XPDL editor. http://www.enhydra.org/workflow/jawe/. accessed on 05/08/2006.

[ETS00]   ETSI. Human factors (HF); user interfaces; generic spoken command vocabulary for ict devices and services. Technical report, ETSI, April 2000. http://www.etsi.org.

[FC95]   Dennis R. Falk and Helen Carlson. *Multimedia in Higher Education: A Practical Guide to New Tools for Interactive Teaching and Learning*. Information Today, Medford, 1995.

[FDM02]   J.L. Franke, J.J. Daniels, and D.C. McFarlane. Recovering Context after Interruption. In *24th Annual Meeting of the Cognitive Science Society*, 2002.

[FG91]   Norman M. Frazer and G. Nigel Gilber. Simulating speech systems. In *Computer Speech and Language*, volume 5. Academic Press Limited, 1991.

[Fro02]   Alexander Fronk. Towards the algebraic analysis of hyperlink structures. Internes memorandum, Universität Dortmund, August 2002.

[Fro03]   Kathy Frostad. The State of Embedded Speech. *speechTECHNOLOGY magazine*, April 2003.

[GHJV92]   Erich Gamma, Richard Helm, Ralph E. Johnson, and John Vlissides. *Design Patterns: Elements of Reusable Object-Oriented Software*. Addison-Wesley, 1992.

[GM97]   J. Gunderson and R. Mendelson. Usability of World Wide Web browsers by persons with visual impairments. In *RESNA Annual Conference*, 1997.

[Goo87]   Dany Goodman. *The Complete HyperCard Handbook*. Bantam Books, 1987.

[Gro05]   The Stanford NLP Group. The stanford natural language processing group. `http://nlp.stanford.edu/index.shtml`, 2005.

[GS01]   Tom Gross and Markus Specht. Awareness in context-aware information systems. In *Mensch & Computer 2001*, pages 173–181, 2001.

[gui]   guidePORT. `http://www.guideport.com`. accessed on 08/28/2006.

[HA03]   Eric Horvitz and Johnson Apacible. Learning and reasoning about interruption. In *Proceedings of the 5th international conference on Multimodal interfaces*, pages 20–27, Vancouver, British Columbia, Canada, 2003. ACM Press.

[HB01]   Jeffrey Hightower and Gaetano Boriello. Location Systems for Ubiquitous Computing. *IEEE Computer*, 34:57–66, 2001.

[HDKC+05]   David Huggins-Daines, Mohit Kumar, Arthur Chan, Alan Black, Mosur Ravishankar, and Alex Rudnicky. Pocketsphinx: A free, real-time continuous speech recognition system for hand-hel devices. Technical report, Carnegie Mellon Unviersity, 2005.

[Hea99]   Marti A. Hearst. Mixed-initiative interaction. *IEEE Intelligent Systems*, pages 14–16, September 1999.

[HKM+03]   Gerd Herzog, Heinz Kirchmann, Stefan Merten, Atlassane Ndiaye, and Peter Poller. Multiplatform testbed: An integration platform for multimodal dialog systems. In Hamish Cunningham and Jon Patrick, editors, *HLT-NAACL 2003 Workshop: Software Engineering and Architecture of Language Technology Systems (SEALTS)*, pages 75–82, Edmonton, Alberta, Canada, May 2003. Association for Computational Linguistics.

[HS95]   M. Hofmann and L. Simon. *Problemlösung Hypertext: Grundlagen, Entwicklung, Anwendung.* Carl Hanser Verlag, München, Wien, 1995.

[HS06]   Melanie Hartmann and Dirk Schnelle. Task Switching in Audio-based Systems. In *Text, Speech and Dialogue, 9th International Conference, TSD 2006*, volume 4188/2006 of *Lecture Notes in Computer Science*, pages 597–604. Springer Berlin / Heidelberg, 2006.

[Hun92]   Melvyn J. Hunt. Speech Technology, 1992.

[IBM06]   IBM. Human Ability and Accessibility Center. http://www-306. ibm.com/able/, 2006. accessed on 08/26/2006.

[Jam96]   Frankie James. Presenting HTML Structure in Audio: User Satisfaction with Audio Hypertext. In *The Proceedings of ICAD 96*, 1996.

[Jam98]   Frankie James. *Representing Structured Information In Audio Interfaces: A Framework For Selecting Audio Marking Techniques To Present Document Structures.* PhD thesis, Stanford University, 1998.

[Jav06a]   Java 3d api. http://java.sun.com/products/java-media/3D/, 2006. accessed on 10/05/2006.

[Jav06b]   Java message service (jms). http://java.sun.com/products/jms/, 2006. accessed on 10/05/2006.

[Jef95]   J. Jeffcoate. *Multimedia In Practice: Technology and Applications.* Prentice Hall, New York, London, Toronto, Sydney, Tokyo, Singapore, 1995.

[Jel01]   Frederick Jelinek. *Statistical Methods for Speech Recognition.* MIT Press, Cambridge, Massachusetts, third printing edition, 2001.

[JM00]   Daniel Jurafsky and James H. Martin. *Speech and Language Processing -An Introduction to Natural Language Processing, Computational Linguistics and Speech Recognition.* Prentice Hall, New Jersey, 2000.

[Jun00]   Jean-Claude Junqua. *Robust Speech Recognition in Embedded System and PC Applications.* Kluwer Academic Publishers, Norwell, MA, USA, 2000.

[Kat06]   Katalavox. Voice Control in Automobiles. http://www.katalavox. com, 2006.

[Kay]   Michael Kay. http://saxon.sourceforge.net/. accessed on 05/12/2006.

[Ker05]   Nicholas J. Kern. *Multi-Sensor Context-Awareness for Wearable Computing.* PhD thesis, TU Darmstadt, Darmstadt, 2005.

[KsTML97]   H. Kochoki, s. Townsend, N. Mitchell, and A. Lloyd. W3C launches international web accessibility initiative. Technical report, W3C, 1997.

[Kub64]   Stanley Kubrick. A Space Odyssey. movie, 1964.

[Kuh91]   R. Kuhlen. *Hypertext: Ein nichtlineares Medium zwischen Buch und Wissensdatenbank*. Springer Verlag, Berlin, Heidelberg, New York, London, SEL stiftung edition, 1991.

[Kum02]   Jean Kumagai. Talk to the Machine. *IEEE Spectrum online*, September 2002.

[Laa03]   Sari A. Laakso. http://www.cs.helsinki.fi/u/salaakso/patterns/, September 2003.

[Lat98]   K. A. Latorella. Effects of the modality on interrupted flight deck performance: Implications for data link. In *Human Factors and Ergonomics Society*, 1998.

[Lin01]   Sumanth Lingam. UIML for Voice Interfaces. In *UIML Europe 2001 Conference*, March 2001.

[Low76]   B. Lowerre. *The HARPY speech recognition system*. PhD thesis, Dept. of Computer Science, Carnegie-Mellon Unviersity, Pittsburg, PA, USA, 1976.

[Luy04]   Kris Luyten. *Dynamic User Interface Generation for Mobile and Embedded Systems with Model-Based User Interface Development*. PhD thesis, transnational University Limburg: School of Information Technology, 2004.

[Man01]   Dragos Manolescu. *Micro-Workflow: A Workflow Architecture Supporting Compositional Object-Oriented Software Development*. PhD thesis, Department of Computer Science, University of Illinois, 2001.

[May92]   J. Terry Mayes. *Multi-media interfaces and learning*, chapter The 'M-word': multimedia interfaces and their role in interactive learning. Springer-Verlag, Heidelberg, 1992.

[MD90]   M. J. Muller and J. E. Daniel. Toward a definition of voice documents. In *Proceedings of the conference on Office information systems*, pages 174 – 183, Cambridge, Massachusetts, United States, 1990.

[MDF02]   Binu K. Mathew, Al Davis, and Zhen Fang. A Gaussian Probability Accelerator for SHINX 3. Technical Report UUCS-03-02, University of Utah, Salt Lake City, UT 84112 USA, November 2002.

[ME92]   Elizabeth D. Mynatt and W. Keith Edwards. Mapping GUIs to Auditory Interfaces. In *5th annaual ACM symposiuum on user interface software and technology*, pages 61–70, Monterey, California, USA, November 1992. ACM.

[Mey05]   Marek Meyer. Context Server: Location Context Support for Ubiquitous Computing. Master's thesis, Darmstadt Univeristy of Technology, January 2005.

[Mic98]   SUN Microsystems. *Java Speech API Programmer's Guide*. SUN Microsystems, 1998.

[Mic05]   Microsoft. Natural Language Processing. `http://research.microsoft.com/nlp/`, 2005. accessed on 08/23/2006.

[Mic06]   Microsoft. Accessibility at Microsoft. `http://www.microsoft.com/enable/`, 2006.

[Mil56]   George A. Miller. The magical number seven, plus or minus two: Some limtis on our capacity for processing information. *Psycological Review*, 63:81–97, 1956.

[Min03]   Lam Yuet Ming. An Optimization Framework for Fixed-point Digital Signal Processing. Master's thesis, The Chinese University of Hong Kong, aug 2003.

[MJ98]   M. J. Mahemoff and L. J. Johnston. Principles for a Usability-Oriented Pattern Language. In *Proceedings of Australian Computer Human Interaction Conference OZCHI'98*, pages 132–139, Adelaide, 1998. IEEE Computer Society, Los Alamitos.

[MOW04]   Mowahs project. `http://www.mowahs.com/`, 2004.

[MPS04]   Giuli Mori, Fabio Paternò, and Carmen Santoro. Design and Development of Multidevice User Interfaces through Multiple Logical descriptions. *IEEE Transactions on Software Engineering*, 30(8):507–520, August 2004.

[MS99]   Christopher Manning and Hinrich Schütze. *Foundations of Statistical Natural Language Processing*. MIT Press, Cambridge/MA, 1999.

[MSAK05]   Max Mühlhäuser, Dirk Schnelle, Erwin Aitenbichler, and Jussi Kangasharju. Video-Based Demonstration: Hands-Free/Eyes-Free Support for Mobile Workers. In *Proc. 2nd Annual International Conference on Mobile and Ubiquitous Systems*, 2005.

[MSzM05]   Carolyn McGregor, Josef Schiefer, and Michael zur Muehlen. A shareable web service based intelligent decision support system for on-demand business process management. *International Journal of Business Process Integration and Management*, 1(3), 2005.

[Nel65]   T. H. Nelson. Complex information processing: a file structure for the complex, the changing and the indeterminate. In *Proceedings of the 1965 20th national conference*, pages 84–100. ACM Press, 1965.

[Neu01]   Amy Neustein. The Linguistics of a Non-Fictional HAL. *ej Talk*, October 2001.

[New90]   A. Newell. *Unified theories of cognition*. Harvard University Press, 1990.

[NHK+03]   M. Novak, R. Hampl, P. Krbec, V. Bergl, and J. Sedivy. Two-pass search strategy for large list recognition on embedded speech recognition platforms. In *Proc. ICASSP*, volume 1, pages 200–203, 2003.

[Nie93]   Jakob Nielsen. *Hypertext and Hypermedia*. Morgan Kaufman Pub, 1993.

[Nie95]   Jakob Nielsen. *Multimedia and Hypertext: The Internet an Beyond*. Academic Press, Cambridge, MA, 1995.

[NN04]   Jan Ole Nødtvedt and Man Hoang Nguyen. Mobility and context awareness in workflow systems. Master's thesis, Institutt for Datateknikk og Informasjonsvitenskap, June 2004.

[Nor88]   Donald A. Norman. *The design of everyday things*. Morgan Kaufman Publishers Inc., 1988.

[Nor91]   Kent Norman. *The Psychology of Menu Selection: Designing Cognitive Control at the Human/Computer Interface*. Ablex, Norwood, NJ, 1991.

[Nyl03]   Stina Nylander. The ubiquitous interactor - mobile services with multiple user interfaces. Master's thesis, Uppsala: Department of Information Technology, Uppsala University, November 2003.

[Ols92]   Dan Olsen. *User Interface Management Systems: Models and Algorithms*. Morgan Kaufman Publishers Inc., 1992.

[OMG06]   Object Management Group. Object Management Group, 2006. Accessed on 10/24/2006.

[Pal06]   Palm. Ways to enter data into a palm handheld, 2006. Accessed on 04/25/2006.

[Paq05]   Frederic Paquay. Image restitution by sonorous signals. Technical report, n/a, November 2005.

[Par89]   H. Van Dyke Parunak. Hypermedia topologies and user navigation. In *Proceedings of the second annual ACM conference on Hypertext*, pages 43–50, Pittsburgh, Pennsylvania, United States, 1989. ACM Pres.

[PE98]   A. Puerta and J. Eisenstein. Towards a general computational framework for model-based interface development systems. *Proceedings of the 4th international conference on Intelligent user interfaces*, pages 171–178, 1998.

[Pea00a]   David Pearce. Enabling New Speech Driven Series for Mobile Devices: An overview of the ETSI standard activities for Distributed Speech Recognition Front-ends. Technical report, Motorola Labs, May 2000.

[Pea00b]   David Pearce. Enabling New Speech Driven Services For Mobile De-
              vices: An overview of the ETSI standard activities for Distributed
              Speech Recognition Frontends. In *AVIOS 2000: The Speech Applica-
              tions Conference*, San Jose, CA, USA, May 2000.

[Rab89]   Lawrence R. Rabiner. A Tutorial on Hidden Markov Models and
              Selected Applications in Speech Recognition. In *Proceedings of the
              IEEE*, volume 77, pages 257–286, February 1989.

[Ram98]   T. V. Raman. *Audio system for technical readings*, volume 1410.
              Springer Verlag, Berlin, Germany / Heidelberg, Germany / London,
              UK / etc., 1998.

[RJ93]   Lawrence R. Rabiner and Biing-Hwang Juang. *Fundamentals of
              Speech Recognition*. Prentice Hall PTR, 1993.

[RSG97]   D. Ross, D. Schwabe, and A. Garrido. Design Reuse in Hypermedia
              Applications Development. In *Proceedings of the eightth ACM confer-
              ence on Hypertext*, pages 57–66. ACM Press, 1997.

[RSY04]   I. V. Ramakrishnan, Amanda Stent, and Guizhen Yang. Hearsay:
              enabling audio browsing on hypertext content. In *Proceedings of the
              13th conference on World Wide Web*, pages 80–89, New York, NY,
              USA, 2004. ACM Press.

[SAKM04]   Dirk   Schnelle,   Erwin   Aitenbichler,   Jussi   Kangasharju,
              and   Max   Mühlhäuser.   Talking   assistant   -   car   re-
              pair   shop   demo.   http://elara.tk.informatik.tu-
              darmstadt.de/publications/2004/taCarRepairShop.pdf, 2004. Please
              also see the associated video at http://elara.tk.informatik.
              tu-darmstadt.de/public_www/dirk/carshop-final.mpg (MPEG,
              170 MB).

[SC90]   Hiroaki Sakoe and Seibi Chiba. Dynamic Programming Algorithm
              Optimization for Spoken Word Recognition. In Alex Waibel and Kai-
              Fu Lee, editors, *Readings in Speech Recognition*, chapter 4.3, pages
              159–165. Morgan Kaufmann Publishers, Inc., 1990.

[Sch96]   Rolf Schulmeister. *Grundlagen hypermedialer Lernsysteme: Theorie
              - Didaktik - Design*. Addison-Wesley, Bonn, 1996.

[Sch05]   Ulrich Schmitz.   Microsoft verbindet Telefonie und Dotnet-
              Webservices. *Computerzeitung*, 29:14, 2005.

[Sel06]   Hans Petter Selasky.   Image sound.   http://www.turbocat.
              net/~hselasky/math/image_sound/index.html, 2006. accessed on
              08/22/2006.

[Ser06]   Shared Web Services. 5 costly mistakes that cause workflow imple-
              mentations to fail. Technical report, Shared Web Services, 2006.

[SFG01]   Bernhard Suhm, Barbara Freeman, and David Getty. Curing the
            Menu Blues in Touch-tone Voice Interfaces. In *CHI '01: CHI '01 ex-
            tended abstracts on Human factors in computing systems*, pages 131–
            132, New York, NY, USA, 2001. ACM Press.

[SG01]   Albrecht Schmidt and Hans-Werner Gellersen. Modell, Architektur
            und Plattform für Informationssysteme mit Kontextbezug. *Informatik
            Forschung und Entwicklung*, 16(4):213–224, November 2001.

[Shn86]   Ben Shneiderman. *Designing the User Interface: Strategies for Effec-
            tive Human-Computer Interaction*. Addison-Wesley Longman Pub-
            lishing Co., Inc., Boston, MA, USA, 1986.

[Shn00]   Ben Shneiderman. The limits of speech recognition. *Communications
            of the ACM*, 43(9), September 2000.

[Shu05]   Jonathan E. Shuster. Introduction to the User Interface Markup Lan-
            guage. *CrossTalk*, pages 15–19, January 2005.

[Sie01]   Daniel P. Sieworik. Mobile access to information: Wearable and con-
            text aware computers. Technical report, Carnegie Mellon University,
            September 2001.

[Sil14]   Herbert Silberer. Der Homunculus. *Imago - Zeitschrift fr Anwendung
            der Psychoanalyse auf die Geisteswissenschaften*, 3:37–79, 1914. Heft
            2.

[SJ05]   Dirk Schnelle and Frankie James. Structured Audio Information Re-
            trieval System (STAIRS). In *Mobile Computing and Ambient Intelli-
            gence: The Challenge of Multimedia, Dagstuhl Seminar 05181*. Schloss
            Dagstuhl, May 2005.

[SK06]   Dirk Schnelle and Tobias Klug. Applying the MVC Pattern to Gen-
            erated User Interfaces with a Focus on Audio. In *Applying the MVC
            Pattern to Generated User Interfaces with a Focus on Audio*, 2006. to
            appear.

[SKHM04]   Dirk Schnelle, Jussi Kangasharju, Andreas Hartl, and Max
            Mühlhäuser. Stairs - navigation strategies. Technical report, Teleco-
            operation Group, Department of Computer Science, Darmstadt Uni-
            versity of Technology, 2004.

[SL06]   Dirk Schnelle and Fernando Lyardet. Voice User Interface Design
            Patterns. In *Proceedings of 11th European Conference on Pattern
            Languages of Programs (EuroPlop 2006)*, 2006.

[SLW05]   Dirk Schnelle, Fernando Lyardet, and Tao Wei. Audio Navigation
            Patterns. In *Proceedings of 10th European Conference on Pattern
            Languages of Programs (EuroPlop 2005)*, Irsee, Germany, July 2005.

[Smaa]   SmartKom. http://www.smartkom.org/. accessed on 05/12/2006.

[Smab]   SmartWeb. http://smartweb.dfki.de/. accessed on 05/12/2006.

[SME06]   S. Shanmugham, P. Monaco, and B. Eberman. A Media Resource
              Control Protocol (MRCP). http://www.rfc-archive.org/getrfc.
              php?rfc=4463, April 2006.

[Spe04]   Speech synthesis markup language (ssml). http://www.w3.org/TR/
              speech-synthesis/, September 2004. accesses on 10/06/2006.

[Spe06]   HandHeld Speech. HandHeld Speech, 2006.

[SR02]   Stefanie Shriver and Roni Rosenfeld. Keyword selection, and the uni-
              versal speech interface projects. Technical report, Carnegie Mellon
              University, 2002.

[SRL98]   H. Schulzrinne, A. Rao, and R. Lanphier. Real Time Streaming Pro-
              tocol. http://www.rfc-archive.org/getrfc.php?rfc=2326, April
              1998. accessed on 05/19/2006.

[SSP98]   T. Starner, B. Schiele, and A. Pentland. Visual contextual aware-
              ness in wearable computing. In *Proceedings 2nd International Sympo-
              sium Wearable Computers (ISWC 98)*, pages 50–57, Los Alamitos,CA,
              USA, 1998. IEEE CS Press.

[ST95]   Ernst Günter Schukat-Talamazzini. *Automatische Spracherkennung*.
              Vieweg Verlag, Braunschweig/Wiesbaden, March 1995.

[Str06]   Christoph Strnadl. Einführung in Business Process Management
              (BPM) und BPM Systeme (BPMS). http://www.bpm-guide.de/
              articles/55, 2006. accessed on 07/28/2006.

[TABM03]   J. Gregory Trafton, Erik M. Altmann, Derek P. Brock, and Farilee E.
              Mintz. Preparing to resume an interrupted task: effects of prospective
              goal encoding and retrospective rehearsal. *International Journal of
              Human-Computer Studies*, 58(5):583–603, 2003.

[Teš05]   Aleksandra Tešanović. What is a pattern. In *Dr.ing. course DT8100
              (prev. 78901 / 45942 / DIF8901) Object-oriented Systems*. IDA De-
              partment of Computer and Information Science, Linköping, Sweden,
              2005.

[The06]   The Apache Xalan Project. http://xalan.apache.org, 2006.

[Tho98]   Edward O. Thorp. The invention of the first wearable computer.
              In *Proceedings of the Second International Symposium on Wearable
              Computers (ISWC)*, pages 4–8, Pittsburgh, PA, USA, 1998.

[Tid05]   Jenifer Tidwell. *Designing Interfaces*. O'Reilly, 2005.

[TWMC95]   The Workflow Management Coalition. Workflow Management Coali-
              tion - The Workflow Reference Model. Technical report, The Workflow
              Management Coalition (WfMC), January 1995.

[TWMC99]   The Workflow Management Coalition. Workflow Management Coalition - Terminology & Glossary. Technical report, The Workflow Management Coalition (WfMC), February 1999.

[TWMC05]   The Workflow Management Coalition. Workflow Process Definition Interface – XML Process Definition Language (XPDL). Technical Report WFMC-TC-1025, The Workflow Management Coalition (WfMC), October 2005.

[Unz00]   Dagmar Unz. *Lernen mit Hypertext: Informationssuche und Navigation*, volume 326 of *Internationale Hochschulschriften*. Waxmann Verlag GmbH, Münster, 2000.

[vDea69]   Aries van Dam et. al. A Hypertext Editing System for the 360. In *Proceedings Conference in Computer Graphics. 1969*, University of Illinois, 1969.

[Voi04]   VoiceXML. http://www.w3.org/TR/voicexml20/, March 2004. accesses on 08/28/2006.

[VR02]   Thomas Vantroys and José Rouillard. Workflow and mobile devices in open distance learning. In *IEEE International Conference on Advanced Learning Technologies (ICALT 2002*, 2002.

[vWvdV03]   M. van Welie and van der Veer. Pattern Languages in Interaction Design: Structure and Organization. In Menozzi Rauterberg, editor, *Proceedings of Interact '03*, Zürich, Switzerland, 2003. IOS Press.

[vWvdVE00]   M. van Welie, G. van der Veer, and A. Eliens. Patterns as Tools for User Interface Design. Technical report, Workshop on Tools for Working With Guidelines, Biarritz, France, 2000.

[W3C06]   W3C. http://www.w3.org/TR/xforms11/, July 2006. accessed on 05/09/2006.

[Whi04]   Stephen A. White, editor. *Business Process Modelling Notation (BPMN)*. bpmn.org, May 2004.

[WRM75]   Gondin William R and Edward W. Mammen. *The Art of Speaking Made Simple*. Doubleday, London, 1975.

[WSSF03]   Alf Inge Wang, Carl-Frederik Sørensen, Eldrid Schei, and Thale Christina Fritzner. Case Study: Use of the Mobile Tool Handyman for Mobile Work. In Marina Del Rey, editor, *IASTED International Conference on Software Engineering amd Applications (SEA 2003)*, USA, November 2003.

[XML99]   Xml path language (xpath). `XMLPathLanguage(XPath)`, November 1999. accessed on 10/05/2006.

[Yan96]   Nicole Yankelovich. How Do Users Know What to Say? *ACM interactions*, 3(6), November 1996.

[Zay06]   Dmitri Zaykobskiy. Survey of the Speech Recognition Techniques for Mobile Devices. In *11th International Conference on Speech and Computer (SPECOM)*, St. Petersburg (Russia), 2006.

[zM04]   Michael zur Muehlen. *Workflow-based Process Controlling. Foundation, Design, and Implementation of Workflow-driven Process Information Systems*, volume 6 of *Advances in Information Systems and Management Science*. Logos, Berlin, 2004.

www.ingramcontent.com/pod-product-compliance
Lightning Source LLC
La Vergne TN
LVHW022306060326
832902LV00020B/3297